The
Social Use of Metaphor

The
Social Use of Metaphor

ESSAYS ON THE ANTHROPOLOGY OF RHETORIC

Edited by
J. DAVID SAPIR
and
J. CHRISTOPHER CROCKER

with contributions by
J. CHRISTOPHER CROCKER
JAMES W. FERNANDEZ
JAMES HOWE
J. DAVID SAPIR
PETER SEITEL

University of Pennsylvania Press 1977

Library of Congress Cataloging in Publication Data

Main entry under title:

The social use of metaphor.

  Enlarged versions of papers presented at a symposium
held during the annual (1970) meeting of the American
Anthropological Association, with one additional paper.
     Bibliography: p.
     Includes index.
     1.Metaphor--Addresses, essays, lectures.
2. Symbolism-- Addresses, essays, lectures. I. Sapir,
J. David. II. Crocker, Jon Christopher, 1938-
III. American Anthropological Association.
PN228.M4S6 1977   301.2'1   76-53200
ISBN 0-8122-7725-2

For

KENNETH BURKE,
  Logologist

Contents

Preface

This collection of essays owes its inception to the dismay felt by the editors at the 1969 meetings of the American Anthropological Association. There, one of us, arriving at his appointed ten minutes to give a paper on a subject related to metaphor, found himself in a small room at the end of a twisted corridor, off in the *other* hotel. Worse, none of the papers, commendable as they were, had anything to do with each other. Due to the distance of one hotel from the other, people coming to hear a paper invariably arrived one too late and were compelled to sit out a discussion of some topic about which they knew nothing and cared less. Ours was a wastebasket session, and metaphor deserved something better.

Strength, or at least conspicuousness, lies in numbers. So, to retrieve metaphor from the wastebasket and to set it out uncrumpled in plain view, we organized for the next (1970) annual meetings a symposium and gave it a title, provided by Peter Seitel: *The Social Use of Metaphor*. Participants, besides the editors, were Fernandez, Seitel, and Peter Stone. Heartened by its success, we went on to prepare this volume which consists of enlarged versions of contributions to the symposium with the added paper by Howe. An exception is Fernandez's presentation which was a small portion of a larger and more basic statement circulated to us in the spring of 1970 (*What It Means to Be Moved: The Operation of Metaphor in Religious Behavior*). After the symposium Fernandez agreed to give us the larger portion of that discussion for inclusion here.

At the meetings we decided to dedicate the volume to Kenneth Burke. We had, in fact, originally planned to invite Mr. Burke to the symposium as a discussant, but lack of funds unhappily made this impossible. Our reasons for wanting to honor Kenneth Burke are plain enough. As anthropologists who take seriously the central place occupied by figurative language in the formation and expression of cultural representations we have been obliged to rise above the parochialism of our discipline and to look elsewhere for appropriate methods and models of analysis. There are two immediate areas of interest: rhetoric, long moribund but now showing signs of being very much alive, and literary criticism. And where else to start but with Kenneth Burke? For more than forty-five years Mr. Burke in his many writings has developed not only a set of analytic terms useful to literature and to rhetoric, but also a theory of language usage that applies directly to the problems of social action. It is through language, as symbolic *action*, that man is able to size up and control—or if not control, at least cajole—his natural, social, and supernatural environment.

This volume divides into two parts: theoretical and particular. Part I, on generalities, consists of two chapters, one on the "anatomy" of metaphor, the other on its use. The former (by Sapir) attempts to describe what metaphor is and goes about this "syntactic" exercise by relating two types of metaphor to each other and to the concepts of synecdoche and metonymy. The latter (by Crocker), on the use and function of metaphor—on its "pragmatics," takes as its point of departure a number of concepts set out by Kenneth Burke, most conspicuously his notion of "perspective by incongruity" and "entitlement." These, among others, are developed, analyzed, and sometimes "discounted" in ways that serve the broad topics covered by symbolic anthropology. Another general discussion appears at the beginning of Fernandez's chapter and in certain ways parallels the arguments of Part I. With Fernandez, however, emphasis is on the more general elements and humanistic motives of figurative language, and his approach is therefore quite different from those developed by Sapir and Crocker. Where it is not different we have endeavored to avoid undue repetition. We defend any overlap that might be present by insisting that in matters as involved as these, two, three, even more, variants are certainly better than one.

Part II consists of five essays, all based on individual fieldwork, that offer interpretations and analyses of particular metaphors or groups of metaphors as they appear in various anthropological contexts. By design each essay deals with a different type of usage: in proverbs, ritual, political discourse, as a cosmological aphorism, and in a folktale. This should give some idea of the *range* of places where metaphors can occur. Partly because of the diversity of the metaphors themselves and partly because of the divergent theoretical perspectives of the contributors each substantive essay is unique in its presentation and argumentation. This is as it should be, for given the relatively recent turn (or, return) in anthropology to questions of symbolism and rhetoric any attempt to enforce some one theoretical ground-plan to be followed by all would be untimely, not to mention utterly uncongenial.

Although we do not expect our readers to agree entirely, if at all, with our analyses and conclusions (we, in fact, do not all agree among ourselves), we do hope that each reader will come to appreciate the complexity and importance of the subject. By argument and example it is our intent to move our colleagues, toward—as A. F. C. Wallace has put it for anthropology generally—precise and "intensive" analyses and away from the "slash and burn" practices common to the study of metaphor.

Our primary audience will be anthropologists, but by chance we might attract the attention of literary critics. That figurative language, especially metaphor, is a subtle and complex topic will not be news to them. If it were otherwise, they would all be out of a job. What we do expect, however, is that our collection of essays will give them some rich examples of figurative language derived from unfamiliar sources and that all this exotica might just afford some fresh *perspectives by* not too much *incongruity.**

Charlottesville, Virginia   J.D.S.
                                J.C.C.

* We would like to acknowledge support from the University of Virginia Small Grants Committee, which on two occasions provided funds that went towards typing different drafts of Part I.

Midway between the unintelligible and the commonplace, it is a metaphor which most produces knowledge.

Aristotle (*Rhetoric*, III, 1410b)

It [metaphor] brings out the thisness of a that, or the thatness of a this.

Kenneth Burke (*A Grammar of Motives*)

PART **I**

Generalities

1

The Anatomy of Metaphor

J. DAVID SAPIR

To talk of metaphor is to talk of *tropes,* those figures of speech that
operate on the meaning (the "signified") rather than the form (the
"signifier") of words.[1] One meaning, or what we will call a *term,* is
related either by replacement, by implication, or by juxtaposition to
another. Tropes always define a relationship between terms, and this
will be important to keep in mind. Tropes are about relationships, never
about a term taken by itself. Moreover, tropes belong to that part of
language that resists strict logical analysis defined by paraphrase,
analytical tautology, truth-value tests, and the like. Their resistance to
such analysis has been an irritant to some logicians and a challenge to
others.[2]

1. I would like to acknowledge a dialogue of several years' standing with Peter
Seitel that has influenced greatly the development of my own position on metaphor.
An earlier version of this chapter was presented during four sessions of Dan
Sperber's seminar on *La Théorie générale du symbolisme* at the Laboratoire
d'Ethnologie et Sociologie Comparative, Université de Paris-Nanterre, where I was
affiliated throughout the 1972–73 academic year. Comments made by the participants, by Sperber, and later Tzvetan Todorov and more recently at the University
of Virginia by Marc Schloss and at the Institute for Advanced Study by Michelle
and Renato Rosaldo were of great help in writing up the final version. Their
interest in the project is acknowledged with grateful appreciation.

2. Because of this resistance many language philosophers have been led to make a
sharp distinction between two types of language and symbolization, one that
responds to logic strictly defined, and the other, including tropes, that does not.
For example, de Saussure (1959) makes a distinction between sign and symbol,
a distinction that in recent times continues in the work of French scholars starting
with Roland Barthes (1957) and continuing with Tzvetan Todorov (1972, 1974*a*,

3

Rhetoricians have defined a large quantity of specific tropes of which four—metaphor, metonymy, synecdoche, and irony—have been taken as the most important, receiving the title of "master tropes."[3] These four either subsume the others (synecdoche subsumes autonomasia) or are directly equivalent to them (irony = antiphrasis). Briefly, and as a way into our discussion, the four can be defined as follows: Metaphor states an equivalence between terms taken from separate semantic domains: George the Lion might be an expression applied to a football player, for instance. Metonymy replaces or juxtaposes contiguous terms that occupy a distinct and separate place within what is considered a single semantic or perceptual domain. Homer will often be used instead of the *Iliad* ("you will read in Homer. . ."), where agent replaces act; or the phrase "deep in his cups," where "cups" as container stands for the sherry or wine that is contained. Synecdoche, like metonymy, draws its terms from a single domain; however, one term always includes or is included by the other as kind for type, part for whole: France for a specific Frenchman, sail for ship. Irony juxtaposes concepts that may come from the same or separate domains and that are felt to contradict each other. It is the subtlest and most complex of the tropes and usually involves whole expressions rather than the simple juxtaposition of terms, although it can be argued that two-term oxymora such as "bright obscurity" and "sweet death" are types of irony.

I first came to the general subject of rhetoric and specifically the *what is* of metaphor when, as an anthropologist, I tried to reconcile Lévi-Strauss's notion of metaphor with a different but equally apt and

---

1974*b*) and Dan Sperber (1974) among many others. A similar distinction is made by Susanne Langer (1942) when she speaks of a contrast between discursive and presentational symbolism. More generally the same kind of distinction is implicit in such opposing categories as Freud's secondary versus primary processes, Levy-Bruhl's civilized and primitive mentalities and Lévi-Strauss's distinction between an "engineer" and a *bricoleur.*

3. Our association of change of meaning with "trope" follows the common practice that contrasts trope with "figure," a device that has to do with changes in formal patterns. Obviously any rhetorical device involves both and its full analysis must account for each type of change. Cf. Lanham's entry (1969:101–3) on *trope.*

Some recent writings on rhetoric and metaphor include the following: Roland Barthes's essay "L'ancienne rhétorique; aide-memoire" (1970) gives a brilliant sketch of the development of rhetoric through the beginning of the Middle Ages. Modern statements on rhetoric can be found in vol. 16 of *Communications* (that includes the Barthes paper) and in Dubois et al. (1970) which gives a systematic analysis of the entire *elocutio* of rhetoric (the part having to do with the choice and ordering of words). A recent number of *New Literary History* (vol. 6, no. 1 [1974]) devoted to metaphor includes several very interesting papers. Warren Shibles's *Metaphor* (1971) is a detailed annotated bibliography. Special mention must be made of Paul Ricoeur's recent book, *La métaphore vive* (1975). It is a very thorough discussion of various treatments of metaphor starting with Aristotle's *Rhetoric* and *Poetics* and continuing to Ricoeur's own version of the phenomenology of metaphor.

usable formulation current in literary criticism and associated mainly with I. A. Richards (1936). This diplomatic mission took me to Aristotle, the clan founder, and to his definition of metaphor in the *Poetics* (chap. 21) where he identified four types: genus substituting for species; species for genus; genus for genus; and analogy. When I discounted the former two, called synecdoches by rhetoricians after Aristotle, it was obvious that Lévi-Strauss considered analogy only, while the literary critics tended to restrict their attention, though never exclusively, to genus for genus metaphors.

My task then was to provide not only a description giving equal weight to the two types, but also a demonstration of how one type develops into the other and furthermore how the two relate to the discounted synecdoches as well as to the related concept of metonymy.[4]

Although my major concern was with typology I was inevitably led both back to the more properly anthropological interest in usage as well as forward to an appreciation of the utter open-endedness of meta- phoric interpretation. That is to say, one cannot really separate rhetori- cal form from usage nor can one affix to any particular example a single necessary and sufficient interpretation. Rhetoric, like its natural home, politics, is a slippery business.

It is interpretation that brings up the major problem of rhetorical, especially metaphoric, forms. If no interpretation can ever be demon- strated as "necessary and sufficient," then at least some interpretations can be shown to be better than others, to be more appropriate, and fuller. But how can we be sure that such is the case, how can we be sure that this interpretation is valid, or at least more so than another? Although none of us has directly and explicitly faced this particular epistemological tangle in this volume, we have nevertheless developed our respective interpretations (and I am referring mainly to the sub- stantive essays in Part II) from the point of view of cultural context. An interpretation is valid if, at some level or another, it shows how the figurative material at hand (ritual, aphorism, folktale . . . whatever) fits into the larger framework of basic cultural understandings, and the more thoroughly and exhaustively it does so the better.

INTERNAL METAPHOR *(Genus for Genus)*

If we say that George the man is like a lion we must also admit, no matter how much we might enjoy this noble characterization, that

4. In contrast, irony in its complexity stands apart. It can be thought of as a derived trope, for ironical expressions can often be analyzed as one of the three other tropes plus the idea of contradiction. To develop this interesting point, how- ever, would lead us away from our immediate concern with the anatomy of metaphor.

at the same time he is not like a lion at all. George might be large, powerful, and deadly, but where is his tail? A metaphor in a variety of ways places into juxtaposition two terms that are, or can be, thought of as both similar and dissimilar. That is, out of the features defining one term and those defining the other, there will be a number shared by both terms.[5]

As a start, then, metaphor consists of three basic constituents, two terms from separate domains (George and a lion) plus the bundle of shared features. These constituents permit us to define a metaphoric process. We start with one term and then move to another by way of a group of implicit or stated intermediary features. This can be diagrammed as:[6]

Departure	Intermediary	Arrival
D	I	A

mammal
strength
courage
etc.

The features involved as intermediaries divide into two rough classes. On the one hand will be a number of features having to do with a strict definition of the two terms: + animal, + mammal. And on the other hand will be more particular features indicating shared conceptual qualities and visual and other sensual similarities. Of the latter features, the conceptual qualities, such as both George's and the lion's courage, strength, aggressiveness, predominate. Sensual features are less important, although, for example, we might liken a man's copious and unruly hair to a lion's mane: "his lion's mane," or simply "his mane." But as

5. The overlap must not be too great, for if it is, the two terms will be considered synonymous (*pail* and *bucket*) and the sense of their being simultaneously alike and not alike will be lost. Thus the line separating synonym from trope can be difficult to establish, and Deese (1974:213–14) has put it well: "The literal and figurative concepts should not share too many important or salient features. It is uninformative to say that the lion is a tiger. It is even not very good to say that the tiger is the lion of India. We are bothered, even though there are close familial resemblances, because it is precisely those features in which lions and tigers differ that are brought to mind by the comparison. The literal and figurative concept must have some features in common. . . , but they had better be neither too numerous or salient nor too obscure and dependent upon a kind of erudition."
6. The diagram is taken from Dubois et al. (1970:108, 118), (cf. below notes 10, 12, 13).

often as not, metaphors that designate sensual similarity tend immediately to imply other qualities. Thus (sticking with hair) "you hairy ape" brings to mind many nonvisual simian attributes. We would apply such an epithet either affectionately or disparagingly to someone who not only is hairy but is also thought to be apelike in other ways, especially in his behavior.

The only example in this volume that makes use of visual similarity is in the Fabricated Child where a womb is equated to a beehive. Both are containers with something inside, but even here a conceptual similarity, internal gestation, dominates. The clearest example showing a contrast between conceptual and sensual metaphors that I have found comes from the Haya of Tanzania where, as Peter Seitel has kindly informed me, *eel* can apply either to a man or a woman. When it applies to a man it is conceptual and refers to his devious qualities of slipperiness and stealth in social interaction; in contrast, when applied to a woman it is sensual and refers more simply and directly to the tactile and visual smoothness of her skin.

To the two terms and shared features that define a metaphor, we must add the topic of discourse, what we are talking about or referring to when we use the metaphor. With certain exceptions that we will get to shortly, one of the terms will be commensurate or continuous with the topic of discourse (I. A. Richards [1936] calls this the *tenor* of the metaphor, we the *continuous term*), while the other will be discontinuous (Richards's *vehicle*, our *discontinuous term*). Thus, for "George the Lion," when the topic is George, we identify George as the continuous term, lion as a discontinuous term. To have a metaphor at all, the discontinuous term (vehicle) must be stated along with the topic and/or the continuous term (tenor). Since the topic will imply the continuous term, and the reverse, only one need be present. We may also add to the metaphor one or more intermediary features. There is thus a continuum of explicitness in the representation of a metaphor:

1. Discontinuous term + topic, the most indirect form of representation and the one to which many people restrict the term metaphor. It is called a replacement metaphor by Brooke-Rose (1958) and a metaphor *in absentia* by Dubois et al. (1972:114). "Willow of the house" (when talking about Judy) and "he will eat his words" are examples of this type.

2. The two terms together, as in the examples "willowy Judy" and "he is like a lion." When the two terms are set out in clear juxtaposition, noun against noun, verb against verb, so that a direct comparison ("is like") is emphasized, the term *simile* rather than metaphor is usually employed.

3. The two terms together plus one or more intermediaries: "Judy, lithesome as a willow."[7]

There is a great variety of expressions often used as examples of metaphor that are nevertheless hardly ever felt as tropes. One common set uses body parts to represent the parts of material objects: "leg of a table," "head of a pin," "eye of a needle," "foot of a mountain," etc. Their representation is that of a replacement metaphor; thus for "head of a pin" we have *pin* as the topic and *head* as the discontinuous term. Unlike a true metaphor, however, it lacks the continuous term, although one might be provided by circumlocution: "spherical or blunt circular and protruding end of a pin," where the supplied phrase is simply an enumeration of the common features linking X with *head*. In most discourses the lack of a continuous term impedes us from sensing the juxtaposition of separate domains essential to a metaphor. We cannot easily answer the question "if it is not a head (of a pin), then what is it?" With a true metaphor we can: "if it is not a willow, what is it?"— "it's Judy."[8]

William Empson (1967:332ff.) prefers to call these expressions "transfers" and Max Black, along with most rhetoricians, considers them as types of *catachresis* which Black defines as "the use of a word in some new sense in order to remedy a gap in the vocabulary" (1962:33). As philosophers of language frequently tell us (cf. Langer 1942) it is just these "transfers" that, through time, provide a language with its abstract vocabularies.

Implicit in our discussion so far is a common view of metaphor as little more than a verbal game. The speaker uses lion when he means George only to make the addressee take the trouble of decoding the message with common features back to George. Metaphor is an ornament that at best breaks up the monotony of "plain talk" and at worst

---

7. Genette (1970:30) in his chapter on "La Rhétorique Restreinte" offers a more comprehensive table where he points out four variables: *comparé, comparant,* and *motif* (respectively equivalent to our continuous and discontinuous terms and shared features), plus *modalisateur* which is a linking term such as "is like," "as." To Genette the only expressions that warrant the title of metaphor are those that leave all but the *comparant* or discontinuous term unstated and implicit, as *ma flamme* (derived from something like: *Mon amour brûle comme une flamme*).

8. As Dubois et al. (1970:95) put it, ". . . the seamstress hardly dreams that the head of her pin resembles her own." This is not to say that the two domains cannot be invoked when called for by the discourse. The seamstress might just dream, in a real dream, that the head of her pin is in fact her own head as it is pushed down "under the thumb" of her malicious employer.

In this regard Paul E. Sapir, M.D., has brought to my attention E. F. Sharpe's (1940) succinct and well illustrated statement on how dreams make use of "poetic tropes." Cf. also, Charles Rycroft (1974).

reduces all communication to little more than fancy babble. This position has been labeled by Max Black (1962:31) as "the substitute view of metaphor" and is of little interest. More profitable is what Black (1962:38ff.) calls the "interaction view of metaphor," a position based on a number of penetrating discussions by literary critics, especially Richards in his *The Philosophy of Rhetoric* and William Empson in *The Structure of Complex Words*. It is the approach we will adhere to here though with some deviations and additions.

As we said, a metaphor is sensed as a trope when we are aware of the simultaneous likeness and unlikeness of the two terms. To put it another way and turn things around, two terms are one in that they are alike, two in that they are not alike. In Samuel Johnson's words, a metaphor "gives you two ideas for one." Herein lies the "interaction" of a metaphor. By replacing a term continuous to a topic with one that is discontinuous, or by putting the two in juxtaposition, we are compelled (both Richards and Black use this emphatic verb) to consider each term in relationship to the other, and it is at this point that we are aware of the metaphor. In establishing a relationship two processes operate: first, the reduction of the terms to their shared features—to what makes them alike; secondly, the transference from one to the other, but mainly from the discontinuous to the continuous, of what they do not share—of what makes them unlike. The first process, which is basic, gives the metaphor its specificity. It allows us to foreground certain features of the continuous term that are felt as being salient to the general topic. On hearing George the Lion we are compelled to consider what we know about lions and to select those features that would apply to George, thus learning something very specific about George. In contrast, the second process gives a metaphor, for want of a better word, its *color*. It allows us to consider the continuous term for what it is not, to assume for a moment that, although George is "really" like a lion only in certain specific ways, he might be a lot more like a lion than in just those ways. We are given the means to imagine George as a real lion, straight and simple, even down to his tail.

Depending on the topic, the intent of the speaker, the nature of the two terms and their respective domains, a particular metaphor emphasizes (or will be understood to emphasize) one or the other process: specificity or the coloration. Take as an example "Put a tiger in your tank," that very successful advertisement for a brand of gasoline. It is a metaphor that certainly stresses color over specificity for there is very little in the way of shared features. The effect of the metaphor has more to do with its coloration, the transfer of a tiger's world to that of gasoline. The advertisement "tigerizes" the gasoline and, by metonymic extension, our automobile and ourselves. All of India, its jungles, its elephants, its tigers are in that gasoline, an exciting though hardly instructive thought.[9]

Other metaphors, in fact all really apt metaphors (those that in Aristotle's phrase "most produce knowledge"), stress specificity. These are the metaphors that with uncanny ability provide a means for making precise statements about their subject, the continuous term. All the metaphors presented and examined in our volume are of this type. The Bororo metaphor "my brother the parrot, or we [men] are macaws" is a striking example. By examining the world of macaws as it exists with reference to the Bororo, Christopher Crocker is able to isolate a cluster of specific features that show the metaphor as a precise statement about the place of men in Bororo society. The macaw, we learn, is a woman's pet. It is kept in her hut and is fed by her. It is also associated with spirit. Other animals might be domestic or associated with spirit, but only the macaw is both. Men in a very real sense live in a woman's world: descent is matrilineal and marriage is uxorilocal; they are, broadly speaking, kept by women. They are also, in contrast to women, associated with spirit, especially in the context of the men's hut that is situated in the center of the village.

What knowledge one has of the discontinuous term and its semantic domain has much to do with the aptness of a metaphor. This knowledge, what Black (1962:40) terms "system of associated commonplaces," can vary considerably from case to case, although presumably it consists of understandings about a particular domain held in common by members of a culture all speaking a common language. The commonplaces can vary, though, even in the context of a single language and culture, by being systematically altered and elaborated during discourse. This frequently happens in poetry where metaphors are developed into extended parables and conceits.

When commonplace knowledge of the discontinuous term and its associated semantic domain is merely perfunctory or has been reduced to the level of almost total ignorance, the metaphor becomes an ornamental cliché. Our English metaphors about animals, especially farm animals, provide good examples: "horse sense," "meek as a lamb," "stubborn as a mule," "a wild goose chase," "an old goat," "cock of the walk," "mother hen," etc. Although an urban dweller might possess a number of "commonplace associations" that he has picked up by hearsay, in reading, or at a museum (Picasso's goats), he will have little direct experience with these farm animals and the metaphors will hardly produce much "new knowledge." Their status as a trope is little

---

9. There is also an unstated sexual allusion in this catchy slogan that we will come to in our discussion of external metaphors.

more than the "head of a pin" type of catachresis, although here what is lacking is not the continuous term but the discontinuous "associated commonplaces." They are at best colorful synonyms: "he is the cock of the walk" is automatically equated to "he is vain and presumptuous"; "he's an old goat" to "he's a dirty old man."

Sufficient backgrounding or direct experience with a barnyard will promptly set matters aright, returning to the animal metaphors their sense of appropriateness. We need only consider the goat: Billy-goats, with their beard and apparent nearsightedness, look like old men. When one of a group of she-goats dominated by a male is in heat, there are great bursts of noisy activity. The whole group of bleating she-goats flee; the Billy pursues. He snorts, advances, makes genital contact with his nose and tongue, at which point he draws in, through mouth and nose, the exciting odor of his mate, all the while emitting in a series of sharp crescendos a penetrating wheeze. The she-goats gain ground; the Billy drops back. He snorts and advances again. The crucial contact, put off to the last moment, is direct and simply accomplished, coming as a distinct anticlimax.

With these associated commonplaces now in mind what was once a colorful cliché has become a highly specific metaphor; not perhaps as philosophically interesting as the Bororo "we are macaws," but nevertheless instructive.

One type of interaction appears in poetry where metaphors can very often be thought of as being bi-directional. Two topics are simultaneously entertained, with each providing the discontinuous term for the other.

The metaphor asserts not only, as Kenneth Burke puts it, "the thisness of a that" but also the "thatness of a this," which makes the distinction between continuous and discontinuous terms (Richards's tenor and vehicle) of little moment. As Brooke-Rose (1958:9–10) argues (and she is talking about poetry), what matters is not what is tenor and what vehicle, but rather the interaction of the two terms and their respective topics with a resulting "new entity." Consider Robert Frost's famous poem "Birches," a pastoral meditation on bent birch trees and the boyhood art of swinging them. In the poem it is impossible to say which is the discontinuous term, "swinging birches" or "getting away from life's considerations." Both are co-present, embedded in their respective topics, and of equal importance to the poem. What we have is an interaction that at once generalizes swinging birches to the level of life's "ups and downs" and at the same time gives a specific shape to our otherwise vaguely felt "life's considerations." We would have to be extremely obtuse and obsessed with a need to generalize if we insisted that the poem was "really" and only about the latter.

Parallel examples illustrating what Brooke-Rose and others mean by "new entity" can be found in folklore. In this volume (Sapir, below) the Fabricated Child's beehive womb is an amalgam created by the interaction of common features and reciprocal colorations. The new entity is built out of the common features: general shape, the gestation of what is contained, at the same time that it is built out of what is transferred: the human fetus from the womb, the container from the beehive. As is pointed out, the stark simplicity of the mixed entity dramatically underscores the mixed and ambiguous social scene encountered by the child. But more importantly, as a new entity, the external beehive womb further defines the whole course of action within the tale, and without its presence the tale would have been something very different.

Folktales using animals to personify human character types illustrate very well these metaphoric "new entities." Thus, in a recent paper by Thomas Beidelman (1975, also 1961, 1963, 1974) Hare and Hyena of Kaguru (Tanzania) folklore are neither natural animals nor the social persona they designate; they are distinct characters in their own right. Looking at the contrasts Beidelman cites as characterizing Hyena and distinguishing him from Hare, we can mention among many (a) the transference from man to Hyena: senior status, selfishness, loyalty to kin only, etc.; (b) from hyena to Hyena: animal shape, large size, eater of carrion, bone-eating, etc.; and (c) the common features that both man and hyena transfer to Hyena: cunning, dirtiness, nocturnal habits (man as witch), insatiable appetite. A similar breakdown can be drawn for Hare, although it is interesting that outside of animal shape and size there is very little that hare, the animal, contributes to Hare the character. We will want to touch this point again in our discussions of both metonymy and analogy.

Our three constituents of metaphor have now become five: not only the two terms and their shared features, but also the topic and the commonplace knowledge that respectively embraces or places the continuous and discontinuous terms. The analysis of any trope identified as a metaphor must take into account these five variables. Only when this is done can we talk of its specificity, transfer and coloration, its directionality and to what extent a "new entity" is formed.

SYNECDOCHE

As we noted earlier the two terms involved in synecdoche and metonymy are drawn from what is felt to be the same semantic domain. Thus, both tropes contrast with metaphor where two separate domains are necessarily brought into juxtaposition. This fundamental contrast—one versus two domains—has led a number of scholars starting as early as the eighteenth century with DuMarsais to reduce synecdoche and metonymy to a single trope. It is a position that has been forcefully stated by Roman Jakobson in his celebrated paper on linguistic aphasia (1956). Here Jakobson not only reduces the two to one (calling them both metonymy) but also argues that the contrast between metaphor and metonymy represents at the level of figurative language a basic contrast between paradigmatic replacement (for metaphor) and syntagmatic continuity or combination (for metonymy) that operates at every linguistic level—from phonology through syntax to semantics. Anthropologists have become familiar with this twofold distinction in Lévi-Strauss's writings on totemism and myth, although there he ignores entirely the kinds of metaphor we have so far been talking about, restricting his interest to the analogic or external metaphors that we will come to shortly.

Synecdoches have to do with the process of replacement within a hierarchical classification. An initial term replaces another that is either more general or more particular than itself. The criteria that classify the two terms vis-à-vis each other may be very precise as in biological classifications or quite loose and ideosyncratic. What is important is that the two are hierarchically arranged.

Two types of classification are particularly relevant.[10] First, a given term may include terms that designate its parts. Thus:

> man = head and hands and feet, etc.
> tree = branches and leaves and trunk and roots, etc.

This type of classification can be labeled the anatomical mode. Secondly, the very same term may also include a set of terms that designate particular varieties of this term. Here a whole is not broken into parts, but rather a whole is replaced by other wholes more precisely defined. Thus:

> man = Frenchman or Zulu or Arab, etc.
> tree = poplar or oak or willow or birch, etc.

This we shall call a taxonomic mode of classification.

Taking into account both taxonomic and anatomical classifications

10. This section draws heavily on Dubois et al.'s discussion of synedoche (1970: 97–106), although here I have made more of the functional differences that exist between the various types of synecdoche.

we get four types of synecdochic processes: taxonomic generalizing (kind for type) and particularizing (type for kind); anatomical gene-eralizing (whole for part) and particularizing (part for whole). The extent to which these processes produce effective tropes depends on whether or not the replacements and associations are "felt." In contrast to metaphor where the juxtaposition of separate domains assures that the trope will be "felt," whether as apt or not, there can be no clear assurance that replacements operating within a single domain will be "felt" at all. As a rule of thumb we can say that a trope, of whatever variety, will be felt, first, when we sense that a replacement or an asso-ciation of terms is indeed being made, and secondly, when the relation-ship, given the topic and context of its occurrence, is in some way marked or, in Prague School terminology, foregrounded as important. Let us keep this in mind as we look at some simple examples of synecdoche:

1. Taxonomic generalizing (genus for species, kind for type).

"Watch out for that beast" or "Watch out for the fauna" where "beast" and "fauna" replace "yellow-jacket."

In a Charles Addams cartoon the sign outside a house "Beware of the thing" which brings to mind the more common "beware of the dog."

Another cartoon, from *The New Yorker* (24 March 1973), by William Hamilton: Two couples converse at a party. One woman referring to the mustache of the man from the other couple says: "Charles? Of course I know Charlie, I've known Charlie since before he grew that thing." Charlie looks annoyed. Here "thing" replaces "mustache."

2. The reverse process, taxonomic particularizing (species for genus, type for kind).

For example, an enthusiast for one variety or another of machine or gadget refers to an object of his admiration with taxonomic precision, "He drove off in his 1935 Dodge DU Six Sedan" when "he drove off in his old car" would serve to make the point.

A much more common example are popular brand names that sub-stitute for the generic product, Clorox for a liquid chlorine bleach, Kleenex for cleansing tissue. But the brand names' status as generic substitutes is not necessarily permanent. We would think someone rather old-fashioned if he still insisted on calling his small hand-held camera a "kodak," even though Kodak remains an important trade name.

3. Anatomical generalizing (whole for part) for which there are few viable examples, although whenever the part has little functional significance a trope can be felt.

"I'm ruined, my fortune is gone," when someone loses twenty-five cents at poker. The whole fortune replaces the twenty-five cents.
"I'm all sore" when one has a sore toe.
"The car has broken down" when the cigarette lighter is out of order. This example recalls the millionaire on one of the 1940s' radio comedy hours who was fond of saying (besides "heavens to Gimbels"), "I must junk my Cadillac, the ashtrays are full."

4. In contrast, the reverse, anatomical particularizing (part for whole) provides a huge variety of tropes.

These are the synecdoches par excellence and are encountered everywhere: in clichés—"all hands on deck," "patter of little feet" (for children); in realistic writing—for example, Pauline Kael's description of Brigitte Bardot (1968), ". . . her smudged, pouty mouth open and the dark roots showing in her yellow hair"; the recorded conversation: A. "Take out the smell." B. "What smell?" A. "The garbage, idiot . . . it stinks"; in slang where Dubois et al. (1970:104) gave us *une partie de jambes en l'air* ("a game of legs in the air") where Elizabethan equivalents would be "the two-backed beast" and "ten toes up, ten toes down," each referring to people making love; and finally, of course, that arch-example appearing in all the books—sail for ship.

The above examples group together because in each case hierarchical replacements have taken place. But if this formal criterion allows us to class them all as synecdoches we may justly query whether or not they go together on functional grounds as well. That is, are these synecdoches doing the same thing? Do we sense that the "patter of little feet" is somehow closer in the kind of information it foregrounds to "beware of the thing" than either is to a metaphor such as "willowy Judy"? We would tend to say no, not at all. This, of course, is a major problem plaguing any discussion that tries to make functional sense out of formal categories. Indeed, the four types of synecdoche are functionally distinct, especially two of them: part for whole synecdoches stress specificity and hence contrast markedly with genus for species synecdoches that imply vagueness and indeterminancy. The remaining two (whole for part, species for genus) are harder to pin down, although they both in different ways at times suggest types of exaggeration or hyperbole. Consider the examples again:

Anatomical particularizing (part for whole). When a part replaces a whole, it serves at least two specifying functions. First, it characterizes the whole as distinct from other objects. Sail substitutes for ship, not simply by force of cliché, but because the sail fully characterizes the boat as something distinct from other objects. For any whole, however, there are usually quite a number of parts that conserve its specificity (as, for example, a boat's keel and rudder as well as its sail, but not its cabin). This leads to the second specifying function: the distinctive part chosen will foreground those aspects of the whole that are not only distinctive but are also taken as essential or directly relevant to the topic. *Hands* in the expression "all hands on deck" characterizes the whole as a person, but so would other body parts, feet for instance. The appropriateness of hands over other parts is determined by the major role traditionally assigned to sailors, that of manual labor.

Certainly ". . . legs up in the air" characterizes the distinctiveness of the whole, for where else but in lovemaking would this position occur? However feet up in the air does not designate the essential parts that are involved in lovemaking. They are peripheral and thus provide an indirect and euphemistic synecdoche. (As will be presently shown, the relationship of the essential to the peripheral parts [but not each to the whole] is a metonymy).

The Bardot example is different from the others, for it is made up of a string of synecdoches rather than a single one. Because of this we might take Kael's description of Bardot's mouth and hair as a straightforward example of realistic writing with nothing being felt at all as a trope. That is, Kael is simply telling us what Bardot looks like, and nothing more. But what is realistic writing if it is not a very great measure the systematic use of part for whole synecdoches with the synecdoches being felt in their total configuration? Realistic descriptions are *selective,* and it is what is selected that gets foregrounded and hence felt as important.[11] In this case Kael chooses to select out for mention those parts of Bardot that are relevant to her immediate topic which is Bardot's relationship to teen-age girls. Thus her description, ". . . her smudged, pouty mouth open and the dark roots showing in

11. I am only reiterating a point made by Roman Jakobson (1956:78) when he writes, "Following the path of contiguous relationships, the realistic author metonymically digresses from the plot to the atmosphere and from the characters to the setting in space and time. He is fond of synecdochic details. In the scene of Anna Karenina's suicide Tolstoj's artistic attention is focused on the heroine's handbag; and in *War and Peace* the synecdoches 'hair on the upper lip' or 'bare shoulders' are used by the same writer to stand for the female characters to whom these features belong." Cf. also Jakobson's note (p. 80, n. 27) giving a sample of the realistic writing of Gleb Ivanovic Uspenskij who uses in the extreme this form of synecdochic description.

her yellow hair," introduces: "The girl who set the style for modern girls to look like teen-age whores." We need only shift the topic, but keep the synecdoches, to appreciate that the latter are very much felt as tropes. Surely it would have been inappropriate for Kael to focus on Bardot's mouth and dyed hair if she had wished to talk of Bardot's relationship to her male, rather than teen-age girl, admirers.

We have included among the examples of part for whole synecdoches those that specify parts or qualities that are not visual, as in "take out the smell" (smell substituting for garbage). They have the same function: to foreground and emphasize for any topic essential or relevant features. To restrict the idea of "part" only to what can be seen and detached (as feet) from a whole implies an exaggerated visual bias that distorts completely what we really conceive any object to be. Our common, if not scientific, idea of a lion's attributes includes not only his head and tail and jaws, etc., but equally well his roar and, for that matter, his so-called courage.

Taxonomic generalizing (genus for species). When the substitution of a genus or type for a particular species or kind is felt as a trope it has the opposite effect to specifying. It generalizes to the point of vagueness. Indeed, if the generalizing is not vague enough, there will be no trope. Thus, in a case where *insect* replaces a *yellowjacket* essential features remain (noxious, small, arthropodal, etc.), we have a substitution similar to that of synonyms, and nothing is foregrounded. If, however, essential features are missing the replacing term catches our attention. It forces us to the context in order to decode the general term, to know that "fauna" or "beast" in our example is about a "yellowjacket," and that the "thing" in the Hamilton cartoon is a mustache. At the same time, because of its extreme generality the generic substitute has the possibility of going beyond the immediate context to include any number of other particular terms it might also subsume. It sets the stage for all manner of associations. How and to what degree we are invited to associate determines the effect and interest of the synecdoche. A particular topic and discourse might offer no invitation at all, as when "thing," "what's its name," "what's his name" simply replaces an unknown word or when "thing" is used as a euphemism. Or the invitation might be entirely open as when "fauna" brings to mind a scientific allusion (implicit contrast with "flora") to all nature's creatures and when "beast" somewhat ironically alludes to a full range of large and perhaps unreliable animals. Particularly apt synecdoches of this sort fall between the two extremes. Their associations are controlled and limited. The "thing" in the Charles Addams cartoon does not extend out to just any thing but only to those strange creatures that occupy Addams's demonic world. The Hamilton cartoon is more restricted. To have a woman say "that thing" for a mustache associates only to the euphimistic and "unknown word" use of "thing." Here the woman is putting the man down by defining his mustache as something that is as unknown to her (hence unappreciated) as say a Stillson wrench and as unnamable as his other "thing."

Taxonomic particularizing (species for genus). It is always the context of discourse that determines to what extent the substitution of a particular for a generic term will be felt as a trope. Someone talking about a collection of old cars will necessarily use a precise term such as 1935 Dodge DU Six Sedan to designate any one out of the group. He cannot indicate a particular car by using the generic "old car" because all of the cars are old. However, in another context where only one old car out of a lot of otherwise recent models is present the use of the same particularistic term: 1935 Dodge DU Six Sedan will be noticed immediately as a foregrounding device. The particularistic term draws attention not so much to the actual referent but to the speaker himself. He is asserting *a fortiori* that he has special knowledge of the object, that he is truly "on the in" when it comes to old cars. Ian Fleming in relating James Bond's own observations in contrast to others' continually uses particularistic trade names. Doing so projects the aura of special knowledge onto his very particular British Secret Service Agent Number 007. From one page of *Goldfinger* Bond notices of his dinner partner: "[a] plain gold Zippo lighter," "It was a Parliament," "dimple Haig and water," and "A whiff of soap or after-shave lotion came across the table. Lentheric?" (1972:9). And when it comes to Bond's own gun: ". . . [he] extracted his Walther PPK in the Berns Martin holster" (31).

The general use of a brand name in place of a generic name can be thought of more as a kind of catachresis than as a trope. A new product is awkwardly named by way of some kind of descriptive wording, "cleansing tissue," "small hand-held camera." Then the trade name of a dominant and conspicuous manufacturer takes over: Kleenex, Kodak. The trade name apparently lasts only as long as the manufacturer dominates the market. Eastman Kodak, though still very much around, is known to photographers today more for its chemicals and film than for its cameras. Thus "kodak" is not likely to be used these days for a small camera, even for Kodak's own Instamatic.

Anatomical generalizing (whole for part). The substitution of the whole for a part will be felt, and as an exaggeration or hyberbole, only when the replaced part is both minute and very secondary with respect to the well-being of the whole: thus body for toe, a whole fortune for twenty-five cents, and a Cadillac for an ashtray. If, however, the part is essential to the whole—body for heart, fortune for $10,000, automobile for differential—the synecdoche will pass without impact.

Out of the group of these functionally distinct synecdoches those which substitute part or quality for a whole are the ones that generate the largest variety of tropes. A device that specifies for any topic essential qualities and parts is bound to be useful when, as in the Bardot example, accurate and pertinent description is called for. And it is just this very process of reduction—from a whole to its pertinent parts—that brings us back to metaphor. We have identified the fact of shared features as the essential element in a metaphor's specificity. Isn't this specificity exactly the same as the specificity of part for whole synecdoches, except that in metaphor it has, to put it loosely, been multiplied by two?[12] The two terms of a metaphor are related to their shared features as part is to whole. Courage, strength, etc. are simultaneously the qualitative parts of both George and the lion, and recognition that this synecdochic relationship applies equally well to George and the lion permits equating the two. This is not to say that metaphor is merely the sum of two synecdoches. Metaphor still has its coloration and transfer plus the simultaneous idea of like and unlike, all of which are factors making it the richer trope.

Take a rather stilted example. With a set of part for whole synecdoches we describe John's face: "He had a long somewhat pointed nose separated from two sharp, prominent and triangular ears, by alert eyes; . . . ." We can then "double" the synecdoche and form a metaphor: "John had a foxlike face" which allows us to develop our description with the aid of a transfer to John of aspects of the fox's social world: "He, John, had a foxlike face, a long somewhat pointed nose separated from two sharp, prominent, and triangular ears, by alert eyes: eyes at once hard and timid as though on the simultaneous watch for rabbit and hound."

METONYMY

Metonymies are usually identified as the substitution of one "cause" (in Aristotle's sense of the word) for another: cause for effect (efficient

---

12. The major point in Dubois et al.'s discussion (1970:108–9) of metaphor. They argue that a metaphor develops linearly via a synecdoche that reduces an initial term to shared features (whole to part, type to kind), then enlarges via another synecdoche to the second term (part to whole, kind to type). Their interesting presentation of this formal position has a number of problems not least of which is its tendency to disregard other more important aspects of metaphor, such as interaction, transference, etc. It nevertheless inspired Todorov (1970:30) to pen this amusing conceit: "Exactly as in fairy stories or in *King Lear,* where the third daughter, continually scorned, at the very end reveals herself as being the most beautiful or the most intelligent, so it is with Synecdoche. It is only today that Synecdoche appears as the central trope, for just on account of its elders, Metaphor and Metonymy, it has until now been long neglected with its existence all but ignored" (my translation).

for final cause), container for contained (formal for material), and such variants as instrument for agent, agent for act, etc. Dubois et al. (1970:119) give a fine example drawn from a newspaper headline announcing the results of the Le Mans auto races: *"Les Ford ont levé le pied."* There are two metonymies here, *"Les Ford"* where instrument substitutes for agent and *"ont levé le pied,"* literally "lifted their feet" where a cause substitutes for an effect: "ran off with the cash," the translation and meaning of the idiom. Since *"levé le pied"* cannot be translated into English without destroying the metonymy, the example would be better if we rewrote it as: "The Fords stepped on it." Here we keep the metonymy: "stepping on the gas" as the cause for "winning the race," which is the effect.

With respect to the notion of shared domain or common ground a metonymy can be taken as the logical inverse of a metaphor. Rather than the relationship of two terms from separate domains that share overlapping features it is the relationship of two terms that occupy a common domain but do not share common features. If metaphor can be diagrammed as:

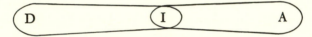

where (I) represents the common features, then metonymy will be like:[13]

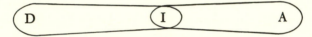

where (I) is the common "domain." We start with the *Iliad*; we then move beyond the *Iliad* to the whole domain that defines the poem and its times, till we arrive at Homer, its author.

When is a metonymy interesting? That is, when does it fulfill some purpose and when is it felt as a trope? This is a difficult question if for no other reason than because few people have attempted much of an answer. Let us make a try, even though it will lead us, as it did with synecdoche, right back to metaphor.

A metonymy, it appears, emphasizes the whole, the entire domain (I) shared by the two terms (D and A), and its success as a trope depends on how fully this idea of wholeness can be conveyed. The causal pairs: cause-effect, container-contained, act-agent, etc. are effective precisely

13. The diagram, once again, comes from Dubois et al (1970:118). Like metaphor they see metonymy as the combination of two synecdoches, though formed by reversing the steps: first generalizing then particularizing, rather than first particularizing then generalizing as with metaphor.

because they, in the abstractness, suggest a complete entity. By substituting one of the two causes in a context that calls for the other a totality is implied that would otherwise not be suggested. When we say Homer (agent) for *Iliad* (act) we extend the world of the poem (*Iliad*) not only to its author but also to his other work (the *Odyssey*) and his times. By substituting "The Fords stepped on it" for "George and the boys won the race" we expand our reference to include the whole event: men in their machines; hard, exciting, and fast action.

Since metonymy foregrounds the idea of "wholeness," it does the very opposite of the more important synecdoches, which foreground a particular quality (smell for garbage) or part (hand for man), and also of those metaphors that serve primarily to specify (we are macaws). This permits us to isolate two basic and complementary functions, or motivations, in the use of tropes and to associate one function, *totalizing*, with metonymy and another, *specifying*, with part for whole synecdohche and with metaphor.

There is, however, functional overlap. Although the replacement metonymies we have been talking about so far do not "specify" in any way, there are instances where metaphors and strings of synecdoches "totalize" at the same time they specify. This is obvious enough for a string of synecdoches that describe a whole. Each synecdoche will foreground a salient part or quality, but, at the same time, the sum of the synecdoches will suggest the whole, though from a particular angle. The synecdoches break down a whole, vaguely conceived, and then reconstruct it into something sharply delineated. There is no mystery here at all in terms of the analysis that we have been following: each part or each quality that represents a given whole, though synecdoches with respect to this whole, are, with respect to each other, metonymies. Each occupies a separate position in the semantic whole. Thus: John's face: S_1 long somewhat pointed nose $+$ S_2 two sharp, prominent, and triangular ears $+$ S_3 alert eyes; where S_1 is linked to S_2 (and S_3) via the common domain: S_1 (pointed nose) $>$ John's face $>$ S_2 (ears) and S_3 (eyes). One of these synecdoches cannot substitute for another, as with the causal pairs (cause-effect), but instead all must be stated together in order to suggest a total configuration, in this case to give a clear image of the whole face.

The sense of a new configuration is even greater if we add the metaphor "John's foxlike face," for added to the specific points staked out by the synecdoches are unstated points suggested by the transfer to John's face of foxlike appearance and character in general.

Looking a little closer and taking seriously the notion that metaphoric interaction forms a new entity, we must conclude that any metaphor implies at once a metonymy. The metonymy comes up at two points, first with respect to the like part of the metaphor, then with respect to the unlike part. We have already considered the "alike": two terms are brought together and an equation is admitted because of overlapping features. The sum of these features, which are metonymies vis-à-vis each other, delineate the new whole. But the "unlike" parts are equally in metonymic relationship to each other for they each occupy separate sections of the new whole that has been created by the equation. It is this metonymic relationship of the "unlike" parts that accounts for what we have already identified as the transference or coloration of one term by the other; a process that serves to augment the new configuration, or "entity" that has already been defined by the overlap. The transference of features from one term to the other can include (if desired) not only those that are in synecdochic relationship to their respective terms, but also those that are related by way of metonymy.

The realization that a metaphor's coloration is established metonymically brings us back to the Fabricated Child's beehive womb and the Kaguru's Hare and Hyena. Although each of these "new entities" is defined by what its two terms (continuous and discontinuous) have in common, it also depends, as we saw, quite as much and perhaps more on what the terms do not share. Considering once again what each side contributes we see that much of the new entity is an amalgam of features that follow closely one of the major types of metonymy: container/contained. The beehive contributes the container, the human womb the fetus. The animals, hare and hyena, contribute their physical shape; the social behavior that Hare and Hyena represent contributes what is contained. Of the two, Hare comes closer to being the product of a pure metonymy. The animal contributes his size and shape, but few if any of the behavioral attributes which are provided by the contained social persona. Hyena is more complex, for the animal contributes besides his shape a large number of behavioral characteristics many of which are shared with his human correspondent. The differences show Hyena as being the more apt creation, with Hare representing something of a logical afterthought.

EXTERNAL METAPHOR *(ANALOGY)*

To this point our attention has been given exclusively to Aristotle's genus-for-genus type of metaphor. What of his analogic metaphor, which he tersely defines as "when one thing is in the same relationship to another as a third is to a fourth," whence the formula a is to b, as x is to y ($a{:}b{::}x{:}y$)? In order to stress an underlying commonality existing between the two types of metaphor, let us say, not that analogy is a variety of metaphor, but rather that analogy is a mode of thought and that metaphor is one product of this thought. This will permit us to say further that there are two types of analogy and two corresponding types of metaphor.

The genus-for-genus metaphors we have been discussing so far, those that state an A = X equation, fall into the first category. Two terms are juxtaposed and, because of the shared features, form a metaphor. The relationship between the terms can be read as an analogy: term A is in the same relationship to the shared features as the term X is to those same features. Thus, George is to courage, etc. as a lion is to courage, etc. We call this kind of analogy an *internal analogy* and its product an *internal metaphor*. The two terms, isolated from their respective domains, have been related via internal identities, their shared features.

But this is not the kind of analogy we usually have in mind when we use the word. We tend to think of analogy as something else, and this something else will be called an *external analogy* or *external metaphor*. Two terms are juxtaposed and, ignoring any shared features they might have, we look instead to their respective semantic domains: A is to A's domain as X is to X's domain. In this arrangement A and X are not thought of as similar; they remain, as Lévi-Strauss has often insisted, in metonymic juxtaposition. The similarity now derives from the relationship each term has to its proper domain.

Each side of an external analogy is stated by a synecdoche: "A is to A's entire domain, as. . . ," which in turn can be developed into a metonymy: "A_1 is to A's domain, $+ A_2$ is to A's domain" becomes "A_1 is to A_2, as. . . ." Both taxonomic and anatomical modes of classification figure in these synecdoches and metonymies.

The taxonomic modes most frequently encountered by anthropologists involve totemic systems and have been discussed at length by Lévi-Strauss (1966*a*, 1963*a*). A set of animals (there can be any number) is set up against a set of differentiated social categories: bear: dear:hawk::clan$_b$:clan$_d$:clan$_h$. The animal set may be extended to include other living, nonanimal beings, for example, plants, and beyond that to anything that is nonhuman, including inanimate objects of great diversity such as machines (airplanes) and natural objects (a particular mountain). The similarity of relationship that pertains between members on either side of the analogy is the abstract notion of difference. Side A is similar to side X because each side is made up of subtypes that are recognized as different from each other. In the domain of animals a bear is different from a deer; likewise in the domain of human groups clan$_b$ is different from clan$_d$.

The terms may be arranged on some sort of scale. On either side of the analogy the terms will be set out in such a way that they will vary along one dimension: from smallest to biggest, from weakest to strongest, from least valuable to most valuable, etc. "George the Lion" can be read as an external metaphor if attention is shifted away from what they share vis-à-vis each other (internal metaphor) to how each relates to its own proper domain. George is to men as lion is to the animals: strongest, greatest of men; strongest, greatest of the animals. "Put a tiger in your tank" can also be thought of in this way: "fiercest of animals, fiercest of gasolines." Implicit in both readings will be other terms: fox, mouse; other gasolines; other men, John for instance.

Any scaling or set of differences, even if it involves several terms on each side of the analogy can, with ingenuity, be reduced to oppositions. The variable feature(s) that differentiates one term from the next is now conceived as set out in an either/or, present/absent opposition. Instead of smallest to biggest we have $-$big$/+$big. "Are you a lion or a mouse?" makes use of the opposition: you_1:you_2::lion:mouse with the criteria for opposition being $+/-$ courage, strength, etc. Lévi-Strauss (1963a:83ff.) uses Radcliffe-Brown's examples of Australian dualistic totemism as illustrations. Eaglehawk is opposed to crow. They are very similar terms but differ in one main dimension. Both are birds that eat meat, but eaglehawk kills its prey while crow eats what has been killed by others. Unlike the "are you a lion or a mouse?" example the criterion that determines the opposition is not the same on each side of the analogy. Moiety A, associated with eaglehawk, is in opposition to Moiety B, associated with crow. The opposition is defined, however, by a variety of social features, such as reciprocal marriage, that may relate only very indirectly, if at all, to eating meat killed by self or by others.

Anatomical synecdoches (part-whole) figure prominently in externally defined metaphors of which the most common make use of body parts. The political state is often equated to the body, where the possibilities for analogy are extensive ranging from such simple parallels as head:heart:hands::monarch:priesthood:peasant, to the complex analogy represented by Hobbes's *Leviathan*.

"Put a tiger in your tank" can be read as being built upon an anatomical analogy. Starting with an implicit correlation between human and automobile domains and adding to it the internal equation tiger = penis, a not infrequent euphemistic substitution (as in the movie title "Tiger Makes Out"), two sexual readings are possible. The first makes the automobile = penis, thus the anatomical metaphor driver:auto:gasoline::man:penis:semen. The second makes instead automobile = woman, a common equation supported by English gender ("she is a beauty") and stresses the verb "put . . . in" of the slogan: auto:gas tank:pump:gasoline::woman:vagina + womb:penis:semen. The two readings contradict each other, with auto = penis in one, auto = woman in the other. But this is an ambiguity that is exploited in advertising where a woman is pictured next to or reclining against the automobile being promoted. And despite the contradiction both instances have identical core associations: tiger equal to penis which is then related to semen metonymically as container + agent is to container + product, and thence, via the overall analogy, to gasoline.

More singular, yet encountered, are external metaphors that arrange terms anatomically on one side and taxonomically on the other. Thus, the Philippine Ilongot (M. Z. Rosaldo, 1972) use the anatomical set of body parts to designate varieties of orchids. Of nineteen varieties identified by the Ilongot, fourteen are called by body parts or by objects associated with the body. Thus, Rosaldo gives as glosses such terms as "their thighs," "their knees," "their necklace," etc. The link between the two domains, orchid and body, is suggested by the descriptive definition of orchids as "plants which stick to trees and have thighs" and is, moreover, rooted in the association between orchids and the body of a spirit called *lampung*.

One example of a complex mix which runs the reverse of the orchid case (the discontinuous side is taxonomic rather than anatomic) is when the sexual organs are designated as independent persons. This occurs in dreams where the penis is the "little man," in many American Indian myths where trickster's penis is his "younger brother" and again in D. H. Lawrence's *Lady Chatterley's Lover* where for penis and vagina we get John Thomas and Lady Jane (the title for the second but not for the third more familiar version of the book). Although this might all be thought of as one of those infrequent synecdoches that substitute whole for part—little man (etc.) for penis, we prefer to read it as an external metaphor mainly because the substitution implies a clear shift in domain; a particular person or type of person substitutes for a particular body part. We start the external analogy with an anatomical synecdoche and finish it with a taxonomic metonymy: trickster:his penis::trickster:his younger brother.

THE INTERPLAY OF EXTERNAL AND INTERNAL METAPHORS

We have been careful to separate external from internal metaphors. For the purposes of presentation this is entirely appropriate. However, given particular cases the possibilities for mixing the two types are unlimited. Almost any equation can be read and expanded either way.

George the Lion, our internal metaphor, becomes an external metaphor as soon as we look beyond what George and a lion share to how each relates to its respective domain. "Put a tiger in your tank" is a highly colored internal metaphor, but it is also, when we choose to make it so, an external metaphor, both taxonomic: fiercest animal/gasoline, and anatomical, when we take into account the implicit human component. Consider these examples:

1. Most of the external metaphors that make use of body parts or house parts illustrate this kind of mix. As soon as we designate the monarch as the head we tend to postulate shared features, primarily those of function, that link the two terms. Head = monarch can now stand alone as an internal metaphor, independent of the notion of the overall domains of which each is a part.

2. An internal metaphor can produce an external metaphor which in turn permits, via opposition, another internal metaphor. The equation "you = a summer's day" immediately implies "someone else = a winter's day," that is, you are to someone else as summer is to winter. By taking certain liberties with our literary heritage, and by systematically inverting the shared features lovely/ugly, temperate/intemperate, May/December, etc. we can produce an inverted "variant" of Shakespeare's XVIII sonnet. Thus:

> Shall I compare thee to a summer's day?
> Thou art more lovely and more temperate:
> Rough winds do shake the darling buds of May,
> And summer's lease hath all too short a date:
> Sometime too hot the eye of heaven shines,
> And often is his gold complexion dimmed;
> And every fair from fair sometime declines,
> By chance or nature's changing course untrimmed;
> But thy eternal summer shall not fade,

. . . .

becomes:

> Shall I compare thee to a winter's day?
> Thou art more ugly and less temperate:
> Warm winds arrest December's cold display,
> And winter's gloom hath all too short a date:
> Sometime too fair the eye of heaven shines,
> And often is his mean complexion dimmed;
> And every foul from foul sometime declines,
> By chance, or nature's changing course untrimmed;
> But thy eternal winter will not fade,

. . . .

It was precisely this form of travesty that Ezra Pound used in the opening lines of "Ancient Music" to change "summer is i-cumen in/ Lhude sing, cuccu" into "Winter is icummen in,/ Lhude sing Goddamm."

3. Usage of the moment will often determine whether a particular example is to be taken as an internal or as an external metaphor. This is especially true for the Cuna when, for instance, chiefs are likened to one of two types of tree, the Ikwa and the Isper. The opposition afforded by the trees: fruit, etc. of limited access/fruit, etc. of general access provides a contrast between the elitest versus the generous and democratic behavior of different chiefs: Ikwa:Isper::elitist:democratic. However, the criteria of opposition in their major dimensions are common to both human and plant domains and as a result each tree and its correlated type of chief can form an independent, internally defined metaphor. A Cuna can talk of an Isper chief without referring to some other Ikwa chief. The opposition is implicit, but if the context of discourse does not require it, it can be entirely ignored. Taken in isolation, in fact, the Ikwa can even lose at least some of its negative associations which would otherwise be present if the Isper was taken into consideration (cf. Howe, Chapter 5, note 11).

4. Hyena, in the Kaguru folktales (Beidelman 1975), provides an interesting case. As we have said earlier Hyena represents a clearly felt internal metaphor. It is a new entity composed of characteristics shared by the animal hyena and a category of unsocial, usually stupid, and entirely bad people. In contrast Hare seems to be the result of a simple container/contained transfer, with the animal providing the container and the clever and tricky, but socially acceptable people providing what is contained. The animal hare and "clever" people appear to share few, if any, features; and the new entity, Hare, rests solely on the overall external analogy, hyena:hare::stupid people: clever people.

Not all metaphors convert easily from one type to the other, a fact that apparently holds true for both totems and proverbs. These are external metaphors where the correlated terms do not share specific features in common. In totemism a particular social group is simply juxtaposed with its totem or placed in some form of metonymic relationship as when a totem is said to be the ancestor (cause) of its clan (effect). If an internal metaphor is so postulated that the social group is said to be like its totem, then the whole totemic system runs the risk of breaking down and of losing its organizing effect. This is the situation Lévi-Strauss refers to in *The Savage Mind* (1966a) where for the Chickasaw members of different clans were said to resemble in behavior the habits of their clan labels: "The Raccoon people were said to live on fish and wild fruit, those of the Puma lived in the mountains, avoided water of which they were very frightened and lived principally on game. The Wild Cat clan slept in the daytime and hunted at night, for they had keen eyes; they were indifferent to women . . . etc." (118). The upshot was that if the Raccoon Clan is so raccoonlike, how could there be any meaningful relationship with the Wild Cat clan? For this reason Lévi-Strauss sees here not so much a totemic system but instead an endogamous caste system masquerading as totemism.

In proverbs two correlated terms share only the kind of relationship each holds with its respective complement. The proverb "where there is smoke there is fire" (smoke:fire) is similar to its contextual referent (accusing people:corrupt official) because each side makes use of a cause and effect relationship: smoke is caused by fire, people making accusations are caused by the presence of a corrupt official. The criteria, however, that make fire cause smoke are not shared by those that make a corrupt official cause accusations. For this reason we cannot speak of smoke as sharing any features internally with accusing people or fire with corrupt officials.

EXTERNAL METAPHOR AS SYSTEM

Once an external metaphor is set out as an opposition, further metaphors can be developed from the original simply by adding to or slightly altering the criteria of opposition. It is precisely this process that Lévi-Strauss has shown to operate in myth, and anyone looking for illustrations need only refer to his monumental work on South American mythology. One example, not from myth but from political rhetoric, will serve our present purposes. Hawk versus dove represents an ideal avicular opposition in that it is based on such clear criteria as: killer/nonkiller, carnivore/herbivore, high flying/low flying, screechy voice/cooing voice, etc.[14] As we all know this opposition has been correlated with differing attitudes toward the United States' military involvement in Vietnam so that those favoring an aggressive warlike policy are linked with hawks, while those favoring peace go with doves, thus hawks:doves::aggressive policy:pacific policy. The correlations, warlike with hawk, peacelike with dove, are founded on internal metaphors and are hence nonarbitrary. Consequently we cannot reverse the

14. The opposition is clearly felt on a purely phonological level as well. The CVC forms [hawk]/[dəv] provide two consonantal, [hk]/[dv], oppositions: voiceless/voiced; back (glottal, velar)/front (dental); plus an opposition in sequence, fricative + stop (h+k)/stop + fricative (d+v).

terms to get a warlike dove and a peacelike hawk without involving ourselves in irony. Both domains share at least one criterion, killer/non-killer, and besides the dove is firmly established in Western thought as equated to peace, quite as the hawk, and its cousin, the eagle, are associated with conquest and aggression.

To this avicular opposition a rather cyincal wag offered the following alteration: "It is not hawk versus dove, but rather vulture versus chicken." We now have a set of four terms which are, as Lévi-Strauss puts it, in varying degrees of opposition and correlation. The domain of birds has been broken down so that each term occupies a position in a fourfold set. The main criterion that correlates hawk with vulture in opposition to dove and chicken is carnivore/herbivore and the one that aligns chicken and vulture against dove and hawk is dependence/independence. Hawks and doves obtain their own food and live completely apart from humans. (We must keep doves apart from pigeons, semantically if not biologically.) Chickens are domestic and are fed by their keepers and vultures eat carrion, meat they themselves have not killed. Also, though wild, vultures in contrast to hawks frequent the periphery of human habitations. Thus, dependence/independence can be also read as associated with/not associated with humans.

In order to maintain the nonarbitrariness of the overall metaphor we must identify types of people who will correspond to chicken and vulture. We have noted already that hawk and dove share the criterion of killer/nonkiller with the corresponding warlike and peaceful people. If we now use the distinction of dependence/independence to locate types of people we can identify vultures as those who are dependent on other's doing the killing (patriotic fathers who send their sons to war) and chickens with those who rely on others to refuse killing (pro-

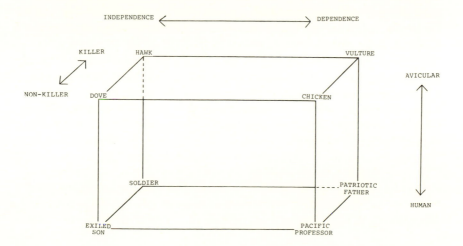

fessors who encourage their sons into exile or jail). Vulture used in this context parallels closely its independent use as an internal metaphor in such epithets that label certain professions dependent upon the misfortune of others. This would not only be undertakers who literally wait for you to die, but also doctors and lawyers who await some physical or social mishap to befall so they may peck your pockets clean. The independent use of chicken = coward fits very well also, and thus a hawk might see a fit linking of the dependent peacemaker with a cackling or crowing professor (cf. the accompanying diagram).

THE REPRESENTATION OF EXTERNAL METAPHORS

An external metaphor has many forms of overt representation, too many to elaborate here in any detail. At a minimum, like an internal metaphor, we can have the topic and one of the discontinuous terms. Many proverbs are of this sort: "one paddle leaves early" ("many paddles leave late" implied), although others give both (or all) discontinuous terms: "when the cat's away/the mice will play." Proverbs never state the continuous terms, which are always implied by the topic (the boss and his subordinates for our latter example). "I am a bear" (i.e., of the bear clan) states two terms, one from each side of the analogy, that are in juxtaposition. The other terms, "he is a fox," etc., are implied by the topic which would be about clan membership. This representation should not be confused (as it was by Levy-Bruhl [1910]) with the full expression of an internal metaphor, as "we are macaws." At the most all the terms, from both sides of the metaphor, can be stated as in the folk song: "Ida Red, 'bout half grown/Jumps on a man like a dog on a bone" (i.e., Ida Red:man::dog:bone). The kind of representation identified by Aristotle for an external metaphor (analogic in his terms) makes a crossover. With the analogy $A_1:A_2::X_1:X_2$, A_1 goes with X_2 and A_2 goes with X_1.

For example, the cup of Dionysus corresponds to the shield of Ares; so the cup will be called the shield of Dionysus, and the shield the cup of Ares. Again, old age is to life as the evening is to the day; so the evening will be called the dying day, or old age, as Empedocles called it, the evening of life, or the sunset of life. (*Poetics*, chap. 21)

This format is commonly used to identify a member of one domain in terms of a corresponding member in another. A philosopher might want to know the precise position among composers of, say, Charles Ives. His informant who knows both domains (of philosophers, of composers) might reply with "he is music's Charles Peirce" which would be based on the analogy Ives:music::Peirce:philosophy, and would imply and also identify for an otherwise unknowing musician that Charles Peirce is "philosophy's Charles Ives."[15]

CONCLUSION

To end with hyperbole:

A package of cigarettes is set out against a background of exciting social activity—lovers running along the beach, cowboys driving their cattle. What are we to make of this juxtaposition? How can we place the disparate terms, the cigarettes and the background, so that the relationship between them is something other than arbitrary? Are the cigarettes the cause (smoke, then go), the effect (work, play, then relax with a smoke), or are they a distinctive *part* of the *whole* scene? Or are the cigarettes the "totem" of the cowboys (lovers), thus forming an external metaphor where Brand X cigarettes:cowboys (lovers):: other Brands:noncowboys (nonlovers). Whatever the relationship chosen (and there are others besides) all are possible.

The more remote the terms are from each other—and cigarettes and cowboys, or gasoline and tigers are hardly close—the greater are the possibilities for making a variety of nonarbitrary connections. This fact was fully understood by the surrealists (the philosophical ancestors to modern advertising) who hold as a major tenet the value of arbitrary juxtaposition as a way of achieving "a spark" leading to a fuller, more than real, insight into reality (Breton 1969:passim). We might mention here a game invented by André Breton (described in Caillois 1968) called "one in the other" which Breton considered a perfect demonstration of the possibility of arbitrary linking. Briefly: a player leaves the room and secretly assumes a name (continuous term)—a staircase. In his absence his friends decide on another name (discontinuous term)—a bottle of champagne. On his return the player must then convey the term staircase to his audience without mentioning staircase and solely in reference to a bottle of champagne: "I am a bottle of champagne that . . . ." This proceeds until the audience guesses that staircase is the word. "Thus in the course of the game a terrier was described as a flowerpot, a lock of hair as an evening gown, a sorcerer's wand as a butterfly, a leer as a partridge, a shooting gallery

15. The implicit grounds for the parallel between Ives and Peirce would include their both being: uniquely American; mainly self-taught; highly original, though sometimes erratic and undisciplined; difficult to understand; largely ignored during their lifetimes, and discovered as truly great only posthumously.

as a church porter, Mme. Sabatier as an elephant's tusk . . . etc." (Caillois 1968:149).

We can conclude from all this that the interpretation and solution of arbitrary (i.e., nonsyllogistic and nonanalytical) juxtapositions is a form of riddle solving where the types of linkages developed follow the processes that we have identified with rhetorical tropes, with metaphor, synecdoche and metonomy. Hardly a new idea since we read in Aristotle: "Good riddles do, in general, provide us with satisfactory metaphors: for metaphors imply riddles, and therefore a good riddle can furnish a good metaphor" (Rhetoric, III, 1405b).

At the onset of this chapter we disabused ourselves of metaphor as a kind of verbal game, and now, with surrealistic insight, we are at games again. But there has been a development. What was then a game of "one *for* the other" has become a game of "one *in* the other." The metaphoric (and by extension synecdochic and metonymic) process is not a simple game of substitution, but rather a creative game where the pregnant (Empson's word) interplay of two disparate terms provides insight that, although it might at times be trivial (Put a tiger in your tank), can also be, as with "we are macaws," profound and revealing of important and deep cultural understandings. So basic is metaphor to creative thought that Ortega y Gasset went so far as to define it cosmologically as "an instrument necessary for the act of creation, which God forgetfully left . . . in the inside of one of his creatures, as an absentminded surgeon sews up one of his instruments in the belly of his patient."[16]

---

16. Translated and cited by Ardener (1971:458).

The Social Functions
of Rhetorical Forms

J. CHRISTOPHER CROCKER*

In this chapter we consider the social uses of the metaphor and of other tropes. Our objectives are twofold: to provide a theoretical background for ethnological inquiry into social rhetoric, such as illustrated by the essays in this volume; and to demonstrate the rewards (and difficulties) of such research in terms of some basic issues in social anthropology. The major problem is just what are the purposes of metaphor, and thus how should we understand the intentions of nonliteral speech? Or, if tropes are very complex semantic means, what social ends do they serve, if indeed we should regard them as "functional"? In trying to answer these questions we first examine the larger issues of the social use of all language, especially as it is employed to further a speaker's motives. We then proceed to search for associations between different kinds of motives, or between different sorts of problems confronted by speakers, and the various properties of specific rhetorical forms, as outlined in the first chapter. We do not attempt an exhaustive survey of either precedent or contemporary work in this muddled field, but indicate, from time to time, how our views relate to various modern anthropological perspectives.

Kenneth Burke has elaborated a systematic vision of the social use of metaphor based on the premise that *all* human action involves

* We would like to acknowledge with appreciation the many valuable insights and comments offered during the preparation of this chapter by Messrs. James Peacock, John Wilson, Peter Huber, Robin Carter, Richard Huntington, Marc Schloss, and Joseph R. Crocker, Jr.

purpose, or motive in the full, classical sense of *Action*. "To study the nature of the term, *act*, one must select a prototype, or paradigm of action. This prototype we find in the conception of a perfect or total act, such as the act of 'the Creation'" (1945:66). Since, in Burke's view, language itself is action, every one of its particular and local manifestations is to be understood as purposive, in all the motivational and "creative" complexity of that term. For any linguistic performance the loci of these motives are to be sought in terms of what Burke calls the "dramatistic pentad," the relation among "scene," "act," "agency," "agent," and "purpose" (Burke 1945:xv–xxiii). These views provide the starting point for this inquiry into the social functions of figurative language. We shall first be concerned with the purposive elements as Burke sees them, in terms of their eminent "classifying" nature, as involving such matters as "entitlement," "perspectives by incongruity," "disguise," "identification," and especially "persuasion."

In his suggestion that "language is equipment for living" (1957: 253–62), Burke draws our attention to the ways in which the applications of categories to particular situations constitute strategies for handling ("acting") these social engagements. In his view, the mere act of defining something through labeling implies certain attitudes and behaviors appropriate to that definition, all the more so when the designation involves the felt, expressive, connotative elements inherent in all tropes. Anthropologists have long recognized this principle in their studies of social classification, and somewhat more recently, certain of us have considered other limited aspects of behavior in such a perspective. Mary Douglas, in her important book *Purity and Danger* (1966), takes a highly Burkean approach toward pollution (or "disorder"), viewing it as disturbance of a society's categorical system. She expresses the not uncommon view that "symbolic enactment. . .provides a focusing mechanism, a method of mnemonics and a control for experience. . . .A ritual provides a frame. The marked off time or place alerts a special kind of expectancy, just as the oft repeated 'Once upon a time' creates a mood receptive to fantastic tales" (1966:63).

According to this approach, symbolic activity does more than merely express reality: it actively structures experience. Without the codified, iconographic ordering of time and place, for example, we become confused, disoriented, unable, in one sense, to act at all.[1] But Burke extends this relatively commonplace commitment to symbolic utility far beyond the point most anthropologists have been willing to accept, through his

---

1. By iconographic we mean those conventional material representations in which meaning and mode (instrument) are nonarbitrary or motivated and inseparable. There is a general difficulty in segregating such concrete "images" and their verbal correlates that we have not treated here.

constant stress that *all* linguistic acts are ritualistic, or symbolic, in this sense of determining experience. In his interpretation, even the simplest, most automatic "naming"—identification—places an entity, a topic, or a context in a semantic perspective which prefigures response. Burke's position requires some amplification if it is to assist us in going beyond the old anthropological truism that cultural values are implicit in definitions, that different languages define the character of reality in different ways.

Burke (1966:44–55) insists that "definitions," or, in his terms, "identifications," "terministic screens," are strategies for handling existential moments, and that the semantic character of rhetorical devices is an intrinsic part of such handling. He would have us recognize that the definitional process is often far from an autonomous, objective matching of labels to events and objects. Such matching, he says, is semantic meaning, which attempts to give a thing's "address" in the universe, or a set of instructions that somehow "point it out." Such unequivocal clarity is the logical positivists' ideal, and is embodied in most scientific languages. Poetic meaning, on the other hand, involves attitudes and has meanings which are not mutually exclusive nor empirically testable. Burke characterizes the difference between the two as congruous with that between "observation" and "participation," a contrast which he admits is difficult to maintain. Social scientists often have a bias toward debunking "poetics" and "participation" as based solely on emotion, and for that reason to be mistrusted. Yet surely we do not believe men are stirred to action by reading some version of the periodic tables, *unless* they take these to be in some way perceived analogies for other kinds of reality. The problem is, as Burke notes, that through the dialectical genius of language we tend to oppose semantic and poetic meaning, whereas they mutually amplify each other, dealing with two dimensions of reality, the classified and the felt (1957:121–44).

In recent years, Burke has suggested that since all classifications imply at least certain attitudes, poetic meaning is basic rather than derived. Or, as he says, "Every perspective requires a metaphor, implicit or explicit, for its organizational base" (1957:132). He proposes to see the problem not so much in terms of "words as signs of objects," but rather, of "objects as the signs of words" (1966:361). He refers to the latter perspective as "entitlement," and urges that by it, "language be viewed, not directly in terms of a word-thing relationship, but roundabout, by thinking of speech as the 'entitling' of complex nonverbal situations (somewhat as the title of a novel does not really name an object, but sums up the vast complexity of elements that compose the novel, giving it its character, essence or general drift)" (1966:361). He goes on to show that even apparently objective "literal descriptions" are more like titles than empirically grounded statements.

For example, it is impossible to "visualize" such sentences as "The man walked the dog around the tree," since we do not know if the man is short or tall, sauntering or dragging the dog or being pulled by it, if the dog is white, brown, or black, who is lurking about in the background, nor whether the tree is in the city or in the country. A purely literal description would have to specify all the "conditions that would be required for the thing named really to happen or exist" (1966:361). This may be the aim of scientific language, but, as noted above, Burke finds it absurd to characterize the entirety of speech sheerly in these purely objective terms. Now, in our and Burke's view, many "key words," entitlements and some tropes can be understood as abbreviations of various titles, or as varieties of "titles of titles." Through a series of such condensations, one gets universals: "man," "walk," "dog," "tree," "with individual men, dogs, and trees serving as particularized instances or manifestations of the 'perfect forms' that are present in the words themselves (which so transcend any particular man, dog, or tree that they can be applied universally to all men, dogs, or trees)" (1966:361). We might note, following points raised in Chapter 1, that while metaphors do "entitle," they do so by shifting domains, by redefining not through generalizing but by *specifying*. They stipulate that while this given man may be an instance of the universal *H. sapiens* class, he also shares certain attributes with other quite distinct forms ("independent carnivore" with "hawks") which delineates his membership in a sub-category of "types of men." Metonymy, on the other hand, entitles by "totalizing" a situation in terms of all the contiguous, nonessential elements which distinguish it from other situations and from generalizations of the distinct components which make it up. Recall the example in Chapter 1, "The Fords stepped on it"; this focuses not on the universal titles "men," "cars," "qualities required to win races," but on particulars that approach a literal description.

THREE LEVELS OF MOTIVES

Burke's notion of entitlement requires us to see situations, or things, as functions of what is said about them, rather than the other way around. Such neo-Platonism enmeshes us with a number of tangled philosophical issues which cannot be unwound in this context.[2] Our

2. Leach, Horton, and Needham have variously considered some of these issues within an anthropological context; in philosophy, the relevant authors appear to be Kant, Wittgenstein and Hampshire.

intent here lies in the implications for ethnographic analysis of Burke's insights concerning the interactive, mutually defining relations between linguistic forms and social contexts. Thus, one such implication is a view of "rhetorical entitlement" as that process whereby actors attempt to provide some linguistic truth about a social situation which summarizes its moral essence in such ways as to define possible actions. Seitel in Chapter 3 seeks to demonstrate how traditional proverbs function in this manner, specifically utilizing Burke's concept of "literature as equipment for living" as a "way in" to the social uses of proverbs. As he clearly shows, the critical aspect of the process involves the matching up of a stock saying to a particular transactional context which is anything but an automatic "naming." The notion of entitlement as strategy for living helps us unravel the complexities of this matching, first by distinguishing three kinds of "strategies" at work in the process.

First, in terms of the social context in which a rhetorical statement is used (Seitel's "interaction situation," Chapter 3, below) we are interested in the "strategy," or "motivation" of the particular speaker. Assuming the most embracing rhetorical motive to be persuasion, the question becomes a quite ordinary one: "What is he trying to get alter to do, and which of his own ends might be served by such action?" As Seitel demonstrates, answers to these kinds of query are far from easy, and depend on understanding precisely the relation of the semantic content of the trope to the interactional situation. He is able to show that, among the Haya, the speaker's strategy is either to sustain peaceful interaction through attaining consensus, or to damage the addressee's reputation and self-esteem, often terminating interaction. The effect of such proverbs as "One paddle leaves early" is to reassure an audience that departure is necessitated by external material conditions rather than by difficulties in the interactive situation itself. It expresses the speaker's attitude toward the relationship between alter and himself, and intends to assure future peaceful transactions.

Second, in terms of the wider social situation to which the statement has reference (Seitel's "context situation"), it is a prescription for action, an answer to the issue, "What shall we do about this?" "This" may be a corrupt politician, or a moral ambiguity, or an intellectual quandry, or simply problems in the maintenance of interpersonal "face" and demeanor, as recently illuminated by Goffman (1967:15–23). But in all cases "this" is the narrated event, not the interpersonal context of the speech event; it is what you and I are talking about. The rhetorical strategy here is a stereotyped "answer" for a general class of situations, an answer which, in intent, codifies social opinion on these problems.

Now, of course, the speaker may be discussing the relationship between himself and his audience, and then no distinction exists between the first and second kind of strategies. Or, more subtly and probably more commonly, the speaker's strategy is to express an attitude toward some "external" context in a trope which at once "entitles" that context, and abets his intentions vis-à-vis the audience. Howe shows in his chapter how many of the sayings employed by a Cuna chief resolve various sorts of social problems and, in so doing, add to the chief's own prestige as a "problem solver," which in turn relates to the first "personalistic" strategy. Finally, we might suppose that if two Haya are discussing a third's abrupt farewell, one might subsequently declare, "One paddle leaves early" to cope with a bit of rudeness in a fashion that has no relevance to the speech event. But this merges on the third tactic.

In terms of the entire cultural system, the rhetorical device itself (Seitel's "proverb situation") is to be vewed as a third and wholly semantic strategy, as a verbal codification of meaning which is part of the society's repertory of semantic techniques for expressing "the truth of things." At their most fixed and universalistic level, tropes exist quite aside from their application to contexts, whether narrated or interpersonal. Riddles are often such cases of "pure meaning," and various word games, puns and other exercises in symboling, likewise are context-free. Presumably most Haya regard "one paddle leaves early" as a universalistic truth independent of any human situation. However, proverbs and most of these "semantic strategies" are applied to both narrated events and interaction contexts. At the same time, most of the things said about these two last situations do not involve the rhetorical "truths" of the third level. Clichés are the best example: compare our "well, I've got to go—it's getting late" to "one paddle leaves early."

We can arrange these three strategies as follows:

Situational Strategy	Speech Event Actors and Context	Strategy of Statement
1. Interaction (Interpersonal)	Me and You	Persuasion of You
2. Context (Narrated)	We and This	Prescription of This
3. Rhetoric (Proverb)	We and That	Proclamation of That

Anthropologists have commonly focused on the third level of strategy in considering certain metaphors as "ways in" to the basic premises and values of a society, but have usually omitted all dimensions of the first, and frequently the second, kinds of strategy, which might be jointly termed as "contextually performative strategies." Our initial point is that analysis of rhetorical entitling involves the examination of the relationships among all three types of strategies. This cannot be sufficiently emphasized. A great deal of past work on this topic has been misleading when not actually mistaken, because one or the other of these strategies has been stressed to the virtual exclusion of the others. We will argue that only an encompassing, "dramatistic" approach can begin to unravel the complexities of how rhetoric socially works, or just as importantly, how it does not work.

Clearly this "work," the social functions of metaphor, tends to revolve around questions regarding the reasons for its being *felt*. It should be obvious by now that only those metaphors (or other kinds of tropes) which are so received can be employed as entitlements. Burke, in dealing with the same issue of how one might determine the "truth" or "goodness" of a metaphor, has a similar view. If there might be a contest among various metaphors, he suggests that we judge them by the degree of their "filling out" the context. "*Let each say all he can* by way of giving body to the perspective inherent in his choice. Let each show the scope, range, relevancy, accuracy, applicability of the perspective, or metaphor, he would advocate" (1957:127). The crucial test of the felt, or in his terms "good" metaphor, is that one can do more with it: "He could integrate wider areas of human relationship" (1957:127).[3] There is more to the issue than this, however, and much of the rest of this commentary involves consideration of just what kinds of summarizing make effective entitlements. That is, we want to explore how a particular trope works in a given social context.

WAYS OF RELATING THE THREE STRATEGIES

While it is not our main purpose to add still more jargon to the already overburdened syntax of anthropological discourse, we find that terminological clarity is nevertheless needed in the tripartite context just raised, which is especially opaque and complex. We find three dichotomies useful for this purpose. The first involves the distinction, derived by Jakobson (1957) from Otto Jespersen, between *shifters* and *non-shifters*. Briefly, in grammar any utterance involves (a) the event being talked about, what Jakobson calls the narrated event or Seitel the context and proverb situations, and (b) the social event of the actual utterance, one person talking to another; this Jakobson calls the speech event and Seitel the interaction situation. Any grammatical

---

3. This criterion obviously replicates the frequently reiterated criterion for "scientific" explanations, that they should be elegant paradigms. The difference, just as clearly, concerns the "felt" quality of metaphor.

device that links the two events, speech and narrated, is a *shifter,* while devices that concern only the narrated event is a *non-shifter.* George talking to John is a speech event, what they are talking about, say the price and purchase of tea at the A & P, is the narrated event. Thus, person and tense are shifters in that they are both relative to who is speaking and when, while gender and number are determined by the topic being discussed. In the latter instance, no matter whether John or George is doing the talking, whoever purchased the tea in the narrated event remains as masculine and as singular. In the former case, person "shifts." If George bought the tea, then in talking about the purchase he will say, "I bought the tea"; if John replies, the "I" of the narrated event becomes "you": "you (i.e., George) bought the tea." Tense also shifts. It indicates when the narrated event took place vis-à-vis the speech event. "I bought the tea" tells us that the tea was bought before the speech event; "I'll buy the tea" tells us that the tea is yet, in relation to the speech event, still to be purchased. Aspect, in contrast, is a non-shifter. It indicates the manner by which the narrated action takes place and makes no reference to the speech event. "I always buy tea at the A & P" tells us that one is in the habit of buying tea, and whether such buying takes place prior, during, or after the speech event is irrelevant.

In terms of the three strategies just outlined, a rhetorical shifter directly relates the rhetorical dimensions of the "context situation" to the "interaction situation," so that some dimension of the relationship between speaker and listener is affected at least in personal intent, or rhetorical principle. A non-shifting figurative term asserts a relationship only between the "proverb (rhetorical) situation" and the "context situation," that social circumstance which is the topic of conversation. Thus, a non-shifter might just assert a rhetorical insight which has the quality of a semantic ("factual") verity: "it is the nature of George to buy tea at good ol' rip-off A & P."

Perhaps the simplest illustration of the difference involves our earlier contrast between proverbs and riddles. The former are usually employed in direct reference to the interactive context between speaker and hearer, as Seitel so copiously illustrates. Haya proverbs "shift" a mundane and highly particularized "me-you" context to the level of "that which must be," so that the specifically unique becomes an instance of the acceptedly universal. But the content of riddles is not conditioned by the social relation between speaker and hearer, nor by the topic under discussion (the "narrated event"). We have only a "riddle-telling situation" ("ask me a riddle and I'll reply. . ."), in much the same way we have a dirty joke-telling situation (the comparison is not idly chosen, as shall be seen below). The implications of the semantic content of the riddle are fundamentally irrelevant to both the "me-you" language event and to any wider topic "we" might be concerned with.

Now, of course, there are societies in which riddles and other nonshifters are employed with specific reference to either or both the interpersonal and the narrated situations, as has been shown in a most perceptive study by Maranda (1971). Further, many societies have contexts in which riddles are told to instruct children or initiates, when such genres are clearly meant to "shift." When riddles are used in this way, they might be called "proverb-riddles." Further, one can imagine social contexts in which a dirty riddle is "inappropriately" told to force a change in the relationship between speaker and hearer. Again, most folktales, myths, metaphorical parables and such are told for their own sake, that is, at the level of universalistic semantic truths, or are applied to some current social situation (second strategy), so that they are usually non-shifters. But, as Rattray with respect to folktales (1930) has demonstrated, a good storyteller frequently manipulates the plot and alludes to immediate situations so that the relationship between himself and the audience is affected. Parents reading bedtime stories to their children often do just the same, with deliberate intent to "shift" attitudes and concepts. Certain kinds of dogmatic figurative expressions such as those discussed by Crocker are in principle independent of any given social context, and are eminently non-shifters, yet they might well be invoked as "entitlements" of especially messy and recurrent social situations. While the rhetorical assertion "we are macaws" has principle reference to the fundamental status of Bororo males in a matrilineal world, it is not inconceivable that one man might employ it to entitle another's woeful account of his existential encounters with the inconsistencies of femininity.

Here we are mainly concerned with "shifters," and in particular those which combine all three levels. In pursuing this concern, another dichotomy is analytically useful, that between "global" and "particular" figures. The former have reference to the major cultural issues: human identity, the premises of effective action, the axiomatic categories of social life, and may bear as well on more "restricted" yet universally valid principles (within that society's range of concerns), such as the attributes of natural entities or the nature of clanship. Particular tropes, on the other hand, tend to be highly restricted in meaning and appropriate to only a few specific contexts. Riddles and proverbs, along with all manner of word games, jokes, puns, magical formulas, and "poetry," tend to be particular figures, while such dogmas as "we are macaws" are clearly "global." Again, the distinction is not an absolute one, since some rhetorical genres fall somewhere between global and particular.

The metaphors utilized by the Cuna chiefs in their counseling of the village have this characteristic, and Howe points out some of the analytic difficulties such ambiguity imposes. But the distinction does allow us to avoid considering *all* figurative language as equally important and socially fundamental. This does not imply that particularizing tropes are trivial, but asserts that their implications are quite different from those of global figures.

The last dyad is not as important for our purposes as the preceding two, and it has been sufficiently recognized in recent anthropological work (e.g., Hymes 1964:215–20) to preclude the necessity of any extended discussion here. It involves simply the distinction between creative and formulaic usages of figurative language, that between poetry and magical formulas. But recognition of this factor does not preclude the necessity of approaching the formula in very much its own terms, quite outside the performative dimensions of how it is utilized in social contexts. This point shall be discussed more fully later, after some other preliminary issues have been disposed of.

THE SOCIAL USE OF RHETORIC

This work, the summation of the strategies, is in the most general sense the purpose of all rhetoric: to persuade. Such persuasions necessarily involve a very wide variety of specific human motives operating in numberless contexts. As Burke says, rhetoric involves "strategies for selecting enemies and allies, for socializing losses,[4] for warding off evil eye, for purification, propitiation, and desanctification, consolation and vengeance, admonition and exhortation, implicit commands or instructions of one sort or another" (1957:262, cf. also 1964:109). Whatever the goals of the rhetorician, his tropes must persuade persons of the *truth* of his position. Most often, as Fernandez points out, this truth is not presented as a known fact, but through a semantic movement or transformation of meaning, as a "revelation" or new comprehension about the nature of things. No additional, previously unknown elements are added to the listener's knowledge of the empirical characteristics of things; rather, he is led to see their *natures* through their *relationships*. But, further consideration of this point would return us to the topics already discussed in the first chapter. We must now examine how the semantic elements in figurative language are related to their

4. This phrase remains obscure to us. By it, Burke appears to mean a semantic process whereby one is able to "discount" evidence counter to that sustained within the actor's position, through referring it to some presumed social necessity.

social functions, which is to say, to the service of those three strategies (interactive, contextual, rhetorical) already described.

We begin with the third (rhetorical) strategy in the service of the second, that related to the "context situation," or the issue: "What shall we do about this?" Burke's general assumption is that metaphors, and to a lesser extent, other tropes, can resolve ethical ambiguity or confusion by pointing up a "moral" through semantic incongruities. He particularly has in mind, at least initially, the curious transformation of meaning (i.e., the import of some situation) achieved by puns, and by extension, all humor. Certainly a great deal of comedy is essentially a rhetorical process which moves us to view things in a startling new way. Puns, for example, semantically "work" by linking two concepts, otherwise quite distinct, through phonetic criteria, thus forcing a recognition of a "two for one" novel truth. Burke utilizes the pun to illustrate what he means by "perspectives by incongruity." That is, "a word belongs by custom to a certain category. . . .The metaphorical extension of perspective by incongruity involves caustic stretching, since it interprets new situations by removing words from their 'constitutional' setting. It is not 'demoralizing,' however, since it is done by the 'transcendence' of a new start. It is not negative smuggling, but positive cards-face-up-on-the-table. It is designed to 'remoralize' by accurately naming a situation already demoralized by inaccuracy" (1964:94–95).

By entitling a difficult situation through applying what might seem an incongruous "metaphorical name" for it, actors can resolve their problems of how to act within its context. The "sublime" and the "ridiculous" are both ways of morally reordering the situation through a falsification of its "real" characteristics, terming it either a good deal more or considerably less than it literally is. Humor, other than the more ironic forms, relies on the belittling technique to save many social moments from utter disaster, which is to say the bewilderment and/or shame of the participants. But the incongruous need not be the ridiculous. Burke utilizes a nonverbal example, interestingly enough, from a painting, that of Grosz's bloated, gross war-profiteer having dinner with a dress manikin. The scene, with diner, chairs, tables, and dishes is quite "realistic" or congruous, but the manikin is utterly incongruous. The perspective afforded is that men of this type relate only to simulacra of women (1964).

Or, to take a somewhat more trivial example, suppose that at a cocktail party a male friend complains, "That son-of-a-bitch is sniffing around my wife," when the lusty fellow occupies some superordinate position toward both of you—your employer, for example. Here the incongruous perspective afforded by a metaphor as a particular shifter derives from the speaker's labeling the activity as inappropriate, sub-human behavior. By acting in such an animal fashion, the boss forfeits his humanly superior position and invites treatment appropriate to his "metaphorical" nature: "kick the cur." But you, tactfully shifting the character of what promises to be a most ambiguous scene, "retitle" it saying, "Oh, he's just an old goat." Dogs, by reason of their anomalous position as half-human, half-animal, are subject to moral rules appropriate to socialized beings which can be enforced by humans, such as not defecating in the house. At the same time, since they cannot be regarded as holding those rights of total moral responsibility characteristic of sentient beings, their punishments for moral infractions may be appropriate for "brute animals," such as beating. But goats occupy a position in the natural order which is parallel to, rather than convergent with, the social order. Since they are much further "out," in the realm of the entirely animal and amoral, they cannot be reproved for "doing what comes naturally."

These examples involve the persuasion gained through a new perspective which forces the recognition of some nonliteral aspect of the situation, a more-than-empirical "truth." Incongruous entitling, as "equipment for living," may arise spontaneously as a reaction to a particular interaction context. Artists, including poets and politicians, attempt constantly to provide new perspectives by devising particular incongruities for troubling situations. The rapid changes in popular slang ("dude," "wasted," "rip off") might be viewed in this manner, as efforts to entitle unique, nonreplicating social contexts and events, rather than as modish attempts to be "in."[5] Such efforts are creative, including the cocktail party caricature. In the societies discussed in this book, though, rhetorical devices tend to be standard elements in the social repertory of actors, and thus more formulaic or traditional, a fact, however, that does not diminish their creative or poetic quality in terms of the circumstances of usage. A proverb may be commonly known, but it still must be applied at a particular social moment. This involves a sense of "aptness," of timing and *gestalt* perception of context, which is just as creative as the coining of a new phrase. This dimension is clearly stressed in the chapters by Howe and Fernandez, where the chief and cult leader derive a fair amount of their prestige from their ability to mesh accepted traditional truths with social circumstances. In other terms, the distinctions between creative and formulaic tend to break down when shifters are utilized, when the alter is concerned not only with how well the story is told, but with its appositeness to the

---

5. Abrahams convincingly demonstrates how such verbal games as "playing the dozens" function to define status, affix guilt, establish the normative parameters of particular situations, and so forth (1970*a*, *b*).

situation at hand (here blending first and second strategies, "I" and "you" in relation to "that").

Such an emphasis on performance raises a difficult issue, since it requires the recognition of different competencies in performing. The joke may fall flat, the poet's writings remain so obscure as to exasperate his readers, the actor is booed off the stage, the chief is ignored. There seem to be at least two dimensions to this issue. The entitlement, the perspective by incongruity, must first be logically appropriate in just how it relates the third (rhetorical) level of strategy (the "proverb situation") to the situation at hand (the context, the interaction, or both). But it must also be "told correctly."[6] These two dimensions of figurative enactment are critical to analysis of the social functions of rhetoric, since auditors may not be persuaded to act in terms of any entitlement by incongruity *either* because it is logically inapposite to the situation, *or* because it is badly performed. But how can one tell which failure vitiates a performance? And still further, as Fernandez has implied in an earlier article (1966), judgments on the performance will vary among the actors, *both* as they perceive (or fail to "get the point of") the congruity of the incongruous, or react to the performance rather than the content. Fernandez resolves this dilemma by invoking a distinction between social ("performative") and cultural ("cognitive") responses, but in our view, as detailed at the conclusion of this piece, this skirts the issue. Finally, we must recognize that many delights of social life derive from the witnessing of highly skilled performances, without any necessary persuasion that the entitlements involved are the least relevant to one's own social context. A good storyteller, whether he is a tribal elder relating a myth, or a father rendering a bedtime story, may be appreciated for his own virtues. Such responses amount to a purely aesthetic judgment concerning how well some standardized text is delivered, without any consideration of its application to either oneself or some external context. The paradoxical conclusion seems to be that good performance makes a crucial difference *either* when it relates the perspective of some traditional universal truth to a parochial individual problem in which one has not been able "to see the forest for the trees," *or* when it elevates a text to the level of art-for-its-own-sake, which takes the audience (presumably) beyond all contexts, "out of oneself."

6. We are aware that such evaluations of "telling" depend partly on the general prestige accorded to the performer. One expects oneself to labor at the nuances of a poet who is generally acclaimed, or one has a predisposition to excuse the banalities of a "successful" comedian. Yet even in these cases entirely performative criteria are not irrelevant, as any critic (and probably nearly all performers) would testify.

Anthropologists have never been indifferent to "performance," considered as the manipulation of relatively standardized verbal forms to gain status and express personality (Evans-Pritchard 1948; J. R. Firth 1950). Nor have they been unappreciative of the delights of language-as-form, of the "poetic function" in which the various attributes of a communication system become exploited for their own sake (Jakobson 1960). There is consequently no dearth of literature on these matters (Hymes 1964:291–381). We have neither the space nor the data to offer any fresh insights into the character of these subtle topics. We would like to suggest that for the most part anthropologists have tended to treat them independently, so that "how" something is said is considered separately from "what" is said. Blending the two raises a number of methodological and theoretical problems, including one especially noted in the preceding two paragraphs: that the "success" of any trope (the degree it entitles) might depend on how well it integrates a figurative truth with the complexity of some social situation. The traditional anthropological wisdom has been to see persuasion as resulting *either* from a "good" performance of a conventional verbal act, *or* from the sheerly expressive power of a verbal formula (or material icon) which somehow states a basic paradigmatic and axiomatic "truth." Once again, we must defer to others to comment on how performance might affect the reception of such dogmas, and concentrate on problems in the latter formulation.

Our approach is predicated on the assumption that the social response to rhetoric is not an automatic, quasi-magical reaction to the "naming of a name," since the whole character of figurative language is directed away from such purely lexical and positivistic concerns. Rhetoric *persuades*; it engages the active intellectual attention, as well as the emotive responses of the listener. This is precisely its fascination and its difficulty, and unless we can demonstrate how a synecdoche or a metaphor can be at once *thought* and *felt,* we cannot show why it might entitle or shift. Our colleagues are surely on the right course when they explore the logical dimensions of the associations on which tropes are based. Yet we would urge them to recognize that rhetoric does something more than just encompass these dimensions: it creates them. If we are to pay any heed to Burke at all, we must acknowledge his insight in proclaiming the programmatic character of metaphor. That is, figurative language does not just *express* the pertinence of certain cultural axioms to given social conditions, it *provides the semantic conditions through which* actors deal with that reality, and these conditions are general to all social contexts and all actors within that society. Our purposes here, however, is not to set any structuralist "dogs" against some contextual "hares," for we must remember that in performance, the mesh connecting rhetorical ground, social context, and interactive situation is always problematic. The great issue remains the *relation* between linguistic/conceptual system and specific contexts/events (i.e., *langue* and *parole*).

METAPHOR AS A SOCIAL CODE

Fernandez, here and elsewhere (1972), has stressed how metaphor seeks to move an inchoate subject (continuous term) to the grounds of a known, choate object (discontinuous term). His examples are drawn from the intense fields of political debate and religious conversions, an entirely valid procedure since rhetoric tends to occur in these states of social and emotional *extremis* which require social confirmation for the continuance of personal integrity. Our extensions of his thoughts into more prosaic realms are intended to extend the range of his analysis.

To begin with, in many situations the inchoate is simply the familiarly dangerous, the implicitly known but explicitly denied, while the choate is a complex series of allusions and rhetorical conceits which provide the highly euphemistic terms in which this hidden area can be openly discussed. As noted earlier, in connection with Burke's position, comic metaphors often simply insist on naming the "truth" through an emphasis on the salient rather than the peripheral attributes of the known-yet-rejected. Such an expression as "thunder-pot" for chamber-pot is a comic metaphor very thinly disguised as a euphemism; it explicitly calls attention to the covert, and thus provides a harmless mode for its realization.[7] But this process occurs not by "naming names," for every society has adequately descriptive terms for those matters it publicly deems "unspeakable," whether these be scientifically objective or coarsely vulgar. Comic metaphors accomplish their social ends, we assume, by providing a perspective in which a threatening "this" can be discussed in terms of an aptly incongruous "that."

But, the allusive trope is by no means invariably a spontaneous one devised or inventively applied for a troubling situation. There are social contexts in which the unseemly *must be* described in terms of the seemly terms of an entirely rhetorical system. Perhaps the best known instances of such analogic systems are those in which aspects of sexuality are correlated with an elaborate cooking-food code. Although one might not wish to go to the extreme of Lévi-Strauss in asserting that

---

7. We wonder why more systematic investigations of indigenous verbal humor have not been made by ethnographers, or if some of the more blatantly illogical indigenous assertions so earnestly demonstrated to be elements in a rational system have not been intended as ironic exaggerations.

"there is a correlation between marriage rules and eating prohibitions" (1966:104),[8] nonetheless such correspondences are found in so many social systems as to pose a challenge for ethnographers (Needham n.d.). The scanty work on the topic so far seems to confirm Lévi-Strauss's suggestions that all metaphors on this theme are "existentially rounded," or "situationally based," in that their logic derives from quasi-ecological associations between the social placement, in socio-geographic terms, of animal/vegetable species, and of pertinent social categories. Generally, the logic seems to be that "near things" (people and living organisms) are "safe but prohibited" while "far things" are "dangerous but preferred."

For example, in his well-known article on "Animal Terms of Verbal Abuse" (1964), Leach constructed a continuum of analogic correspondences relating the physical spaces occupied by various domestic and wild animal species, to those spaces occupied by the household and by various social categories "near" or "far" from it. He could then form logical sets such as dog:fox::sister:sister-in-law, with the latter half (fox/sister-in-law) as not only good, but "fair game." Domestic pets are thus correlated with household members, barnyard creatures with such kinsmen as "cousins," and so forth. Of course there are complex reasons why certain species are associated with one area and not with others. Such indigenous reasonings involve a penumbra of connotative metaphorical elements, such as a domesticated animal's resemblance to a wild counterpart. Bulmer's (1967) analysis of why the cassowary is a metaphor for cross cousins as well as Crocker's and Sapir's essays here, further demonstrate that ecological/spatial association is only one aspect of the metonymic associations utilized in food-sexuality metaphors.

Thus, we should stress the flexibility in food, zoological, and even, for that matter, botanical reference systems. This is due to the changing, fluid nature of analogic, anatomical, and taxonomic logical relationships discussed in Chapter 1. It is a matter of definitional perspective just what parts are essential and invariant members of a whole, what is classified with what, what is "like" something else and in what ways. For example, a "dog" may be viewed as an essential part of the household, giving rise to whole series of metonymic associations. Or "dog's" taxonomic status can be emphasized, as with distinctions between pure-bred aristocrats and mongrels, to afford a series of metaphors. The

8. To be fair, Lévi-Strauss does not mean this as narrowly as it appears when taken out of context. He appears to stress the notion that there is a formal correspondence between taxonomic species which are culturally stressed in some manner, as by restrictions on the manner, place, and time of their consumption, and those relational categories similarly hedged about by "negative prescriptions." He does not claim, in our reading, that such correspondences *always* form a consistent analogic system.

symbol "dog" consequently breaks down into a wide range of figurative relationships, such as "man's best friend," "faithful as a dog," "cowardly cur," "bitch," and "puppy love."[9] Social and semantic context determines just what definitional perspective is involved in the figure, and it would be a fatal error to insist on any single association as primary.

In short, food, animal, and plant codes can be employed as metaphors for many inchoate and often unspeakable aspects of social nearness and distance besides those dimensions of exogamy, endogamy, and proper sex. The classic example of a dietary rule-social category analogic set is, of course, the Indian caste system, which we may assume Lévi-Strauss had very much in mind in his writings. As Mayer shows (1965: 33–52), the explicit rules determining which group can eat food prepared by another group express very neatly their respective ranks and degrees of classificatory pollution. In this case, the analytical utility, even necessity, of an understanding of the metaphorical code in deciphering the logic of the relationship system is quite obvious. But all too often, ethnographers seized with a touching faith in the objectivity of biological facts and perplexed by the complexity and subtlety of such semantic figurations have not bothered to explore them systematically. However, the postulation that the allusive range and flexibility of the figures just discussed can be compressed into formal analogical sets poses a real problem.

ANALOGIC SYSTEMS AND RHETORICAL PERSUASION

The preceding formal and ethnographic considerations raise a number of issues which we have chosen to ignore until now. Involved are the relationships between external and internal metaphors,[10] and systematic (semantic) and situational (interactive) strategies. It would be nice if we could discover a neat correlation between the first and second terms of these two dichotomies: that is, if we could assert that internal metaphors are commonly used to entitle limited personalistic situations, while external analogic systems are employed for recurrent major problems faced by the society. But such is by no ethnographic means the case. The tropes which entitle persistent social difficulties are sometimes drawn from a well-defined and restricted domain, such as those involving anatomical synecdoches, or other functionally integrated universes (such as cockfights [Geertz 1972]). But there is no

9. Burke has some deservedly famous comments on this issue (1966:73–75). Turner and Beidelman raise similar considerations (1966 and 1967 respectively).
10. We use here the distinction made by Sapir (above) between internal (genus-for-genus) and external (analogic) metaphors.

good reason to assume that, because of this, such metaphors form an analogic system, that the felt resemblance between the continuous and discontinuous terms is a matter of metonymic juxtaposition rather than perceptibly shared attributes.[11] Sapir raised this problem above in the consideration of totemism, which may or may not develop internal links between corresponding terms depending partly on context and frame of reference. Further, in every essay gathered in this volume, with the exception of Seitel's proverbs, internal metaphors predominate and the various authors demonstrate the surprisingly large range of situations that these can entitle.

The postulation of analogic systems as "codes," whereby the complexities of relationships between social entities can be manipulated in terms of paradigmatic unities, has served as an impetus to structural analysis in recent social anthropology. We have talk of transformations, the generative quality of the logical models embodied in myths, dazzling symbolic "equations" between all manner of highly distinctive entities. In keeping with the generally contextual emphasis of this volume, our concern is not with the elaboration of these conceptual systems as such, but with their relevance to people, situations, and things. Granted that the logic of any analogic system is a fascinating and seductive entertainment for sophisticated minds, such forms still must be demonstrated to have some relevance for those dull clods who have not had the advantage of advanced training in symbolic analysis. This is by no means an uncommon complaint. The usual structural demonstration of a logical matrix in which a "this" can be dealt with in terms of a "that," and where both are shown to be derivative from some basic logical model, has been roundly criticized for its irrelevance to the interactional setting. Southall, for example, objects to structural analysis in this way: "nor is there any suggestion of how, or whether, such transformations relate in any meaningful fashion to the societal interaction of groups of human beings or to the process of establishment, differentiation, and modification of ethnic and cultural identities" (Southall 1972:79). Our position is that metaphors and other tropes are the semantic modes through which such relationships and identifications are accomplished. Consequently we suggest that metaphor must be viewed not just as a way into the generative logical models of a society, but also as a way out, as ways people come to "understand" and, then, act.

But this is just where the problem of analogy intervenes. It is easy enough to comprehend why an internal metaphor is "felt" to entitle

---

11. Continuous and discontinuous term (tenor and vehicle) are defined by Sapir, above (p. 7).

some social puzzlement. The specification of common attributes in distinctive entities produces knowledge, while the awareness of what they do not share colors that understanding with connotative associations. To explain how this socially works involves exploring the figures' synecdochic and metonymic associations, as the following essays try to do. But what about analogic systems, based not on "first-felt resemblance" but metonymic contiguities? Are these felt, do they entitle in the same way, or are they merely "conceits?" Our initial response is that there are great differences in the social functions of the two forms of metaphor, but that for a variety of reasons, some of which have already been discussed, the metonymic relationships on which external metaphors are predicated tend to be transformed into relations of shared attributes, creating internal metaphors. The mechanics of this and the whole issue of the social efficacy of such hybridized analogic systems are exceedingly complex.

It has already been noted that often powerful analogies are built up on the basis of some especially apt internal metaphor. Let us first examine how an internal metaphor provides a "felt entitlement" in terms that might generate a more extensive analogic set. For an example that will not prove obtuse, we go to an extreme that runs counter to the usual canons of academic delicacy. By using a related series of sexual "entitlements" from our own culture, we can emphasize how the "felt" quality of metaphors depends very much upon their semantic complexity, not upon their "naming a name." Our example is the masculine entitlement for a perennially troubling situation: "I want pussy." Such a statement is usually restricted to male conversations, which is not without significance. This figure, in our view, is a combination of all three basic tropes. The initial demand is for sexual satisfaction through vaginal means, but a blatant statement of this in literalistic terms is not a satisfactory strategy for both social and psychological reasons. The situation can also be, and sometimes is, entitled as "I want a woman," which would be itself a generalizing synecdoche (whole for part) or metonymy (container for thing contained). The cat, through metonymic association, is commonly perceived as a part of a woman's world. Within the taxonomic class of cats, a small cat is commonly a "pussy cat." This sets up the analogy cat:pussy cat:: woman:vagina, in which the large/small dichotomy combines with the generalizing synecdoche (whole for part). This metonymic juxtaposition allows the metaphorical establishment of pussy for vagina, through the (again) synecdochically shared attributes of things small, furry, and, above all, vocally responsive to being stroked.

Another metaphor (derived, we think, from this basic one rather than the other way round), "making her purr with pleasure," is a quite proper and widely used entitlement for the consequences of various masculine gifts and services. But this phrase suggests that the reason why the "pussy" metaphor is felt as an appropriate entitlement is that the desired object is not a female organ, nor less the whole woman-person, but a highly responsive yet somehow "dehumanized" thing. Starting with this association, an analyst would have to go on to explore the entire range of shared attributes linking women and cats in American society. Clearly these shared attributes are complex and numerous enough to sustain great numbers of particular internal metaphors.

Now, given that an almost equal wealth of associations exists between men and dogs, and the ubiquitous metonymic propinquity of cats and dogs in American domestic experience, the analogy, man:woman::dog:cat is virtually unavoidable. The internal metaphors dominate so strongly that it is difficult to shift attention to how each set of terms relates to its own domain, the prerequisite for an external metaphor. Such a shift must be accomplished by stressing the logical dimensions of the terms, rather than dwelling on the "felt" transfers of the internal metaphors. That is, analogies must be "thought" rather than "felt." "Thinking" an external metaphor is a process that ignores the complex associations that identify two disparate terms and instead looks out to see how each term fits with others within its own proper domain. It establishes critical dimensions that are developed out of logical oppositions, correlations and the like, to produce a paradigm that is abstractly and globally "true" man:woman::dog:cat.

Clearly few anthropologists will wish to go to the trouble of puzzling out in such detail every bit of figurative language that comes their way, let alone trying to establish the complex relations between "internal" and "external" metaphors. The traditional, and entirely reasonable, tactic has been to select material which is at once appropriate to the ethnographer's analytical concerns, but restricted or circumscribed in import (Southall 1972:76–77). If one wishes to examine certain tropes that seem expressive of the society's attitudes toward such recurrent, global issues as the nature of clanship, one concentrates on tracing the semantic complexities of such internal metaphors as "blood" and "bone." Alternately, one's interest might be caught by a body of verbal materials which seem to have some extended logical order, so that an analogical structure can be elaborated as a pure "code" or "system of meaning," without much reference to its social correlations and applications. But what if one wants to do both, to examine the persuasive efficacy of an analogic system in terms of how it brings about felt identifications?

This problem involves one of the fundamental theoretical difficulties in the study of figurative language. Insofar as we concentrate on internal metaphors, we can equate the "persuasive" and "expressive" dimensions of tropes. Thus far in examining the social use of metaphor, we have tried to demonstrate the utility of such figures in defining situations so that attitudes are transformed and guidelines for behavior are established. But what of the "programmatic" capacity of metaphors, their function as *langue* through the capacity to form analogies in which a whole range of discrete "thises" are understood in terms of a series of metonymic "thats"? The problem with internal metaphors is that they are not systematic, they do not participate in any paradigmatic logical structure, so that analysis of a single figure must be worked out independently of any others, as with our "pussy" example. And once this has been done, what are the results? One special case has been illuminated, we understand one way in which the members of a society go about coping with one set of problems, but this comprehension may have no relevance to any other behavioral/epistemological premises entertained by the society. Surely a culture achieves consistency not by treating things and situations constantly in their own terms, but by signifying the character of their participation in a system.

Now, as we said earlier, this is not to deny that anthropologists have been able to demonstrate the social impact of certain analogic systems. But usually they have focused on these analogic sets based on internal metaphors, preeminently those with reference to the human body. Social scientists are far from the only humans to appreciate the systematic, functionally ordered "organic analogy" for the convincing rhetorical portrayal of social categories. It is by no means coincidental that some of the first insights concerning the social necessity of metaphor, and its analytical utility, derived from studies focusing on the human body as the discontinuous term for social principles (the continuous terms). Not only does the body provide systematic analogical categories, its functioning generates liminal entities which can serve as models for those processes which relate distinctive categories. Finally, the body is most surely "felt," an obvious dimension which helped those writers who emphasized its importance in social paradigms (Hertz, Douglas, Turner, not to mention Hobbes and other social philosophers) to convince their colleagues of the power of analogy. Things are not so easy for those artists or scholars who would explore the social impact of analogies based on nonorganic systems. The usual critical reception for them (we have Lévi-Strauss particularly in mind) has involved much complaining about the "arbitrary," "formal," and "remote" character of the analogic systems they postulate. Such a reaction doubts that "objective" logical parallels can be a socially effective base for persuasive rhetoric (a position that might have some merit if it were developed in these terms). The unexamined epistemological/ cultural assumptions that may be involved here deserve examination; perhaps some fundamental differences in Gallic and Anglo-Saxon attitudes toward mind and body might be clarified. But the general point is that most anthropologists have been skeptical about the social utility of figurative language unless it could be clearly shown to utilize "convincing," "bodily felt," internal metaphors.

But there is more than the critics' human proclivity for good (that is, internal) metaphors confusing the understanding of rhetorical logic. The fundamental issue in assessing the social impact of analogic systems is the formal possibility of their "reversibility." In nearly all internal metaphors, the continuous and discontinuous terms cannot be substituted for one another without a profound change in meaning. What is true about one for the other is not so when their positions are exchanged. "George the lion" means something entirely different from "the lion George"; by way of the transfer George is animalized but the lion is humanized, each with very different semantic results. Bororo men compare themselves to macaws, not macaws to themselves; but if they did, a whole new set of associations would be involved. Geertz says that, among the Balinese, an elaborate metaphor transfers perceptions from the realm of fighting cocks to that of men. "Logically the transfer could, of course, as well go the other way, but like most of the rest of us, the Balinese are a great deal more interested in understanding men than they are in understanding cocks" (1972:26). This appeal to the human propensity for egocentrism does not entirely resolve the issue. For one thing, in many social contexts the continuous term (the "inchoate tenor") is very often some eminently "natural" subject, with a known cultural object as discontinuous term ("vehicle"). Just as often, especially in such technological societies as our own, social categories provide both terms, as when we try to entitle an ambiguous political personage as a "used car salesman." The point is that the "inchoate," the topic one seeks to clarify by some sort of figurative airs above the literalistic ground, can involve practically any area of human concern. We speak of the lion as the king of beasts, of male and female electrical plugs. Perhaps the most entertaining instances in English of employing human attributes as vehicles for natural tenors are the old "nouns of venery," the collective terms for animal groups, such as the familiar "a pride of lions," a "school of fish," a "colony of ants" and some unfortunately dropped from vernacular usage: "murder of crows," "parliament of owls," "building of rooks," and "congregation of plovers" (the last examples are from Lipton 1968).

Now, the problem is that theoretically, rhetorical figures have the capacity of reversibility when they derive from, or participate in, an analogic system founded on external metaphors. Such reversals and substitutions need not be constant elements in the society's verbal codes; rather, they provide a fund of challenging possibilities to be elaborated in discourses and novel speculations. In Lévi-Strauss's analysis of totemic systems, for example, the logical contrasts between clans correspond formally to those between totemic systems; what a native or an analyst can say about relations between the bear and eagle clans applies just as well to contrasts between bears and eagles. For a metaphor is truly reversible only when what is said about one term is exactly the same as what is said about the other. This can occur only with external metaphors that preclude transfer and that are devoid of directional bias; for once any kind of identification of two corresponding terms creeps in, the entire system breaks down. The possibilities of reversal and substitution derive from the way that whole systems of differences are juxtaposed, with every one co-substantial with the others and thus "open-ended." Once the bear:eagle::clan B:clan E analogy is established, any number of additional terms can be added; the only requirement is that any new series involve logical contrasts among its own elements comparable to those already functioning. Not just animal species, but geographical orientations, physiological conditions, and entire cosmological orders can be included to form a multileveled system (as in "La Geste d'Asdiwal," Lévi-Strauss 1958). For these reasons external metaphors form a true paradigm which has the virtue of relating sets of discontinuous terms to one another, so that continuous ("inchoate") terms cease to exist, at least in terms of the analogic system itself.

The social utility of the analogic capacity derives, implicitly, from its ability to handle a virtually unbounded range of recurrent issues within a single paradigmatic formula. This systematic quality of analogies contrasts with the completely nonsystematic, narrow (but complex and intense) qualities of internal metaphors. In the example elaborated by Sapir (above, p. 29), the addition of the "vulture-chicken" contrast to the "hawk-dove" metaphor transformed it into an extended analogy and in so doing developed its capacity to entitle many types of contemporary political encounters, if not wider issues in American life. But now the question must arise, is this not really a case of internal metaphors, in which certain characteristics of vultures, hawks, and warmongers are perceived to congrue? And, if this is so, can the features of reversibility and substitution continue to operate? Just as importantly, can the analogic formula be fully systematic if it involves internal, "closed" metaphors?

Perhaps the whole issue can be summarized in the following way. External metaphors are theoretically systematic, reversible, and "thought";

internal metaphors are nonsystematic, irreversible, and "felt." The problem is the degree to which each of the three pairs of contrasting attributes is independent of the others, so that one might encounter a metaphor that was at once, say, felt, systematic, but irreversible. The crucial point seems to be the characteristics that cause an internal metaphor to be felt. As was shown in Chapter 1, internal metaphors involve the identifying of attributes of two usually segregated entities, a process which is termed "transfer" and is associated with the expressive "coloration" of these figures and with the way the terms are simultaneously apprehended as like and unlike. Since external metaphors involve no such equating of the two terms, they do not "transfer." It is just this lack of "color" which make many analogies appear so pedantic and formal, or at best, as in the case of many proverbs, somewhat abstract and remote "parallels." We deduce from this that when there is no identification (no transfer, no color), the metaphor is not felt but only "thought," which fits in with the programmatic, cognitive, systematic and "cold" characteristics of analogy that we have already noted. But, to reiterate a point from Chapter 1, once the external analogy is established all sorts of internal resemblances between the juxtaposed terms can be "discovered": to put it much too simply, "thinking" can generate "feeling," here as in other dimensions of human behavior.

But then the analogy seems to lose its systematic, reversible, and paradigmatic qualities. Once we know (or rather, "feel") just how similar hawks are to warlike men, and doves to peace-lovers, it becomes much harder to talk about the avicular universe in terms of human beings. It also becomes difficult to transform hawks into vultures, and doves into chickens. On the other hand, if attention is focused on the system qua system, the abstract binary dimensions (killer, nonkiller, dependent, independent) that define the paradigm are stressed, at the cost of specificity and, of course, transfer. For it is only at this level of generalized logical contrasts that the prerequisite for reversibility, that what applies to one term is exactly the same for the other, can be satisfied. And by maintaining thought on this level further systems or terms can be incorporated. Adopting Beidelman's Kaguru Hare and Hyena (1975) and our own "are you a lion or a mouse?" we can generate a reversible "thinking" paradigm that is devoid of the felt transfers and entitlements of internal metaphors:

	birds		mammals	
	dependent	independent	dependent	independent
killer	vulture	hawk	hyena	lion
nonkiller	chicken	dove	mouse	hare

$\longleftrightarrow$

Here *en pleine mythologique*, or at least the myth logic of Lévi-Strauss, is a process of cerebration that manipulates contrastive dimensions to form correlations and inversions, all in an effort to define and systematize categories of thought.

Since the new mammalian series could be added when the criteria for reversibility were stressed, one possible conclusion might be that the systematic attribute of analogic schemes is indissolubly bound up with their reversibility. Now, in Sapir's chapter we saw that a "transfer" is basic to feeling an internal metaphor, and we might therefore conclude the internal metaphors' three attributes of nonreversible, nonsystematic, and felt are in fact mutually dependent. But things are not so simple. Analogies may be formed from some kind of combination of internal with external metaphors, and just such examples are provided above by Sapir (pp. 25–27).

Nor is this the extent of the problem. There appear to be perfectly good external metaphors which are not capable of being meaningfully reversed or even systematized. Most proverbs involve such figures. Take the sentence "Where there's smoke there's fire," used to entitle scandal about corrupt politicians. Here smoke:fire::scandal:corruption, with the terms in each domain being related as cause-effect rather than as oppositions. Since the attributes of fire which cause smoke are completely different from the conditions which generate gossip about corruption, the terms do not share any common elements. These might be discovered however. For instance, someone might characterize a densely smoking pile of rubbish as "a Watergate," but then we would have a reasonably good internal metaphor, not a proverb. Now, proverbs might be considered peripheral to the issues raised here, since these figures usually concern quite particularized and isolated situations, while we are chiefly occupied with encompassing analogic systems of the totemic variety. The original question remains: can such systems retain their paradigmatic reversibility and systematization, and yet transfer, color, and "move"?

ANALOGY AND THE FIGURATIVE
REPRESENTATION OF POWER

To explore this problem further, we draw upon anthropological treatments of the social understanding of power and personal identity. These areas are selected because of their eminently mutable and inchoate character. If external metaphors are to be credited with a social function, then surely we might expect to find them relating such diverse manifestations of power as thunder, gunpowder, the police, ancestral spirits, atomic fission, stratified status, economic coercion, lust, and even the power of expressive speech itself. It would seem that if rhetorical speech can be treated as at once "persuasive" and "programmatic," then its characteristics should be manifest in magical formulas, chants, prayers, exorcisms, curses, and other formulaic verbal forms. Ever since Malinowski, anthropologists have assumed that if "felt analogies" of more than restricted and particularistic relevance exist, they might be found in ritual language. Surely when a people wish to confront effectively the "truth of things" so as to effect a transformation in that truth, they might be expected to employ paradigmatic models in the form of ritual dogmas (Turner 1967:359–93, Lévi-Strauss 1963*c*: 186–205). But is it enough merely to cite the analogy for it to be instrumentally functional, in terms of not just redefining one social context, but defining it in such a way as to relate its essence to those of dozens of other contexts? The problem is well known to ethnographers: the rote quality of much ritual performance, the very obligation to perform, would indicate that the verbal forms are merely expressive of analogic verities, without that quality of felt aptness that characterizes internal metaphors and, perhaps, endows these latter with persuasive power. Consequently the tendency has been to stress either "programs" (analogic systems) or "persuasions," not, with the exception of a few studies of rites of affliction, the nexus between them.

Following Burke, to the degree his perspective can be translated into anthropological terms, we would like to have it both ways. Certainly a ritual is very much a "dancing of an attitude" (his definition of a poem), a communication which tries to express some sense of the nature of things in terms of their manifest attributes. At the same time, such communication *defines* the situation in terms of its relation to other contexts and entities. Generally, we would view rhetorical entitlement in ritual (including magic) as that process whereby actors verbally establish the present (or future) truth of a whole series of social contexts. Analogic tropes thus are persuasive self-fulfilling prophecies, instrumentally expressive, or expressively instrumental.

Now, all this sounds promising, but we are right back at the beginning: how do tropes do all this? We think it is the capacity for analogies to slip from metaphor to metonymy and back again that enables external metaphors to become internal and fully persuasive. Such slippage involves not just the semantic attributes of the figures, but the fact they are utilized within a context of action partially determined by the words themselves. For example, two terms from separate domains juxtaposed in an external metaphor might be brought into actual physical conjunction, so that the metaphor literally becomes a metonymy. To illustrate we choose an example from magical formulas, notoriously a tricky area. Unfortunately, we lack an essay on this topic, and so we refer to a brilliant article by Tambiah (1968).

The particular merit of his article is the demonstration that the analogic systems employed in Trobriand magic are a combination of both metonymies (where contiguity and mechanical contagion predominate) and metaphors, which link different semantic domains (the metonymies) so as to transform the entities in one or both. Tambiah shows, in other words, that the functional relationship between two modes of thought once considered complementary and separate (e.g., Jakobson) is basic to the accomplishments of ritual.[12] He states that often food taboos for persons in liminal states (e.g., pregnancy) derive from metaphorical relationships which are perceived as having undesirable synecdochic attributes, in contrast to the desired elements secured by the ritual manipulation of the metaphors involved in garden magic. "Normally edible things that suggest an analogy [in our terms, felt resemblance] to the condition of the mother in some respects (. . .fish in holes are like the child in the womb) but are also antagonistic in certain other respects (. . .fish in submarine holes do not easily emerge) are tabooed" (1968:196). Here the point is to avoid contagious contact, a metonymic transfer that might make the figurative resemblance true in fact. This is the reverse of an arbitrary metonymy. There are certainly cases well known to anthropologists in which a semantic congruence is so marked yet so negative in its connotations that even visual or mental ("thinking about it") contact is prohibited for vulnerable statuses. For example, butchers in Western Europe were for centuries required to fix a silver muzzle over the snouts of hares displayed in their windows so that pregnant women who might view the horrible naked spectacle would not deliver "hare-lipped" children (Crocker and Crocker 1970:126–27). In such cases, the distinction between the contagious power in the metonymic conjunction of powerful substances, along with the conceptual force of metaphorical similarity in totally different entities, breaks down completely, and testifies to the point that, finally, metaphor and metonymy are perspectives.

Tambiah does not explore such ramifications of "perfect" internal metaphors, nor does he seek to relate them, in either their positive (sought) or negative (prohibited) nuances, to the analogic systems he documents so well.[13] What he does emphasize is the programmatic and creative impact of these verbal and behavior performances on the actors. Tambiah dwells on the way magical formulas provide a "blueprint and a self-fulfilling prophecy" for all kinds of tasks, both in the mnemonic sense of a formulaic memory aid for a series of technological

12. Lévi-Strauss, of course, makes the same point (1966:105–6, 204–8), but not so lucidly or to such analytic effect as Tambiah.

13. These observations are not intended as any criticism of Tambiah, since he does not make the "internal-external" distinction and consequently cannot be faulted for not considering the problematic elements in their relationship.

accomplishments and as a creative paradigm clarifying the essential mechanistic relationships which must be accomplished on *all* levels for a garden to grow, a car to be built, and a woman bedded. It would appear that we often find a literal account of a mechanical process inadequate as a plan for behavior. Instructing a neighbor in the mysteries of a balky furnace, coaching a novice in some sport, and paying court to some desired person (including a political superior) also require the elaboration of metaphors.

Our point is not that anthropologists have been unappreciative of the pragmatically creative powers of figurative language and especially metaphor. From Malinowski's magnificent documentation of its programmatic virtues, these have been sensitively described in numerous ethnographies, notably those by Goody (1962), Freedman (1967), Middleton (1960), Spencer (1965), and especially Richards (1956) and Peacock (1968). However, nearly all of these accounts have focused on the "power" of the tropes themselves, considered within the context of ritual and, largely, as varieties of "felt" entitlements, as internal metaphors and other figures in which the associative logic was perceived and not enjoined. The utility of analogic systems in this connection, which one might expect to be the most truly "programmed" of all, has not been explored save by some of structuralist persuasion, and even these have dealt largely with nonverbal symbols. Fernandez and Sapir in this volume set about to remedy this lack, each specifying the semantic characteristics of two different sorts of analogic paradigms which have the capacity to fuse system and context. In the next section of this chapter we offer a brief outline of how analogies, internal metaphors, and other tropes are basic to an anthropological field in which "programs" and "persuasions" are essential: politics.

SYSTEM, POWER, AND RHETORICAL IDENTIFICATION

While anthropologists appear to be willing to credit metaphor with various instrumental and aesthetic accomplishments within the context of ritual action, they are more skeptical of its virtues within the political context. Here its intentions are not so noble, nor its efficacy quite so automatic. It may well be that such is a measured response to the naive overestimation of the instrumental functions of political rhetoric sustained by traditional anthropologists, who were concerned to locate the mechanisms whereby social conformity was accomplished. But the pendulum has swung too far the other way. Nowadays it seems fashionable to regard the problem as nonexistent, assuming, as Howe so vividly complains, that all political behavior takes place in a completely

amoral void, where words relating to moral values are so much epiphenomenal glitter. Why not regard political metaphors as just metaphors,
and proceed in the general manner recommended here?

Such a tactic encounters a major objection within the terms of the
classical understanding of political rhetoric (Burke 1969:55–59). This
perspective holds that persuasive language concerning power has a
dimension which, although not lacking in other figurative usages, is of
less central importance to their mechanics. This is "identification,"
which Aristotle held to be that basic process whereby a speaker
attempts through metaphors, other tropes, and the whole bag of rhetorical tricks to cause an audience to align their goals with his objectives, and ultimately to merge their selves with his self. Now, the need
to be lucid on this topic is very great, since recently there has been a
good deal of anthropological discussion of what "identification" might
be (Firth 1966; Evans-Pritchard 1956*a*; Rigby 1969; Beidelman 1966;
Hayley 1968; Gourlay 1972), much of it muddled and at cross-purposes.
The basic problem, it seems to us, comes from a confusion involving
two different but interrelated meanings of the term "identify." The
first, a technical term employed in psychoanalysis, involves the psychological process whereby an actor fails to differentiate the boundaries
of his own self from that of another person, so that two states of being
become affectually merged. The second sense of "identify" is that of
"to name, specify, or characterize" the uniqueness of some entity. As
used in the analysis of rhetoric the two meanings tend to overlap. Burke
puts it very well. "A is not identical with his colleague, B. But insofar
as their interests are joined, A is *identified* with B. Or he may *identify
himself* with B even when their interests are not joined, if he assumes
that they are, or is persuaded to believe so. Here are ambiguities of
substance. In being identified with B, A is 'substantially one' with a
person other than himself. Yet at the same time he remains unique, an
individual locus of motives. Thus, he is both joined and separate, at
once a distinct substance and consubstantial with another" (Burke
1969:20–21).

This suggests some of the reasons anthropologists have had so much
difficulty handling "identification," especially when the psychological
dimensions are relevant. Yet it is useful to remember that metaphor
postulates the "identity" of two different entities only in highly specific
senses, and that these vary along the dimensions of internal, external,
analogic and so forth. As I try to show in my essay below, the Bororo
identification of themselves as macaws must be interpreted as a complex internal metaphor if any sense is to be made of the trope. Similarly,
arguments concerning whether or not the Nuer "completely" identify
with their oxen so as not to differentiate between animal and owner

(e.g., Gourlay 1972:249–50), become vapid once it can be established that metaphors and not metonymies/synecdoches ("man" and "ox" as parts of a single whole) are being employed. The issue clearly involves the nature of "distinction" and "consubstantiality," to employ Burke's felicitous terms. However one might view the components of identity— as psychological, sociological, cosmological, economic, historical, cultural, national, or what-have-you—one must recognize the figurative "situatizing" of self, context, and content as essential to action. Even the utilitarian perspective which predicates the universalistic omnipotence of a "what's in it for *me*" orientation for actors (e.g., Barth 1965:1–4) must cope with the content of that egotistic "sense of self." (Not, of course, that such a perspective ever recognizes the possible existence of any problematic dimension to "identity.")

The first point to recognize, in coming to terms with the character and function of "identifying" political rhetoric, is that such figurative specification of common attributes or juxtapositions does not imply any mystical sense of union. Burke stresses that all identifications are founded on opposition. "Identification is affirmed with earnestness precisely because there is division. Identification is compensatory to division. If men were not apart from one another, there would be no need for the rhetorician to proclaim their unity. If men were wholly and truly of one substance, absolute communication would be of man's very essence" (1969:22). Rhetoric, then, in Burke's view, so functions as to accomplish an "acting together," which in itself establishes that men do share "common sensations, concepts, images, ideas, attitudes that make them consubstantial" (1969:21). If there were absolute separateness, he argues, there would be likewise no mediational ground for division; but given a confusion of "identity" and "division," there is an invitation to rhetoric such that no one quite precisely knows where his own "interests" (self, social, or economic) end and begin. Burke follows Aristotle by insisting that rhetoric seeks to reconcile opposites (1969:25).

The second point is that the figurative "situatizing," which leads (theoretically) to consubstantial "acting together," does involve specifying what things (actors, entities, and so forth) *are*. Such entitling defines the attributes of identity, not in the narrow semantic definitional sense, but in terms of moral attitudes toward such "real" elements as character, ability, and the attributes of situation. We have made this point repeatedly, but it deserves to be emphasized in this context. The problem here is that such specification is by definition empirically "false"; political metaphors make simplifying, felt identifications which attempt to overcome quite real differences of substance or interest through modes which are not subject to empirical confirmation. Consequently, the identifications felt by one group to reveal something of the moral essence of situations are rejected by other social entities as the most hideously wrong and distorted warpings of reality. When one is confronted by such material, a typical analytical response is to focus on the manipulative qualities of leaders, the gullibility of the public, or the epiphenomenal quality of verbal artifice. Within this response the only identities which are explanatory are those founded on such "empirical" conditions as mutual economic/political interests. These reactions ignore the self-deceptive qualities of rhetoric, at the very least, and its essential place in the political process, at the most.

For figurative language to transform politics requires subleties of the kind elaborated by Burke. First, concerning the self-deceptive elements in rhetoric, he perceives these as involving more than just a simplistic "mistaken" metaphorical identification of one's own attributes with those of some other entity. They result from the excesses of what Burke labels the "synecdochic fallacy," mistaking the part for the whole. This amounts to assuming that, because entities A and B have a few common attributes, especially when these are qualities, they must be generally similar in terms of the preeminence of these particular selected attributes as determinant of their whole character. Such mistakes may involve one's own identity or that of the "other," and are very common in synecdoches based on such anatomic relationships as residence and descent. "We New Yorkers should stand up to those people in Albany." The rhetoric of social class within this society provides numerous examples of the negative effects produced by characterizing a social group by some "part": the farmer's "clod-hopping clayey boots," implying a certain "stickiness" and "earthy reality," a Southern millworker's "beefy red neck" with its connotations of a "thick head" occupied with irrational passions; an intellectual's "effete snobbery" which denies the hard, complex realities experienced by "real men." Closely related to these confusions are what are termed metonymic misrepresentations, common in the substitution of social effect for deterministic causes (as when blacks are characterized by any or all ghetto conditions). From these basic self-deceptions metaphors which entitle the nature of class relations are formed, including those which seek to overcome the divisiveness between such (mistakenly founded) grossly different social "natures."

Burke sees the identifications involved in political rhetoric as a form of "courtship," and suggests all attempts to achieve "consubstantiality" begin at home, or at any rate, as intentions to achieve physical union. In Burkean language, identification seeks to convert a "yours" and "mine" into an "ours," and it is not surprising that the same figurative representations which identify the mutuality of body parts might serve as models for those that seek to merge properties, whether these are "real" possessions or metaphysical attributes. Burke insists that most such efforts end with the conversion of "mine" into "thine," and that courtship rhetoric involves a "range of mountings," including prostitution, masochism, sadism, rape and bestiality. Such distorted outcomes of the rhetorical motive should not disguise, in his view, the human proclivity to define self in terms of a mysterious other, and to sharpen this definition through a courtship which must exacerbate the differences to justify its own excesses. The embarrassed fascination we have in the awkward posturings of adolescent love is very close to our shame in hearing the maudlin phrases of political campaigns, but can we deny that very occasionally we are *moved* by such efforts to "overcome"? We do not assume such insights to be proven, but suggest that a fruitful analysis of political movement might be undertaken with this scheme in mind.

In concluding this section, it is helpful to recall yet another Burkean theme, that the purposive strategies of political rhetoric must be initially comprehended in terms of their intentions rather than their effects, that what they reveal concerning their author's motives and the fund of perceived "truths" embedded in the specific tropes is far more illuminating than speculations about their functional merits in maintaining social solidarity. These latter questions must be asked, but their answering depends on acute analysis of the performative dimension stressed earlier, as well as on the accurate appraisal of the relevance of such nonverbal factors as structural, economic, and material systems. Burke has never offered his vision of rhetoric as any miraculous alchemic transformation of the intransigent conflicts rooted in all political hierarchies and the inequalities inherent in economic systems. He merely proposes to deal with the verbal means through which such things are endured or ignored.

CONCLUSION

The major issue seems to be just how to reconcile appreciation of (a) what might be termed linguistic politics, the subtle ways in which rhetoric persuades actors of the character of situations, and of (b) a more general concern for those logical structures, economic systems, or psychological forces which might underlie the surface flux of contextual motivation. The former perspective stresses the dimensions of performance, the character of "shifters," and those relationships between actors, situations, agencies, and the like which Burke sums up in his "dramatistic pentad." These interests hardly preclude appreciation for the formal semantic characteristics of particular tropes, on the contrary; but there is, understandably, less concern for the systematic character of a series of linguistic figures. As we remarked earlier, rhetoric within this view tends to be treated as purely *expressive*, and its instrumental effects explained by reference to relative merits in this respect. In the other perspective, figurative language is taken to be often fully *programmatic*, in that as it expresses the structural paradigm which generates behavior within a given social tradition, it dictates action. The two are not antithetical, although there does seem to be the tendency for the first performative view to be associated with a sort of behavioral empiricism and the second to coincide with a rationalist (or idealist) position.

It is by no means easy to integrate these two dimensions of social metaphor. All the essays in this volume attempt an uneasy mediation between them, how successfully each reader must judge for himself. At least we feel there is an inherent virtue in trying to reconcile the "performative" and the "structuralist" approaches to rhetoric insofar as it avoids another analytical approach which we believe misleading and ultimately false. This approach involves a somewhat covert substitution of "symbols" (or "rhetoric") for "culture," in all the complex ways this term has been employed by American anthropology. Admittedly, it is seductively easy to treat the recurrent figurative images used by a society as deriving from some transcendental sphere of values which prefigure but never fully reflect or express the peculiarly social conditions of action, and all the easier when these images have to do with the nature of "us," the members of that society. But even the most expressive identification is eminently situation bound, to the extent that it is difficult to find any one, or even a logically integrated set of them, that is consistently employed through all social contexts to express (and persuade) what "we" might be. The analyst, however, may find it convenient to forget this, and to focus instead on some central trope, or series of "key metaphors," that are either indigenous or imported for the occasion, and that can be offered up as constituting in themselves a summary of the "total truth" for the society he is investigating. This was the legacy from the cultural anthropology of the thirties and forties that gave us Gregory Bateson's classic *Naven* (1936), where "Naven" became one extended metaphor through which all the sociological and psychological elements within Iatmul society can be apprehended; and that also gave us Ruth Benedict's characterization of "Appolonian" Zuni and "Dionysian" Kwakiutl. And the legacy persists today, but in subtler hands and better documented studies: the

Balinese's "cockfight" and the Ndembu's concept of "Whiteness" are but two outstanding examples. These are all anthropological "perspectives by incongruity," entitlements in a very real sense.

The danger in utilizing rhetorical devices as a springboard into some nebulous land of "values," "configurations," "ethos," and the like, is that these all too easily become tautological self-fulfilling prophecies irrelevant to the mass of contradictions, ambiguities, and befuddlements which is the essence of social life. Further, such rendering of a set of "transcendent" yet unique metaphors as the fundamental expression and explanation of a society's character risks negating any hope for systematic comparisons. The other extreme, the contextual approach, is just as limiting: it has a tendency to collapse into the particularizing, idiosyncratic focus on the inexhaustible complexities of specific acts characteristic of all historical perspectives. While there is no facile way to resolve the problem, it would seem at least interesting to utilize a sort of Burkean analysis of the general in the particular, rather than the reverse, or of the particular taken as something uniquely itself. At least that has been our strategy, as it is the strategy of the chapters that follow. We hope that if the reader is not himself moved and persuaded in his reading he may at least gain some new "titles," for none of us, anthropologists and human beings, can have too many of those.

PART II

Particulars

Introduction to Part II

The substantive essays to follow can be set out according to the distinctions made by Crocker between shifter/non-shifter and particular/global, taking into account the inevitable slippage existing between a simple taxonomy and empirical fact.

	Shifter	*Particular*
Haya Proverbs	+	+
Bwiti Ritual	+	−
Cuna Political Metaphors	+/−	−
"We Are Macaws"	−	−
Fabricated Child	−	−

Proverbs are shifters par excellence; they exist only to be used in specific situations obtaining between interacting individuals. And it is this highly fluid and contextual quality that also tends to make them particularistic. They entitle the small truths of face-to-face interaction; not the general truths of cosmology. Their particularistic tendencies are responsible for the contradictions so often remarked upon in the repertoire of any culture's proverbs, as, for example, the apparent logical incompatibility of our "haste makes waste" versus "the early bird gets the worm." It was this fact that seemed to have annoyed Alfred de Musset when he wrote, *"J'aime peu les proverbes en général, parce que ce sont des selles à tous chevaux; il n'en est pas un qui n'ait son contraire."*

69

The pervasive and self-conscious use of proverbs in Haya social life has given Seitel the opportunity to develop, within the general framework of the "ethnography of communication" approach (Hymes 1962; Gumperz and Hymes 1972), a novel and original method for describing the use, not only of proverbs, but of other similar rhetorical shifters as well. Emphasizing interaction and situation Seitel puts to work an "etic" frame that he originally developed for the Igbo proverbs appearing in Achebe's novels (Seitel 1969). He shows us how to describe any single proverb as it is used in interaction; whether one or both terms in the proverb text are or are not applied to the addressor, the addressee, or some third party. This leads Seitel to a contrasting set of terms, *enfumo/omwizo* (an "emic" pair) that are used by the Haya to label a proverb as it is used at a particular time. In one context a proverb will be an *enfumo*; it will assert accord between the speaker and his addressee. In a different context another proverb, or perhaps the same one, will have the opposite effect; it will be an *omwizo* that terminates interaction on a note of discord. *Enfumo* and *omwizo* are but part of a much larger Haya vocabulary that labels varieties of speech acts, and Seitel ends his chapter by placing the two terms in this wider field.

Rituals, like proverbs, are shifters. They put into action for any group of individuals at a particular point of time the global truths of religious belief. By performing a ritual the actors themselves are absorbed into and become a part of these truths. One important result from Fernandez's studies of modern syncretist movements in Africa has been his elaboration of a model of ritual action that gives serious attention to the expressive content of ritual representations. From this perspective, which he first began to work out in "Microcosmogeny and modernization" (1969b), ritual becomes a form of metaphoric process, where the underlying vehicles of cult metaphors not only "entitle" otherwise inchoate and undefined participants, but also "move" them to a new state of involvement and social incorporation. A ritual will entail a group of key metaphors which combine to make an ordered set, a *metaphoric progression*, where one metaphor leads to the next. The participants "actualize" the first metaphor, which prepares them to actualize the next, continuing until all the steps have been completed and the desired final state, itself metaphorically defined, has been achieved. A metaphor is actualized by the performance of specific ritual acts, *scenes*, such as prayers, dances, songs, parades, sacrifices, and the like. And it is by means of these performances and the *chains of associations* implied by them that the participants become cognitively and emotionally involved with and transformed or moved by the metaphors.

This complex, and just because of its complexity, interesting and challenging model for ritual as metaphor has been applied by Fernandez, in a preliminary way, to aspects of the Christian communion (1974). In his present discussion Fernandez now, after a brief summary of his general theoretical position, gives it a fuller presentation using it to analyze the extremely rich material of the Bwiti cult as it is practiced by the Fang of Gabon.

The Cuna metaphors, described and analyzed by Howe, are splendid examples of the rhetoric of political discourse. Sometimes used as non-shifters for the general good and edification of the audience without immediate application, and sometimes, and perhaps more frequently, pronounced as shifters to comment on some current event; these global metaphorical conceits serve very well the needs of the Cuna chief. As Howe tells us, the chief's role is to represent the moderating and conservative influence of Cuna tradition, propriety, and good sense, and it is imperative that he maintain a respectable distance from the squabbles and ambiguities of day-to-day living. The metaphors provide him with one means for keeping this distance. As a variety of indirect speech, which is seldom interpreted by the chief himself, but generally only by his assistant and then rather vaguely, the metaphors permit the chief to express his opinions by innuendo and without "naming names."

Howe's discussion follows three major lines: first, to describe the various metaphorical texts (discontinuous terms) and their "commonplace associations" (cf. above p. 10); second, to describe how the metaphors are deployed in the context of social gatherings; third, to inquire how, as a "sort of metaphorical constitution," they might be interpreted with respect to the underlying principles of Cuna politics. Howe opens his paper by making the observation that, although "anthropology may have given the concept of culture to social science," anthropology itself has made little use of concept when turning its attention to the problems of politics and of political socialization. Certainly, one conclusion to be drawn from his study is the poverty of such a perspective. An analysis of Cuna political life without a close investigation of the rhetoric of Cuna politics, in this case Cuna metaphors and the cultural understandings they imply, would be an analysis devoid of subtlety, insight, and, in fact, devoid of much interest at all.

The Bororo aphorism "we are macaws" is an old anthropological chestnut if there ever was one. First described by Steinen in 1894, it was soon taken over by Levy-Bruhl who used it as a prime example for his "mystical participation" theory of primitive mentality. From then on anthropologists of various theoretical persuasions have picked it up from time to time to do service for one polemic or another.

During his fieldwork with the Bororo, Crocker took the opportunity to take a new and close look at this bit of global cosmological dogma.

Taking the aphorism as a non-shifter, a justified position considering its context free and general import, Crocker focuses on the complex place held by macaws in Bororo social life and thought. Since the Bororo have many ideas that can be subsumed under the broad topic of totemism and since Levy-Bruhl originally identified the aphorism as a variety of totemism, Crocker's interpretation necessarily takes into account what can and what cannot legitimately be called totemic in Bororo cosmology. Although, from Crocker's analysis, "we are macaws" is not, in any strict sense of the word, a totemic statement, it is near enough to warrant close comparison with other Bororo statements that are, and a large portion of Crocker's efforts are devoted to this end.

Beyond the problem of totemism, by following out the "associated commonplaces" implicit in the aphorism, Crocker is able to demonstrate the kinds of rewards to be gained when a study of this kind of rhetorical device takes little for granted and pursues subtle clues wherever they lead. And this is all the more true when the study, as this one, resists the temptation of assuming that the device, in some ineffable way, sums up all there is to know about the society being studied.

On another matter, there is one interesting conclusion that develops from Crocker's analysis. Precisely because he has tried to take into account the full range of cultural and social implications of "we are macaws," Crocker is, surprisingly, led to rehabilitate part of Levy-Bruhl's original interpretation, quite as he, at the same time, finds himself "discounting" to some extent the rigid analogics associated with Lévi-Strauss's structuralism.

Although there are exceptions, folktales are generally non-shifters. The plot, content, and import of a tale seldom pertain directly to the situation of its telling. Whether or not the subject matter of a tale is global, particularistic, or somewhere in between will obviously vary. Since the "Fabricated Child" has to do with basic issues in Kujamaat belief, their notions of legitimacy and the problems of sexual identity, it can surely be thought of as having a global import.

In my analysis of the "Fabricated Child," I take an approach that answers to the question, "how might the 'Fabricated Child' and its beehive metaphor be interpreted by the Kujamaat themselves?" That is, the analysis offered here operates under the assumption that the tale is meaningful, in other than a trivial way, to the tellers and their audience. In this instance the tale is taken as a symbolic comment (a temporalizing of essence, in Kenneth Burke's terms) on problematic aspects of Kujamaat social reality. Analysis of this variety necessitates looking beyond the tale itself to relevant understandings and beliefs held by the people who tell the tale. Thus, a fair portion of my discussion is devoted to Kujamaat ideas about legitimacy, procreation, bee-hives, honey, and sexual roles.

The kind of interpretation that I make can be labeled as "con-textual," and complements the comparative studies of the structuralists. For the latter a tale such as the "Fabricated Child" is but one mani-festation of an underlying symbolic structure. It is, to use one of Lévi-Strauss's optical metaphors, but a single twist of the structural kaleido-scope. Other variants of the tale exist, either among the Kujamaat or among their neighbors, and each may be related to the others by a number of "transformations" that involve a variety of limited analogic manipulations. To get at the underlying structure a whole set of diverse variants must be examined. But if comparison can instruct us about an underlying structure, it cannot tell us much about why a particular tale, in a particular cultural context, takes the shape it does. That is, com-parative structuralism cannot tell us why at this place and point in time the kaleidoscope produced this pattern and not another. For this to be explained, one must have recourse to the "contingent" cultural essences of the sort examined here. Hence the complementarity of the two, comparative and contextual, approaches. The former has to do with a general structure that is perhaps universal to human imaginative thought, while the latter shows how this imaginative capacity gets put to use to entitle, within a particular context, various cultural truths.

J.D.S.

Chapter
3

Saying Haya Sayings:
Two Categories of Proverb Use

PETER SEITEL*

Observers of society who have analyzed proverbs at all have most often dealt with them in terms of some larger notion. They have taken them for evidence of a general theory, fed them as grist to the mill of already established technique, or employed them as guides to wider areas of interest. The content of proverbs has been taken as evidence for a society's collective personality (Whiting 1931:73–74, n. 5); worldwide patterns in the distribution of proverbs as evidence for unilineal evolution (Loeb 1952); their formal structure as evidence for archetypical patterns in thought (Milner 1969). Proverbs have been analyzed as Rorschach protocols (Shimkin and Sanjuan 1953); they have had the "ethnography of speaking" technique worked upon them (Arewa and Dundes 1964). Anthropologists have used proverbs in field research to lead informants into a discussion of other areas of culture (I. Kopytoff, 1967: personal communication). Moreover, in literary criticism Kenneth Burke has discussed English proverbs as an easy "way in" to the idea of literature as "equipment for living" and ultimately to a general sociological criticism of literature (Burke 1957).

In his essay, Burke notes several things about the work proverbs do in society, and these observations lead naturally to a discussion of the social role of literature. Although he employs proverbs only to reach literature, Burke has said important things about proverb usage. In

* I thank David Crabb, Dell Hymes, and J. David Sapir for their many helpful comments and criticisms of previous drafts of this paper.

this essay, I shall adopt concepts from his discussion of proverbs as a "way in" to a description and analysis of one aspect of proverb usage among the Haya. Burke's insight into proverbs, although designed to serve literary criticism, will lead us to an explication of a category distinction between two types of proverb usage which are recognized by the Haya: *enfumo* and *omwizo*.

The Haya, a Bantu-speaking patrilineal group of approximately 350,000, live in West Lake Region, the northwestern-most section of Tanzania. Their political organization in former times was a centralized form of state bureaucracy, with seven distinct chiefdoms based upon the institution of clientship in landholding (Reining 1962). Haya oral tradition is very rich, including not only proverbs, songs, and folktales but also genres found in royal milieu—praise poems and epics.[1]

Kenneth Burke observes that "proverbs are *strategies* for dealing with *situations*. Insofar as situations are typical and recurrent in a given social structure, people develop names for them and strategies for handling them." (Burke 1957:256) It is the situation to which a proverb is applied that makes that proverb something more than a literary text. A proverb applied to a certain situation can be said to be used by the speaker, rather than recited. Furthermore, the speaker implies a certain way in which the situation should be handled. This prescription for dealing with the situation Burke terms "strategy." Adding that proverbs are usually metaphorical, we can begin to articulate an analytical framework that suits Haya proverb usage specifically but is also more generally applicable.

AN ETIC FRAME[2]

There are three separate domains involved when a proverb is spoken: the one inherent in the text of the proverb itself taken literally; the one to which the proverb is intended to be applied; and the one in which the proverb is in fact being said. They are termed, respectively, the *proverb situation,* the *context situation,* and the *interaction situation.* (Note that *context situation* corresponds to Burke's "situation.") A

1. Examples of songs, folktales, and proverbs may be found in Rehse (1910) and in Cesard (1928–29). A collection of proverbs has been made by Rascher (1967–68). For detailed explanations of usage the best collection is the unpublished manuscript "Emiizo!" in Haya by an anonymous author, in the Hans Cory Collection at the Library, University of Dar es Salaam. Data for my own study were collected during field research in Tanzania, 1968–70, sponsored by the National Institutes of Mental Health.

2. Etic and emic are employed here as developed by Pike (1967).

proverb speaker asserts that the relationship that obtains between the things in the *proverb situation* is analogous to the relationship between the entities in the *context situation.*

The three domains entailed in explicating proverb use can be illustrated by an application of the proverb "where there's smoke there's fire" to a context situation in which certain people have been making accusations of corruption against a public official. The proverb speaker

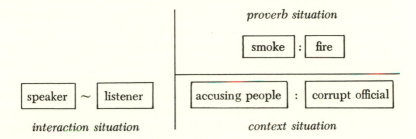

proverb situation

smoke : fire

speaker ~ listener | accusing people : corrupt official

interaction situation | *context situation*

intends the hearer to interpret the accusation as a true sign of the official's corruption. Here the speaker and the listener are part of the *interaction situation*; the *proverb situation* is someone perceiving smoke and knowing therefore that there must be a fire present. People who make accusations and the official whom they accuse constitute the *context situation.* In analogical form, the speaker says—smoke:fire:: people who make accusations:official who is corrupt. That is, in both sets of terms the first (smoke, people who make accusations) is a true sign of the second (fire, official who is corrupt). The terms of the proverb situation are substantives that are related by analogy to the terms of the context situation. The terms of the context situation are also substantives—usually persons.

The "strategy" for handling the context situation might be stated, "Believe the accusations." The concept of "strategy" may also be applied to the interaction situation in which the proverb is spoken where it refers to the speaker's reason for using the proverb. Here the strategy in the interaction situation might be called simply "persuading," or trying to effect agreement of hearer with speaker. The speaker's strategy in using the proverb as a technique in interaction will be shown to be a criterion by which Haya speakers differentiate two kinds of proverb usage—*enfumo* and *omwizo.* Before we come to analyze how the Haya make this distinction, let us first consider in detail how a speaker applies a proverb to a context situation.

A proverb in conversation can refer to the speaker himself, to the addressee(s), or to a person who is not addressed (and may be present or absent). When we say that a proverb refers to an individual, we mean that the individual in question is included within, or part of, the context situation to which the proverb is applied. Thus, if the proverb refers to the speaker himself, then the speaker is included within that situation. If the proverb refers to the intended hearer, then he is included within that situation.

The speaker and hearer are, of course, also within the interaction situation in which the proverb is spoken. In any given case, the persons in the interaction situation may or may not be those referred to in the context situation. To describe a specific proverb use, we thus must specify which person, if any, within the interaction situation is referred to in the context situation. Each possibility of matching individuals in context situation and interaction situation (speaker[s], hearer[s], third person[s]) constitutes a possible type of usage. Let us call both the process of matching individuals and the types of matching "correlations." We may say that a speaker correlates a term in the proverb situation with an entity in the context situation and also (possibly) with a person in the interaction situation. Each resulting configuration of these items can be called a correlation. Both the process of correlating and its result are given the same name because they are in fact the same thing. The necessity of exposition causes them to be distinguished.

In a proverb in which only one term in the proverb situation can be correlated with a person in the context situation (henceforth, a "single correlation proverb"), these possibilities exist: the person who is correlated with a term in the proverb situation may be the speaker, or the hearer, or someone else—who may be absent or present but not the addressee. If the *speaker* correlates himself with the term in the proverb situation, I call this a "first person correlation." If the *addressee* is correlated with a term in the proverb situation, I call this a "second person correlation." If *someone other* than the speaker or the addressee is correlated with a term in the proverb situation, I call this "third person correlation." For our present purposes there is no need to distinguish singular from plural. Therefore, a "first person correlation" may be a "we," that is, speaker speaks on behalf of a group. This limitation in the notation for correlation is made here to simplify the presentation of the proverb use data by reducing the number of possibilities for each proverb. Empirically, excluding the singular/plural dimension does not alter the Haya system of classification for proverb use (i.e., the *enfumo/ omwizo* distinction). The person-number paradigm may be elaborated in the study of proverb speaking in other cultures to accommodate complex pronomial systems.

The person-number problem raises an important issue: the relationship between the analytic framework proposed for proverb use in general and the Haya system in particular. The frame—consisting so far of three related domains and a system of correlating entities within these domains (more etic principles will be introduced below)—generates all the theoretically possible uses for a single proverb. Haya proverb speakers, however, do not accept as proper uses all those etically possible. These culture-specific limitations within the analytic framework articulate an emic system of Haya proverb speaking.

The investigation of acceptable uses for proverbs is, in fact, the basis of the proposed analytic method. But for the purposes of this essay— which focuses on the application of two categories of proverb use in general rather than the system of usage for specific proverbs or classes of proverbs—the question of acceptable and nonacceptable uses of single proverbs does not directly concern us. The reader will, however, note several important instances of limitations in application below as part of the discussion of related areas.

THE ETIC FRAME APPLIED

A single correlation proverb that is used frequently by the Haya is "One paddle leaves early." The proverb situation consists of a comparison between two canoes—one in which there are many men with many paddles and one in which there is but a single man with only one paddle. Now, because the many men can propel their canoe much faster than the lone man can, they are able to stay longer at a given place and still return before dark. The lone paddler, compensating for his slower pace, must leave earlier. This proverb may be used to say metaphorically that one must be going. An example of a context situation to which the proverb is applied in a first person correlation is the following. A man meets another on the road and they begin to converse. The time is approaching sunset and one of the men must travel some distance to reach his home. He explains that the hour is late, and he must travel far. Then he might add, (1)* "The Haya have a proverb, they say, 'One paddle leaves early.'" This is a first person correlation because the speaker is correlated with the lone man in the canoe of the proverb situation.

A second person correlation might occur when a host advises a guest that if he is to reach home before dark, he should set out now. He would explain that the way is long and so on, and add, (2) "You know, you should leave now. The Haya say, 'One paddle leaves early.'" There the hearer is correlated with the lone man in the canoe.

A third person correlation of this proverb might occur when a woman

---

* Numbers in parentheses mark and index specific uses of given proverbs.

is discussing with another woman the behavior of a third woman at a wedding. The third woman, the speaker says, had to leave the celebration early because she has no co-wife to help her do the housework. The others, who have co-wives, could stay but she had to go home to prepare dinner. (3) "The Haya say, 'One paddle leaves early.'" Here the lone man in the canoe is correlated with a person referred to—neither the speaker nor the hearer.

More complex than the single correlation proverbs are those in which two terms in the proverb situation are correlated with two people in the context situation. To specify this type of correlation, one must state which person is correlated with which term in the proverb situation. The use of this "double correlation proverb" will become clear in the following example.

The text of the proverb reads, "An *enfula* who does not borrow shames his sub-clan." To understand the proverb situation, one must know something of the social and political structure of Buhaya as it existed about twenty-five years ago. There were seven chiefdoms ruled by chiefs and administered by a state bureaucracy. The clans were divided into two groups—the ruling clans and the nonruling clans. The upper group of clans controlled the apportionment of land for the cultivation of plantains—the staple crop—and were the main owners of cattle. Cattle were used for hides, meat and milk products, and also for manure that was used to fertilize the banana plants. In order to gain access to land and cattle, members of the nonruling clans had to form client relationships with members of the ruling clans. Hypergamy was practiced between the otherwise endogamous groups of ruling clans and nonruling clans; that is, a man of a ruling clan could marry a woman of a nonruling clan but not vice versa. Thus, one way of forming alliances with a ruling clan was to provide a wife for one of their members' sons. The sub-clan section of the clan that provided the wife would receive cattle in bride-price payment and could perhaps obtain more land through their new alliance. The members of the wife-giving sub-clan could assume a semiroyal status called *enfula*. A person of this status could legitimately take on the markers of the ruling clans—a certain dress, cosmetic attention to the body, and "refined" behavior. One could identify an *enfula* by his high status appearance and manner. The *enfula* sub-clan did not, of course, have the resources of the ruling clans and often appearance had to be kept up through borrowing clothing and butterfat to rub on the skin. The poor behavior or bad appearance of any one *enfula* shamed the other members of the sub-clan who were trying to appear of as high a status as possible. This is the proverb situation of the proverb, "An *enfula* who does not borrow shames his sub-clan."

A context situation to which the proverb may be applied is a man's asking the members of his family for aid in some project—a trip, a marriage, or some economic venture. Here there are two social entities to be correlated with the *"enfula"* and his "sub-clan" of the proverb situation. (4) If the man himself speaks the proverb, he will explain his request and then state the proverb. In this usage, the analogy between the proverb situation and the context situation may be stated— I (man asking):you(his family)::*enfula*:sub-clan. He persuades his family to help by saying that if an *enfula* has nothing to borrow, he shames his sub-clan; but (he implies) if an *enfula* has something to borrow, he does not shame his sub-clan. So (he implies) let me not shame you—give me what I ask for. Because the analogy can be stated— I:you::*enfula*:sub-clan—I call this type of correlation "first person– second person." Recall that I (we) = first person = speaker; and you (you pl.) = second person = hearer, etc.

In the same type of context situation, in which the man has requested aid (but he has not used the proverb), the family can say, (5) "Yes, we will help you. The Haya have a proverb, 'An *enfula* who does not borrow shames his sub-clan.'" The analogy between the context situation and the proverb situation here can be stated—you (asker for aid): we(family)::*enfula*:sub-clan. This type of correlation I call "second person–first person." Note that in this usage and in example (4) directly above, both the speaker and the hearer appear in the context situation. The two examples are differentiated by the way the terms in the proverb (*enfula* and sub-clan) are correlated with the speaker and the hearer. In example (4), *enfula*:sub-clan::speaker:hearer (first person– second person correlation). In example (5), *enfula*:sub-clan::hearer: speaker (second person–first person correlation). Note that the terms of the proverb are consistently written "*enfula*:sub-clan" rather than "sub-clan:*enfula*" because this is the order in which they occur in the proverb text.

Consider a similar context situation—one in which a man needs the help of his family for some project. Suppose he has asked for it but has been turned down. A person who is well known to both the man and his family—a neighbor perhaps—can intercede on behalf of the man. He may try to convince the family to help. The neighbor explains why he believes the request to be a just one and then says to the family, (6) "You should help him. You know they say, 'An *enfula* who does not borrow shames his sub-clan.'" In this usage, *enfula* is correlated with the man, but he is neither speaker nor hearer. Sub-clan is correlated with the family, which is the intended hearer. Thus, the analogy can be written—*enfula*:sub-clan::he(man):you(family). This I call a "third person–second person correlation."

Suppose a man refuses to request the aid of his family to do a cer-, tain project, and his friend knows that it will not turn out well without the family's help. The friend might advise him he had better ask for their help. After explaining his reasons for thus advising him, the friend says to him, (7) "You know they say, 'An *enfula* who does not bor- row. . .etc.'" *Enfula* is correlated with "you," the hearer, and sub-clan is correlated with "they," the family, not present. The analogy can be stated—*enfula*:sub-clan::you:they. I call this a "second person–third person correlation."

If a family is deciding whether or not to help a kinsman with his undertaking, one member of the family may say, (8) "We should help him. You know they say, 'An *enfula* who does not borrow. . .etc.'" This would be a "third person–first person correlation." The analogy can here be stated—*enfula*:sub-clan::he(kinsman):we(family).

Of the two remaining types of correlation, first person–third person and third person–third person, the former is not acceptable to the Haya. That is, to all hypothetical situations constructed on this type, Haya speakers responded that they were not possible. "I might bring shame on them" or "they have to help me because" are not regarded as reason- able feelings to express with this proverb. (Recall the discussion of etic to emic at the end of the preceding section.) A third person–third per- son correlation might be used by someone who has no part in the situation to describe it to someone who also has no part in it.

In Burke's terms, the strategy for handling the context situation to which the proverb is applied is the same in all the usages described above—namely, that a man should ask for and receive aid from his family for certain undertakings. The strategy that the proverb serves in the special context of proverb use is also the same for all the above usages. In all cases, the speaker uses the proverb to persuade the hearer. He uses the proverb to try to effect an agreement between the hearer and himself.

THE FRAME DEVELOPED: TEMPORAL RELATIONSHIPS
BETWEEN DOMAINS AND RELATED FEATURES

In all of the proverb uses described so far, the project or event that the man is planning has not yet occurred. This proverb can also be used *after* the event. In this case, the proverb may be used in certain correlations but not in others, depending on whether the event in ques- tion went well or badly. Thus, for this proverb there is not only a second person–first person/before correlation (5); there is also a second person–first person/after/bad correlation. This last correlation points to the distinction between *enfumo* and *omwizo*.

A second person–first person/after/bad correlation would look something like this: (9) A man's son marries against his father's wishes. The son tries to perform all of the requirements of the marriage rituals and payments himself, but he is unable to. His failure is known throughout the community. The father reviles his son with this proverb. He uses it to cut off the conversation with his son and make it known to him that their relationship has been damaged, if not completely broken, by the son's inept and disobedient action. In this usage, the father speaks the proverb without prior explanation and without introductory phrases. The son knows without being told literally what the father means when he says, "An *enfula* who does not borrow shames his subclan." In the form of an analogy, this usage can be stated you (son): I(father)::*enfula*:sub-clan; further, the proverb is spoken *after* the event, which (because of the son's disobedience and inability) was *bad*. Thus, the usage is characterized as second person–first person/after/bad.

The strategy for handling the *context situation* is the same here as in the other examples of possible usages. The father states that the proper way to handle a marriage is to ask for and receive help from kin. The strategy that the proverb serves in the *interaction situation* differs, however, from the previously discussed usages. In all of the examples except (9), the second person–first person/after/bad correlation, we noted that the speaker uses the proverb to effect agreement between the hearer and himself. In this instance, the speaker uses the proverb to break off the conversation, to upbraid the hearer for his wrongdoing, and to signal that the relationship between the speaker and the hearer is not a peaceful one. In short, it can be said that in all usages of this proverb except second person–first person/after/bad, the proverb serves to draw the speaker and hearer together. In this one exception, the proverb is used to separate the speaker from the hearer because of something the hearer has done. In general, when a proverb serves the former strategy in an interaction situation, the Haya call it an *enfumo*. When a proverb serves the latter strategy, the Haya call it an *omwizo*. An *enfumo* is a proverb used to bring together the opinions of speaker and hearer. The speaker tries to effect an agreement between the hearer and himself. An *omwizo*, on the other hand, may be used by the speaker to signal that there is not a peaceful relationship between the interlocutors. In sum, an *enfumo* draws the speaker and hearer together; an *omwizo* can be used to drive them apart.[3]

3. Evans-Pritchard (1956*b*, 1962:337) notes a similar distinction made in Zande proverbs.

ENFUMO AND OMWIZO: EXAMPLES OF USE

It may be difficult for a non-proverb-user to imagine how a single text might alternately serve each purpose, depending on the circumstances of its use. In fact, there are some texts which are always used as *emiizo* (pl. of *omwizo*) and other texts used only as *enfumo* (pl. of *enfumo*). But there are many texts (including "An *enfula* who does not borrow. . .") that may be classified as either one or the other. These proverbs afford a good opportunity to investigate differences in speaking an *enfumo* and in speaking an *omwizo*. By viewing a single proverb alternately as an *enfumo* and as an *omwizo*, we can isolate the minimal differences in usage which constitute a change in classification. Each of the five proverbs discussed below illustrate one such feature.

One of the criteria of an *omwizo* is that the person who committed the wrong be among the hearers of the proverb usage.* For example, (10) an old woman was living with her grown son. One day he became drunk, verbally abused her, and in the end drove her from the house. She went to live with a married grandson. After a day or two, the son came to where she was living to apologize and to ask her to return to his house. She agreed and said she would follow him home later. The son left. The mother's friends then questioned the wisdom of her decision to go back—the son was known to have a volatile temper. She replied that after all he was her son and added, "What can I do? They say, 'It nauseates but it does not cause vomiting.' " That is, her son had caused her much pain (it nauseates) but she still could not bring herself to separate from him (it does not cause vomiting—i.e., separation). Because this was said in the son's absence, it was an *enfumo*. Had the son been present, (11) it would have been an *omwizo*.

Often the type of correlation is important in determining how a proverb is classified. The difference between a first person and a second person correlation in a single correlation proverb is often the difference between *enfumo* and *omwizo*. For example, (12) someone comes to a man and asks to borrow some money. The man may explain that he has none to lend, and then may add, "You know, the Haya have a proverb. They say, 'There are real women who cannot have children; how can Nyante, who doesn't even menstruate?' " That is, there are rich men who lack money to lend; how can I, a poor man, have money to lend you? The correlation here is first person, and the usage is an *enfumo*.

In a large group discussion, a person begins to offer an opinion. Before he can speak, however, someone else interrupts him saying,

---

* There are exceptions to this rule which will be dealt with below.

(13) "There are real women who cannot have children; how can Nyante, who doesn't even menstruate?" The speaker means that there are wise people who have no opinion on this matter; how can this person have one who is not at all wise? The correlation here is second person and the usage is an *omwizo*.

In a double correlation proverb, the distinction can be between a first person–second person correlation and a third person–second person. Consider, for example, the proverb, "I-thought-it-would-be-good-for-myself (a man's name) saved the wife of Mulalo." The proverb situation is this: one day a man came to the canoe-crossing on the bank of a river (this man was to become known as 'I-thought-it-would-be-good-for-myself'). He boarded the canoe along with a woman. In midstream, the river's current overturned the canoe. The woman, who could not swim, was close to drowning. Just in time, the man was able to save her by pulling her to the bank they had been headed for. She thanked him greatly, of course, and they went on their way. Later, the man heard that the woman he had saved was the wife of Mulalo, a cattle herder, and furthermore that she had a marriageable daughter. He went to Mulalo to ask to marry the daughter. Mulalo agreed and arrangements were made. When Mulalo's wife heard of it, however, she absolutely refused to allow her child to marry the man. The reason she gave was that when the canoe overturned, the water billowed her skirt above her waist exposing her genitalia. Now, because it is a great taboo for a man to see the genitalia of his mother-in-law, the marriage could never take place. The man said, "But when you were in the river you almost drowned. And I pulled you out. I did good and now you return me bad. Truly, I-thought-it-would-be-good for-myself saved the wife of Mulalo." Many people who know this story add that the wife was really lying. She refused to give her daughter to the man because he had been her own lover for some time—beginning with when she "thanked" him for saving her.

This proverb might be applied to a context situation in which one man lends money to another, but when the time for repayment comes, the borrower causes trouble. He argues and disclaims knowledge of the debt, or disputes the amount. The lender can say, (14) "If I had known you would have acted like this, I would not have lent you the money. Truly, they say, 'I-thought-it-would-be-good-for-myself saved the wife of Mulalo." This is a first person–second person correlation because I-thought-it-would-be-good-for-myself:wife of Mulalo::speaker(lender): hearer(borrower). This is an *omwizo*.

The proverb might also be said (15) by one friend to another about a third person. If the speaker knows that the hearer has treated someone ungratefully, he can advise him to change his behavior. He explains to the hearer why he feels he has done wrong and how to rectify the situation. He may add the proverb to clinch the argument. The proverb here is an *enfumo*. The correlation is third person–second person because I-thought. . .etc.:wife of Mulalo::a third person (not present): hearer. The shift in correlation from first person–second person to third person–second person is accompanied by a change in the classification of the proverb from *omwizo* to *enfumo*.

Sometimes two uses of the same text can have identical correlations but be of different sub-types. The proverb "Not looking in on food causes it to spoil" is an example of this. The proverb situation consists of someone who does not look in from time to time on food which is cooking. This negligence causes the food to burn and be spoiled. The proverb is often used when someone comes to pay a visit. Visiting confers status upon the host and is an important social obligation among friends, neighbors, and kinsmen. When someone comes to pay a visit, the host can use this proverb to thank him for coming. He might say, (16) "Thank you for visiting me. The Haya have a proverb, 'Not looking in on food causes it to spoil.'" The correlation is second person, there is no wrongdoing present, and this is termed an *enfumo*.

If a person fell ill and was confined to his house, his friends or relatives would be obligated to visit him. If a friend or relative failed to visit, the aggrieved party at their next meeting might say, (17) "You know, 'Not looking in on food causes it to spoil.'" This would be an *omwizo*. The correlation is a second person, like the *enfumo* above; but unlike the *enfumo* usage, here the speaker has been wronged by the hearer.

Interpreting whether a proverb is an *enfumo* or an *omwizo* often depends on whether the proverb is spoken *before or after* the situation to which it is applied. "He who was not warned set out in a clay canoe" is a proverb which has these possibilities. The proverb situation is the story of a young man who was not told that clay canoes are not seaworthy, and so built one and set out onto Lake Victoria. When he had gone some distance from shore, the canoe disintegrated and he drowned. The proverb is usually spoken to warn someone to take the advice offered him, for if he does not, disaster will follow. For example, if it is during the rainy season and the roads are very muddy, one does not ride his bicycle in areas which are known to wash out. If one advises another that the section of the road in question has washed out but the would-be traveler says he can ride his bicycle through anyway, the adviser can say, (18) "I have warned you that if you go you will have trouble there. You should listen. You know they say, 'He who was not warned set out in a clay canoe.'" This usage is an *enfumo*.

On the other hand, suppose a man has been warned by another that the road is washed out in a certain section, but he sets out with his bicycle anyway. After a few hours he returns without having reached his destination. He is wet, dirty, and his bicycle is fouled in mud. His adviser looks at him, laughs through the nose (*ensheko omunyindo*), and says, (19) "He who was not told set out in a clay canoe." This is an *omwizo*.

ENFUMO AND OMWIZO: TOWARD DISTINCTIVE FEATURES

The preceding usages exemplify four features which distinguish an *omwizo* from an *enfumo*. The features are: First, the matter to which the proverb refers (the context situation) is considered a wrongdoing. Second, the person who has committed the wrongdoing is the hearer. Third, the person who has been wronged by the hearer is the speaker himself. Fourth, the context situation to which the proverb is applied obtains in the present or occurred in the past. These four features are necessary conditions for a proverb to be classified as an *omwizo*. If one or more is lacking in a proverb usage, the proverb is classed as an *enfumo*. There are exceptions to this rule which will be dealt with later.

Consider the alternate uses described above for the proverb, "I-thought-it-would-be-good-for-myself saved the wife of Mulalo" (henceforth to be known as the "wife of Mulalo" proverb). Used as an *enfumo* (in a third person–second person correlation, example [15]), the "wife of Mulalo" proverb may be described by the following features: First, the context situation is a wrongdoing. Second, the wrongdoer is the hearer (he is correlated with the wife in the proverb situation). Third, the person wronged is not the speaker but a third person, not present. Fourth, the social situation occurred in the past. Note that the third criterion is not met, and so the proverb is an *enfumo*.

Taking the example of the "wife of Mulalo" proverb used as an *omwizo* (that is, in a first person–second person correlation in example [14]), we may note that first, the social situation is a wrongdoing. Second, the wrongdoer is the hearer (he is correlated with the wife). Third, the person wronged is the speaker (he is correlated with I-thought-it-would-be-good-for-myself). Fourth, the social situation occurred in the past. All four criteria are met, and the proverb here is classified as an *omwizo*.

In the *enfumo* use (10) of "It nauseates; it does not cause vomiting," (henceforth, the "it nauseates" proverb), first, the social situation is a wrongdoing. Second, the wrongdoer is *not* the hearer (the son is absent). Third, the person wronged is the speaker (i.e., the mother).

Fourth, the context situation occurred in the past. In the *omwizo* use of the "it nauseates" proverb (11), the son is present and thus a hearer of the proverb. This alters the second feature of usage: the wrongdoer is a hearer (the son is present). The other features remain the same. Thus, all of the criteria are met and the proverb is called an *omwizo*.

In the *enfumo* usage (16) of "Not looking in on food causes it to spoil" (henceforth the "not looking in on food" proverb), the first feature marks the proverb as an *enfumo*. The context situation is not considered a wrongdoing. Recall that here the speaker has been visited and uses the proverb to thank the visitor. The second, third, and fourth features, however, are consistent with *omwizo* usage: the actor in the context situation is the hearer; the person acted upon is the speaker; the context situation occurred in the past.[4]

In the second instance (17), the usage is the same as above except that the proverb is applied to a situation in which wrongdoing has occurred. The four criteria are met, and the "not looking in on food" proverb becomes an *omwizo*. In this usage the speaker alludes to the hearer's failure to pay a visit. The features are then, first, the context situation (hearer's failure to visit the speaker) is considered a wrongdoing. Second, the actor in the context situation (i.e., he who does wrong by failing to visit) is the hearer. Third, the person acted upon (i.e., the person wronged by not being visited) is the speaker. Fourth, the context situation occurred in the past. The "not looking in on food" proverb in this usage is an *omwizo*.

The proverb, "He who was not told set out in a clay canoe" (henceforth the "clay canoe" proverb), is classified as an *enfumo* or as an *omwizo* depending on whether the context situation will occur in the future or has occurred in the past. Thus, the four features of the *enfumo* usage (18) are first, the context situation is considered a wrongdoing (rejection of the advice through action contrary to it; this leads to trouble). Second, the wrongdoer (he who rejects the advice) is the hearer. Third, the person wronged by the hearer is the speaker. Fourth,

---

4. Here we have changed the term which describes the hearer from "wrongdoer" to "actor" and the term for the speaker from "person wronged" to "person acted upon." This change is necessary because the *enfumo* usage of the "not looking in on food" proverb (16) is applied to a situation in which no wrong has been done. The terms "actor" and "acted upon" for the hearer and speaker respectively might be used in all of the examples and in the statement of features 2 and 3. The second feature would then be "the actor in the social situation is the hearer," rather than "the person who committed the wrongdoing is the hearer," as it now stands. The third feature would read "the person acted upon is the speaker" rather than the present "the person who has been wronged by the hearer is the speaker himself." The latter statement of each pair, although less general in application, was selected because its meaning is more readily apparent.

the context situation does *not* occur in the present or the past—it will occur in the future. When the "clay canoe" proverb is spoken after the headstrong person has got into trouble for his contrary actions (19), all of the features except the fourth are the same as those in the *enfumo* usage. The context situation shifts from future to past. The fourth criterion is met. The "clay canoe" proverb becomes an *omwizo*.

The following table summarizes the analysis of examples:

TABLE 1

Features:

1. The context situation is a wrongdoing.
2. The actor (i.e., the person who committed the wrongdoing) is the hearer.
3. The person acted upon (i.e., the person who has been wronged) is the speaker.
4. The context situation occurs in the present or the past.

	1.	2.	3.	4.
An *omwizo* usage of any of the four proverbs	X	X	X	X
The given *enfumo* usage of:				
"clay canoe" proverb	X	X	X	O
"wife of Mulalo" proverb	X	X	O	X
"it nauseates" proverb	X	O	X	X
"not looking in on food" proverb	O	X	X	X

X = present, affirmative
O = absent, negative

If we pause here to view proverb use in the more conventional linguistic scheme of "text and context," the results of the analysis so far will be seen as evidence for an important principle of language use in general. Translating from our tripartite system to "text and context," we see "text" as the proverb (situation) plus the context situation; that is, respectively, the symbol and its referent. "Context" in our system is "interaction situation," which, as will appear below, has a linguistic component in addition to the nonlinguistic features considered so far.

We may note, then, that to classify a given use of one of the four proverbs one must take into account both text (criteria 1, 4) and context (criteria 2, 3). The *enfumo/omwizo* distinction demonstrates the principle that *meaning*—here the process of interpreting and classifying a specific use of a particular proverb—is the product of the interaction between text and context. This principle of the interdependence of message and context, the central perspective of the "ethnography of speaking" approach to language use in general, is demonstrated here with regard to a specific conventional genre of speech. This perspective on the study of meaning in speech unites the ethnography of speaking and sociolinguistic approaches to language with the study of folklore as communication.

THE CRITERION OF *OKU-GAYA*

Returning to the "clay canoe" proverb, we might ask in what sense can the speaker think himself wronged if his advice is not taken? To answer this, we must refer to the Haya concept of *"oku-gaya."* The closest English equivalent of this is "to put down" in the sense of to denigrate, to scorn, to treat something as being of low status or of lower status than it really is. In Buhaya status consists of, among other things, the right to be obeyed. Furthermore, wisdom, polite behavior, fastidious eating habits, careful attention to dress and grooming, as well as economic means, are all said to be directly related to high status. Thus, to *gaya* (the stem form) may be to disobey someone, to disparage his wisdom, his eating habits, his dress and grooming, or his wealth. In the example of the "clay canoe" proverb, the intended hearer has *gaya'*d the speaker. He has disparaged his knowledge by setting out against his advice. When he gets into trouble because of his refusal to be advised, the speaker says the *omwizo* to him.

A proverb itself may be used to *gaya*. When it is used in this way, the Haya classify it as an *omwizo*. This is the case in example (13) of "There are real women who lack children; how can Nyante, who doesn't even menstruate?" (henceforth the "Nyante" proverb). This proverb is used in a second person correlation to disparage the wisdom of a person offering an opinion. The proverb is spoken to *gaya* the would-be speaker. It is therefore an *omwizo*. Note that the four criteria used to classify the other proverbs do not apply here. The proverb is not used to refer to the intended hearer's wrongdoing. It is used to assert his low status—here with respect to knowledge. Moreover, this proverb is classified as an *omwizo* even when it is spoken about someone who is not an intended hearer.

The "Nyante" proverb might also be used to *gaya* someone's personal wealth. If a man boasts that he will accomplish some task requiring a large sum of money—a marriage, a land purchase, a cattle deal—someone may *gaya* him with the "Nyante" proverb. In effect, the speaker says, "There are wealthy men who cannot do these things; how can X who doesn't even have a little money?"

The "Nyante" proverb used in a first person correlation (12) is not an *omwizo* because it does not convey a status-related insult. Recall that in this example the speaker uses the proverb to emphasize his own lack of money. The proverb is spoken not to lower another's status (*oku-gaya*) but to assume for oneself the attributes of inferior status. The Haya term this act *okw-etohya*, literally "to make oneself small," that is, to affect a humble stance, to be self-effacing. Thus, the "Nyante" proverb in a first person correlation is an *enfumo* spoken "to make oneself small"; in a second person correlation it is an *omwizo* spoken to convey a status insult (*oku-gaya*).

Another proverb that follows this pattern (first person/"make oneself small"/*enfumo* and second person/*gaya*/*omwizo*) is, "He who hasn't his own wealth doesn't travel." This proverb can be spoken in a first person correlation "to make oneself small"; one uses the proverb to explain his decision not to undertake some enterprise for lack of funds. On the other hand, if one person asks another for a loan to finance an undertaking, and if the person asked neither wishes to grant the loan nor cares to maintain a peaceful relationship with the petitioner, the person asked can deny the request with this proverb. This is an *omwizo* and is used to *gaya*. The speaker *gaya*'s the hearer for his lack of funds. Further, he uses the *omwizo* to break off the conversation and, very probably, most social relations with the hearer.

SEQUENCING

When an *enfumo* is spoken, it is almost always accompanied by a literal (that is, a nonfigurative) statement of speaker's view of the social situation in question. The *enfumo* usually comes after this account (see examples [1]–[8], [10], [12], [15], [16], [18] of *enfumo* usage). The Haya say that adding the *enfumo* makes the words of the literal account "hard"; it "tightens" them. One man told me, "An *enfumo* is like a wrench—it tightens your words." Spoken *after* an explanation of its application, the *enfumo* is an attempt to convince the hearer that the speaker's view of the social situation is correct. And if it is correct, the speaker hopes that discussion of alternate views will then be left off. Concluding an explanation with an *enfumo* is an attempt to close the discussion of a topic—in agreement.

An *enfumo* can also be used before the literal explanation of its application. In this case it serves as a "way in" to a discussion. Spoken before, it introduces the topic of a conversation in which the speaker expects the hearer to voice an opinion. Introducing the *enfumo* first shows that the speaker is very sure of the correctness of his view of the social situation. He is so sure, in fact, that he invites discussion.

Whether the *enfumo* is spoken before or after the literal explanation, the interaction is a peaceful one. There are many words spoken. The hearer may even laugh—an *enfumo* often evokes this response. The conversation passes back and forth, especially when the *enfumo* is used to introduce the topic. All these are signs of peaceful interaction. The word *enfumo* comes from *"oku-fumola"* which means "to converse peacefully."

On the other hand, an *omwizo* is usually spoken without explaining its application (see examples [9], [13], [17], [19] of *omwizo* usage). As one Haya defined the difference between *enfumo* and *omwizo*, "The speaker interprets an *enfumo* for you. An *omwizo* you interpret for yourself." An alternate meaning for the word *omwizo* is "insides" in the sense of a person's insides or viscera. To speak an *omwizo* is *"oku-tela omwizo,"* literally "to strike (someone's) insides."

A proverb use is classified as an *omwizo* when it meets the four criteria in Table 1, and it is spoken without a literal explanation. A proverb use that *gaya*'s is likewise an *omwizo* and is spoken without explanation.

The questions may now be asked: Can an *omwizo* be spoken *with* an explanation? The answer is yes, but if it is so used, further specification must be made in regard to the sequential position of the proverb relative to its explanation and relative to the terminal parts of the conversation. There are two possibilities: *"omwizo"* precedes explanation to begin a conversation; explanation precedes *"omwizo"* to end the conversation (I am using *"omwizo"* here in the sense of a proverb which meets the four stated criteria of usage). If an *"omwizo"* is used to begin a conversation (20), it will be preceded by an introductory phrase like, "I have come to speak a proverb* to you. The Haya say. . ." or "I have come to hit you an *omwizo*. The Haya say. . . ." After the proverb, the speaker explains its application to the context situation. Because it is an *"omwizo"* the context situation involves a wrong which hearer has done the speaker. By inviting discussion about the situation, the speaker clearly intends to reconcile the differences between himself and the hearer. This usage is like an *omwizo* in that it meets the four criteria (the proverb refers to a wrong done the speaker by the hearer in the past). But it is also like an *enfumo* in that it is used as a way into a discussion that will draw the speaker and

* The Haya word is *omugani* which may be translated either as "tale" or "proverb."

hearer together. Haya speakers do not classify this usage unequivocally. They say it is "like" an *enfumo* or "like" an *omwizo*.

When an *omwizo* is spoken at the end of a discussion following an explanation of its application (21), it is used to close off verbal interaction. The speaker states the wrong he feels has been done to him and "tightens" his words with a proverb. The proverb shows that there is no peaceful relationship between them. Spoken at the end of a discussion, after an explanation of its meaning, the proverb is an *omwizo*.

SEMANTIC CONSIDERATIONS

An *omwizo* indirectly states something about the referent that he would not want said about himself. What is "inside" and alluded to by the proverb is inconsistent with and damaging to his public self. An *omwizo* "hits (the referent's) insides" by pointing to an inconsistency between what he thinks, feels, or knows inside and his outward behavior.

The examples of *omwizo* usage given above (excluding those in which a status insult, or *gaya*, is conveyed) point up the inconsistency between the referent's actions and what he knows or should know is proper behavior. This latter knowledge is said to be inside the wrongdoer. When a proverb is used to *gaya*, its implication is that the person is *really*—that is, on the inside as opposed to the way he outwardly tries to present himself—a low status individual.

One may also use an *omwizo* to imply that the referent's real intentions are opposite to the ones which he has expressed. Of the five proverbs of this kind collected, two constitute exceptions to the criteria for classification in Table 1. They are exceptions in that they are classed as *emiizo* (pl. of *omwizo*), although they are not spoken in the presence of the person to whom the proverb refers (cf. feature 2 in Table 1). The two exceptions may be used *only in the absence of the referant*, that is, only in a third person correlation.

As a group, the five proverbs that point up the inconsistency between expressed and real intentions have unusually restricted applications. Most other proverbs have more than one type of possible correlation; each of these proverbs is restricted to a single type of correlation. Three of them may be used only with a second person referent. The two proverbs under discussion may be used only in third person correlations.

One of the proverbs thus restricted is (22), "The person who surpasses the mother in mourning is the one who killed the child." This proverb is used as an indirect accusation of witchcraft against a person who, according to the speaker, is trying to cover her guilt by an outward display of grief at a child's death. Such accusations are made against women who are said to bewitch a child out of envy for its mother's good fortune. The outward/inward inconsistency pointed up is between mourning and practicing witchcraft. The proverb is used only in the absence of the referent, and it is classed as an *omwizo*.

The other proverb restricted to use in the third person (23), "When the ant kills is when he sees his relatives" describes people who visit only when they hope to gain some benefit, never out of social obligation. Outwardly, the ant's relatives appear to be behaving in a proper way by visiting, but they actually do it only because they hope to get some food (they have heard that the ant has "killed"—i.e., been successful in getting food). When a man's cow dies, he is visited by neighbors and relatives who perhaps visit only rarely. He might use this proverb to describe their behavior to his best friend. He would use the proverb only in their absence, but it would be classed as an *omwizo*. The outward/inward inconsistency pointed to is between socially proper visiting and selfish gluttony (in Haya, *obululu*). One could not accuse his neighbors and relatives of this fault directly without grave social consequences.

RULES OF USAGE AND CULTURAL VALUES

Let us now reconcile the exceptions—*emiizo* which convey status insults (*gaya*) and those two described above which allude to witchcraft and gluttony—with the *emiizo* that meet the four criteria given in Table 1. It will be recalled that the two *emiizo* regarding witchcraft and gluttony do not meet the criterion (no. 2) that the referent of the proverb be present. The *emiizo* used to *gaya* do not meet the criterion (no. 1) that some sort of wrong has been committed. Moreover, these latter proverbs may be used in a third person correlation, with the referent absent, or present but not spoken to; this does not meet the criterion that the referent be present (no. 2). The process of reconciling all of these types of usages into a single system may be begun by considering the actual terms *enfumo* and *omwizo* more closely.

Although *enfumo* and *omwizo* are taken as a contrasting pair, each lexical term in fact refers to a different domain of proverb use. The word *enfumo* refers specifically to the interaction situation in which the proverb is spoken to effect an agreement between the hearer and himself. The *enfumo* helps the interlocutor "to converse peacefully"—*oku-fumola*. The word *omwizo*, in contrast, refers specifically to the context situation about which the proverb is spoken. The person in the context situation to whom the proverb is applied is "hit inside" by being exposed; that is, by having the alleged inconsistency between his internal state and external behavior overtly pointed to. By hitting him inside, the speaker damages the referent's social persona. In another idiom, he causes the referent "to lose face."

An *enfumo continues* or aids the conversation of the participants. An *omwizo* points to an *inconsistency* and *damages* the social persona of the referent. This is represented in the following table.

TABLE 2

	Interaction Situation	*Context Situation*
enfumo	continue	*a*
omwizo	*b*	inconsistency-damage

Because the two terms are in a sense opposites, we might wish to complete the paradigm by adding (in position *a*) that an *enfumo* does *not* point to an inconsistency or damage the person referred to in the context situation, and by adding (in position *b*) that an *omwizo* does *not* continue (that is, it *disrupts*) the conversation in the interaction situation. Such a completed paradigm would be valid for the first group of proverbs considered—those for which the four features in Table 1 characterize an *omwizo* usage. But exceptions have already shown the matter to be more complex. To account for all of the usages, first, the dimensions continue/disrupt and no damage–no inconsistency/ damage–inconsistency must be considered independent of each other. Second, usages in which the correlation is second person must be separated from those in which the correlation is third person. This may be represented in two fourfold tables:

TABLE 3:
Second Person Correlation

The pluses and minuses specify values on each of the two-value dimensions. The pluses signify the former values on each dimension (continue and no inconsistency, no damage) and the minuses signify the latter values (disrupt and inconsistency, damage).

		Combinations			
		1	2	3	4
interaction situation:	continue/disrupt	+	+	−	−
context situation:	no incon./incon.				
	no damage/damage	+	−	+	−
	usage classified as:	*enfumo*	mixed	(see text)	*omwizo*

TABLE 4:
Third Person Correlation

		Combinations			
		1	2	3	4
interaction situation:	continue/disrupt	+	+	−	−
context situation:	no incon./incon.				
	no damage/damage	+	−	+	−
	usage classified as:	*enfumo*	*omwizo*	(see text)	?

In the second person correlation table, combinations 1 and 4 are clearcut instances of *enfumo* and *omwizo* as described by the four features in Table 1. Combination 1 characterizes a proverb usage that continues the flow of conversation and does no harm to the person referred to by the proverb—the addressee. A proverb used in the manner specified by combination 4 would break off the conversation and damage the persona of the addressee by pointing to an inconsistency between his outward actions and his inner thoughts. Combination 2 is a proverb usage that serves to continue the conversation but at the same time points to an inconsistency between inward and outward states. This is example (20) above of a proverb characterized by the four features necessary for an *omwizo* but used to *begin* a conversation. It is said to be "like" an *enfumo*—in that it continues the conversation. But at the same time it is "like" an *omwizo* in that it points to an inconsistency. There is a genre of speech which can be described by combination 3; that is, that causes conversational disruption without pointing to an inward/outward inconsistency or doing personal damage. Some examples of these direct insults, called *ebijumi*, are: "drop dead," "be struck by lightning," "lick an anus."

In the third person correlation table, the first combination is easily recognizable as an *enfumo*. The proverb usage continues the conversation and does no damage to the referent, who is not present. The second combination, in which the proverb continues the conversation but points to a damaging inconsistency in a third person referent, is classified as an *omwizo*. This combination characterizes the two examples (22) and (23) that allude to witchcraft and selfish gluttony. These proverbs may be spoken only in a third person correlation and are used to promote agreement between the interlocutors. Combination 2 also includes proverbs that convey a status insult (*gaya*), when these proverbs are used with a third person referent. An example of a proverb that *gaya*'s is the "Nyante" proverb. The *emiizo* in combination 2 of Table 4 are thought to be damaging to their referents even when not spoken in their presence.

Combination 3 of the third person correlation table, like its counter-part in Table 3, is not accomplished through proverb use. The genre of speech that combines disruption in the interaction situation with not pointing to an inconsistency in the context situation is the same genre described in combination 3 of Table 3, the insults known as *ebijumi*. Here the reference is to a third person so that the insult is less direct. An example of a third person *ekijumi* (sing. of *ebijumi*) is, "The rats of your house are lying down and fighting." This was told to me as an example of what young boys say to one another when they are away from the village herding goats. The sentence is a metaphorical way of saying, "Your parents are lying down and having sexual intercourse." This was said to be "like" an *omwizo*, but definately an *ekijumi*. It is like an *omwizo* in that the insult is indirect, but unlike an *omwizo* in that it does not point to a socially disapproved or shameful state of affairs. The fact that parents engage in sexual intercourse may seem like an inconsistency between outward appearance and inward reali-ties to adolescent boys, but it is not "really" so. The expression, there-fore, is not "really" an *omwizo*. It is mere verbal abuse, that is, an *ekijumi*.

Proverb usages described by combination 4—a third person correla-tion that points to an inconsistency in and damages the referent, and at the same time disrupts the conversation—do not occur in my data. On the basis of my knowledge of Haya proverb use, I can state that such usages are improbable. But knowing the verbal agility of Haya proverb speakers, I would not say that such usages are impossible.

Comparing the two tables, we now ask the question, why are some proverbs damaging to their referent *only* when spoken to his face (i.e., in a second person correlation) while other proverbs are damaging *even* when spoken behind the referent's back (i.e., in a third person correlation)? The former group is represented by the "clay canoe" proverb, the "wife of Mulalo" proverb, the "it nauseates" proverb, and the "not looking in on food" proverb. The latter group is composed of the witchcraft proverb (22), the selfish gluttony proverb (23), and proverbs that convey a status insult (*gaya*) when they are used in a third person correlation.

An answer to the question may be found by considering the kinds of faults that are pointed up by each group of proverbs. The misdeeds committed by the referents of the first group of proverbs primarily effect the relationship between the guilty party and the victim. The action referred to can be considered a wrongdoing primarily with respect to this two-person set. For example, the "not looking in on food" proverb used as an *omwizo* involves a person who fails to visit (the guilty party) and a person who is not visited (the victim). Although there are cultural prescriptions for proper visiting behavior, the fault of not visiting is a fault only with reference to the person not visited. This same relativity characterizes the faults of the other proverbs representative of this group. The "clay canoe" proverb points to one person's refusal to follow the advice of another; this is regarded as an insult to his knowledge. As such, it is a fault but the matter is solely between wrongdoer and victim. The "wife of Mulalo" proverb used as an *omwizo* (14) refers to a matter of nonreciprocity between two individuals. The "it nauseates" proverb involves a mother and her son's unfilial behavior. In all the *omwizo* uses of these proverbs, the matter referred to is a fault relative to the relationship between two people. The frame of reference employed in judging the action a misdeed is a two-person set, rather than the society as a whole.

In contrast to this, the witchcraft, gluttony, and status insult *emiizo* point to faults that are judged with respect to the society as a whole rather than merely to a two-person relationship. An *omwizo* that conveys a status insult (*gaya*) points to traits on the part of the referent that are considered to be low status judged with respect to a shared system of status-related traits. Similarly, witchcraft is an offense of such severity that it affects not only the parties directly involved, but also the entire community. The frame of reference used in judging witchcraft an offense is therefore not a two-person set; it is rather the society as a whole. Selfish gluttony (*obululu*) is not so immediately apparent a case of "crime against society" as witchcraft, but evidence can be marshaled to this point. As Beidelman has pointed out with respect to another Tanzanian people, selfishness in regard to food is considered a serious offense in a society dependent upon a subsistence economy (Beidelman 1975). Both leopard and hyena are depicted as selfish gluttons (*abalulu*) in Haya folktales, and stories are told which explore the consequences of this character trait in human beings as well. The frequent appearance of this theme in folktales would seem to confirm that gluttony is a fault with respect to society rather than merely with respect to two individuals.

In sum, we have the *emiizo* in combination 4, Table 3, that refer to a relative fault on the part of the referent. These *emiizo* are thought to "hit inside" (i.e., do damage) only when spoken by the person wronged in the presence of the wrongdoer. On the other hand, we have the *emiizo* in combination 2, Table 4, that refer to a fault on the part of the referent which may be called "absolute" in the sense that it is a fault with respect to the society as a whole. These *emiizo* do damage even when the person referred to is not present. A proverb that alludes to an "absolute" fault hits the referent "inside" without regard to context. A proverb that alludes to a "relative" fault hits the referent "inside" under certain contextual conditions; namely, that it is spoken by the person wronged in the presence of the referent.

We began by focusing on the proverb as a specific genre of speech; we have concluded by explicating a category distinction made by Haya proverb speakers. To move from a focus on a folkloristic genre to an explication of indigenous categories, first, an etic framework was developed that sees proverbs as speech *used* in social interaction. This implies that the metaphoric relationships between proverb situation and context situation must be described and related to the interaction situation of proverb use. Second, examples of proverb use were adduced to illustrate that a single proverb has many applications, how these applications are logically related to one another, and how some are termed *enfumo*, others *emiizo*, by the Haya. Finally, the criteria for the *enfumo/omwizo* distinction were developed and were shown to include context as well as text, sequencing as well as semantics.

Many questions about how the Haya use proverbs have not been fully dealt with here. Questions regarding who uses proverbs, when a proverb is used instead of or to complement nonfigurative discourse, the ritual uses of proverbs, thematic content, structural features of proverb texts, the relationship between proverb use as a speech act and other speech acts—all of these are components of an ethnographic account of Haya proverb usage, and are dealt with in a larger format (Seitel 1972).

Chapter

4

The Performance of
Ritual Metaphors

JAMES W. FERNANDEZ*

Finally a few examples may be given of cases in which the use of descriptive terms for certain concepts or the metaphorical use of terms has led to peculiar views or customs. . . .More convincing are examples taken from the use of metaphorical terms in poetry, which in rituals are taken literally, and are made the basis of certain rites. I am inclined to believe, for example, that the frequently occuring image of *the devouring of wealth* has a close relation to the detailed form of the winter ritual among the Indians of the North Pacific coast. . . .

FRANZ BOAS (1911)

This insight offered to anthropology by Franz Boas has largely lain fallow in the sixty years since. Kenneth Burke, however, in his wide-ranging and insatiable inquiry into man and all his works, has made that insight central in his task. And he would appear to have carried it far beyond the bounds of religious ceremony. He writes:

Indeed as the documents of science pile up, are we not coming to see that whole works of scientific research, even entire schools, are hardly

* The field research lying behind this discussion was supported by the Ford Foundation Foreign Area Fellowship Program (1958–61) and the Social Science Research Council–American Council of Learned Societies Joint Committee on African Studies (1965–66). Versions of this paper were presented at colloquia at Duke University (March 1968, December 1969), The Philadelphia Anthropological Society (October 1968), and Brown University (April 1970). John Lanzetta, Robert Kleck, James H. Spencer, Jr., and Edward Yonan have provided valuable commentary for which I am grateful.

100

more than the patient repetition, in all its ramifications, of a fertile metaphor? Thus we have at different eras in history, considered man as the son of God, as an animal, as a political and economic brick, as a machine, each such metaphor, and a hundred others, serving as the cue for an unending line of data and generalizations. (1954:95)

Of course as Burke has worked out his theories of "dramatism"—for him any discussion of human affairs is dramatic criticism—the symbolic actions singled out again and again take the form of ancient collective ritual. In Burke's analysis ritual dramas emerge in the most contemporary and mundane literary materials. However widely he searches for central metaphors, therefore, the problem of their relation to ritual remains.

In anthropological theory we recognize a progression of central metaphors: the growth metaphor of evolutionism, Frazier's "struggle over succession," the Durkheimian mechanical-organic typology, the Kroeberian superorganic, the diffusionist "pebble in a pool." Histories of anthropological theory are usually silent on these central metaphors although literary anthropologists influenced by Burke (Hyman 1959) are quick to point them out. While we may resist seeing in them a whole system of thought (Pepper 1942) we can recognize their fertility. A new metaphor does plant before us a new frame of reference which is felt to be more apt and to make better sense of the materials than previous perspectives.

If an awareness of metaphor is important because of its presence as an organizing element in inquiry, one is equally moved to its study by the frequency of figures of speech in natural discourse. Unless we give some explanation of how metaphor—the essential figure of speech—operates, we risk making what Garfinkle calls "judgmental dopes" out of our informants. We risk ignoring in our intellections the comprehension they have of their situation as a result of more subtle "sign functions." He points out: "Available theories have many important things to say about such sign functions as marks and indicators but they are silent on such overwhelmingly more common features as glosses, synecdoche, documented representation, euphemism, irony and double entendre." (Garfinkle 1967:71)

If Garfinkle finds such devices of representation common in the natural discourse of the mass society in which he works, how much more common must they be in the societies studied by anthropologists which are proverbially reliant upon indirection and analogy rather than upon direct analysis. Although an interest in the relation of metaphor to ritual is nothing new a theory of that relationship is in need of elaboration. It is proposed here that metaphors provide organizing images which ritual action puts into effect. This ritualization of metaphor enables the pronouns participating in ritual to undergo apt integrations and transformations in their experience. The study of ritual is the study of the structure of associations brought into play by metaphoric predications upon pronouns.

METAPHORIC PREDICATION AND METAPHORIC MOVEMENT

How can one give an account of metaphoric statements? They are slippery and appear to be something of a swindle. In what way is one to be critical of them. . .affirm or deny their use by reference to the distinctive features of the event or object to which they are applied? Metaphorical statements—our leader is a foxy grandpa—"cannot be corrected by reference to proper usage nor by the way things turn out" (McClosky 1964:216). In what way can one say of them that they are right or wrong? They can only be shown to be inappropriate or inept. Can inquiry satisfactorily probe anyone's sense of ineptness or propriety? It is difficult to specify the set of rules or principles of distribution by which the decision to associate our leader and a foxy grandpa can be anticipated. That decision rests upon a multitude of experiences with these words in contexts which overlap in some respects but contrast in others.

Rather than a grammatical definition of metaphor, I will propose, to guide us, a two-part semantic definition. A metaphor is (1) a device of representation by which a new meaning is learned (Von Steenburgh 1965:678) and (2) a strategic predication upon an inchoate pronoun (an I, a you, a we, a they) which makes a movement and leads to performance.

First, a metaphor is a predication to some subject that changes the meaning of that subject. Thus George is a muffin. Metaphoric usage is to be contrasted with literal usage in the sense that when we make a literal predication about some subject we do not really learn anything new about it. We merely identify it by applying a name to it according to its characteristics (the distinctive features it gives evidence of) at some level of the domain to which it belongs. Thus George is an animal, George is a man, George is an adult, George is a father, etc.

Any subject or any set of subjects is literally assigned a name (a predicate) according to a set of characteristics which ordinarily characterize it in common parlance in relation to the domain in which it belongs. Any subject or any set of subjects is assigned a metaphoric predicate according to a set of characteristics which do not literally characterize it, except at a very high level of abstraction. This can be illustrated with Venn diagrams (Figure 1). In that sense metaphor makes a false attribution and it is in that sense that we learn something new about the subject. And it is also in that sense that Aristotle defined metaphor as the extension of a name from that to which it usually belongs to some other object.

It is sometimes said that literal predication singles out the essential or important features of the subject while metaphoric predication singles out striking but not essential or important features (McClosky 1964:219). This may be the case by reference to logical rules of classification and denotation but it does not hold when we have connotation in mind. It is in the realm of connotation primarily that metaphoric predication teaches us something new. What we are taught there, I mean to point out, may be essential and very important. Although Locke, from the logical point of view (*Essay on Human Understanding*), criticizes such eloquent and artificial invention as metaphor obtains for "insinuating wrong ideas and moving the passions," it is precisely this insinuation and this movement which are behaviorally of greatest interest.

The fact that there is movement in our understanding, that we do learn something new in metaphor, is well recognized by Wheelwright who speaks of that imaginative process of outreaching (epiphor) and combining (diaphor) that characterizes the metaphoric process. Wheelwright (1962) makes a sharp distinction between epiphor—the extension of meaning by unusual comparison—(life is a dream) and diaphor—the creation of new meaning by juxtaposition—("The Emperor of Ice-Cream"). This is not easily borne out by analysis, however, for metaphor generally combines both processes. Wheelwright's emphasis upon the etymology of the term—*meta* (change), *phora* (motion)—

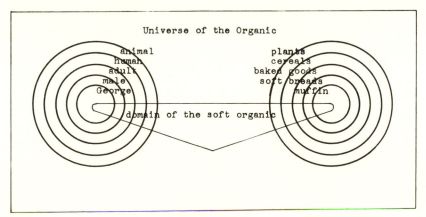

FIGURE 1

hence change in motion, captures, however, the dynamic to be emphasized. Indeed the term "vehicle," emphasized in the humanities for the
metaphoric predicate, expresses the dynamic as well.

It is necessary to distinguish varieties of metaphor. The distinction
is to be made first according to the relationship of the metaphorical
predicate to its subject. As Aristotle advises, "To adorn, borrow metaphor from things superior; to disparage, borrow from things inferior."
Metaphor will thus vary as it adorns or disparages its subject, and this
is fundamental. But metaphor as vehicle must also be distinguished
according to the clarity with which the subject is held in mind. Thus,
if the subject is held clearly in mind, metaphoric comment has a rather
different effect than when the subject is vaguely conceived. Here metaphor accomplishes a notable illumination of the obscure and inchoate.
This difference has been made in terms of perspective metaphor (my
arm, clearly conceived, is a lever) and prescinding metaphor (hate,
obscurely conceived, is a smoldering fire) (Van Steenburgh 1965). In
general, the semantic movement accomplished by metaphor is from the
abstract, and inchoate in the subject to the more concrete, ostensive and
easily graspable in the metaphoric predicate. Thus "mercy droppeth as
a gentle rain from heaven." The gentle rain gives to the abstract and
vaguely conceived "mercy" a concreteness that literal definition is hope-
less to achieve. Metaphor obtains in such cases what has been well
called by T. S. Elliot an "objective correlative" of what is subjectively
inchoate in perception and reflection.

Metaphors, like language generally, can serve a variety of functions:
informative, expressive, declarative, directive, etc. They can be put
forth in an attempt to bring additional information to bear on a subject
where logical processes of superordination or subordination seem inadequate. They can serve merely to express the speaker's feelings vis-à-vis
the subject or to declare his intentions vis-à-vis the subject, or, in an
indirect way, to give directions to the subject. The metaphors to be
discussed have, in varying degrees, all these uses but their particular
use approximates the last in that they give directions. We will call them
performative metaphors because, as we shall see, they bring about
actions appropriate to their realization. They imply performance.

There are many distinctions to be made in figures of speech. We will
remark on one only: the distinction between analogue or structural
metaphors (Black 1962:222) and textual metaphors (Berggren 1962–
63).[1] The difference hinges upon the principle of association, the rule

---

1. Both Black (1962) and Berggren (1963) make finer distinctions in the varieties
of these metaphors than we feel it necessary to make here. For example, Black
distinguishes among scale models, analogic models, mathematical models. He also
prefers the term *archetype* to metaphor probably because of the association of
metaphor exclusively with poetics.

by which there is assimilation of metaphoric predication to its subject. In the case of structural or analogic metaphor, a metaphor is assigned to its subject on the basis of some isomorphic similar structure or pattern of relationships. Thus we say the *branch* of the stream, we use *tree* diagrams in logic, and we speak of the *mechanical* relationship of self-sufficient parts in traditional societies and the *organic* relationship of mutually dependent cells in bureaucratic societies. Black warns with good reason that "identity of structure is compatible with the widest variety of content—hence the possibilities for construction of analogic models are endless. . . .the risks of fallacious inference from inevitable irrelevancies and distortions in the model are present in aggravated measure" (1962:223).

By textual metaphor one means that metaphor in which the assimilation made is on the basis of similarity in feeling tone—glowering clouds, a brooding landscape, a dyspeptic bureaucracy. It is, of course, the intent of science to eradicate mere textual or emotional association and capitalize as much as possible on the analogic mode of metaphor attempting to develop more systematic precision in the structural analogy by experimental verification. [The textual/structural distinction is roughly similar to that made between internal and external metaphors in Part I. (eds.)]

In the analogic mode of metaphoric reasoning, however, there may often be emotional reasons behind the assimilation. Take the Durkheimian mechanical and organic metaphors. As has been frequently pointed out, they have a different emotional weight—the former an objectivity, an exteriority, a detachment, the other a subjectivity, an interiority, an attachment. These metaphors move by a kind of "principle of compensation." One can speculate that the assignment of the mechanical metaphor to traditional societies objectifies societies in which the emotional subjectivity of kinship is the characteristic feature. On the other hand, the assignment of the organic metaphor to the impersonal and rational bureaucratic societies subjectifies them and gives them an interiority they do not, in fact, possess. In our analysis of metaphoric usage we stress the importance of the emotional movement accomplished by the metaphor whether textual or analogic in emphasis.

We can now identify the kernel metaphoric statement with which we will be preoccupied: the inchoate subject and metaphoric predicate out of which, by a series of transformations, we see arise the thick and complex surface structure of cult ritual. One need not apologize for employing a modish transformational metaphor for it fits the phenomena very well. Kernel metaphoric statements involve pronouns as the inchoate subjects (tenors, continuous terms) and any of a virtually limitless range of nominal attributes as the metaphoric predicates (vehicles, discontinuous terms). The general movement of kernel metaphor is from the abstract and inchoate in the subject to the concrete and ostensive in the predicate. What is more abstract and inchoate and in need of predication than a pronoun? Personal experience and social life cry out that we predicate some identity upon the I, the you, the he, the she, the they, the it. These are the "generalized others" which social experience singles out for us but does not meaningfully identify in any particular way.

Hence:

> I am a lion or a parrot.
> He is a mouse or a muffin or the King of Kings!
> We are friendly giants a bit clumsy in our paternalism.
> They are calculating machines who know the price of everything and the value of nothing.
> She is a common scold.
> It is an organism which was born and will die.

From all these kernel metaphoric statements, we learn something new about the subject in the sense in which we have above discussed learning as movement.

When faced, in short, with the inchoate pronoun men have several options. Most reasonably they can appeal to the principal domain to which the subject belongs and offer a predicate definition by super-ordination within that domain. He is an investment officer. He is a banker. He is a businessman. He is a father. He is an adult. He is a homo sapiens. We see here immediately that men in social life belong to a number of domains and hence in qualifying the inchoate pronoun we must always choose one domain or another of his activity. Of course, we learn something by the very choice of domains and by ordination within it but not in the sense that we learn something by the metaphoric choice of a domain to which the subject does not legitimately belong and within which he does not legitimately act. The other alternative in the pursuit of a forceful and clear predication to the inchoate pronoun is the tautological one upon which great works of the imagination, in pursuit of ultimate definitions, often end, viz. *The Divine Comedy*. The subject, perhaps out of phenomenological despair that no predicate is not in some sense metaphorical, is simply reiterated, neither confirmed nor denied in the predicate: I am I, he is he, it is itness, etc. The subject like Dante finds himself, itself, themselves, looking into a mirror. In fact, this tautology of the mirror exists in the cult to be examined.[2] But this alternative, an aspect perhaps of the mythological

2. The initiates, sometimes in Bwiti and almost always in the sister cult of Mbiri, eat the alkaloid *eboga* (*Tabernenthes eboga*) while looking into a mirror painted

motif of eternal return, is not so interesting as the metaphoric predicate which entails, as I now want to point out, ritual performance.

A RITUAL PROGRESS: BWITI

I would like to demonstrate the operation of kernel metaphoric statements in relationship to the Fang reformative cult of Bwiti (Fernandez 1964, 1965, 1966). This cult offers one of the most complex liturgical structures that we know of among African religious movements, which must be today numbered in the many thousands (Sundkler 1960; Barrett 1968).[3] It is correspondingly richer in metaphor. But metaphor is an organizing element in all these cult movements and I have elsewhere attempted to give an account of these metaphors—the militant metaphor of Christian soldiering in the *Apostles Revelation Society* in Ghana, the pastoral metaphor of the bull that crashes in the kraal, in the *Church of God in Christ* in Natal, South Africa, the sylvan metaphor of the parrot's egg in *Bwiti* itself, and the atmospheric metaphor of the circumambient holy wind (or ghost) in Christianism Celeste in Dahomey (Fernandez 1966, 1967, 1969, 1970).

The cult of Bwiti in the Gabon Republic is polymorphous with more than six sub-branches. The data presented here are taken from the *Asumege Ening* (New Life) branch which appeared after the Second World War in the Region of the Estuaire and in the early sixties was principally located in Kango, Medounu, and Oyem districts. But Bwiti itself is much older. It appears about the time of the First World War as a result of the contact between the Fang and the southern Gabonese people in the lumber camps of the Gabon estuary and the lower Ogoowe. The Fang adapted their own ancestor cult Bieri (then failing) to Bwiti, the more aesthetically compelling ancestor cult of the southern Gabonese people, notably the Mitsogo and the Baloumbo. At its inception Bwiti represented the syncretism of two northwest Bantu ancestor cults. More recently there has been considerable syncretization of Christian elements.

In the Asumege Ening branch of Bwiti we can identify the following distribution of ceremonial scenes (Frake 1964) in the all night cere-

---

with abstract designs. After some time, under the influence of the narcotic and the ritual, they "see" their ancestor come out of the ground (actually their own face reflected). It is an essential first step of initiation. But it is a crucial step for, visually, the I is transformed into the other by a simple tautology.

3. This judgment is based on field work in ten religious movements in various parts of Africa in 1959–60 and 1965–66. See, for example, the ritual parsimony that characterizes the *Apostles Revelation Society* in Ghana (Fernandez 1970).

mony held once a week. The distinctions may be made according to the Bwitist's own ritual vocabulary.

Introduction
1. *Minkin:* ceremonies of entrance into the chapel and invitation to the ancestors. Intermittent, beginning at 3:00 P.M.
2. *Njimba:* ceremonies of personal prayer, preparation, and fore-gathering. Held en masse in a hut outside the chapel, 6:00 P.M. to 8:00 P.M.

Zen Ngombi Part I (Road of the Cult Harp)
3. *Zen Abiale:* the ceremonies of the birth of the spirit into the after life (syncretized to the birth of Christ). From early evening until midnight. Interspersed with *obango*—vertiginous dances in which the spirit is shaken free from the body.
4. *Nkobo Akyunge:* "evangile," the ceremonies of final reunion with the ancestors. Final and most direct and powerful prayer to the supernatural. Direction of the "miraculous word" to the membership from the cult leader—*nima na kombo.* Includes a small *minkin* in which the membership exits to go out into the forest on narrow pre-cut trails in order to invite in any lingering ancestor spirits. Midnight.

Zen Ngombi Part II (Road of the Cross)
5. *Zen Awu:* the ceremonies of the death of the spirit from after life into this life (syncretized to the death of Christ). From midnight to first light, interspersed with *obango.*

Conclusion
6. *Minkin:* ceremonies of exit from the chapel and farewell to the ancestors. First light until sunrise.
7. *Njimba:* ceremonies of euphoric aftergathering of the member-ship for ritual food and relaxed conversation. 8:00 A.M.

The scenario is not absolutely fixed in any cult house, and scene development tends to vary with season and with the leaders responsible for the particular seance. Some leaders are more given to creative and unscheduled ceremonial elaboration than others. Now that a Christian calendar has been adopted, the particular ceremonies are even more susceptible to shift in spiritual and practical focus. But we may define four major categories of the scene:

1. *Minkin:* ceremonies (songs and dances) of entrance and exit.
2. *Njimba:* ceremonies (song and prayers) of group cohesion, inter-communication, and appeal to the powers.
3. *Zen Ngombi:* ceremonies (songs and dances) particularly cele-brating the primordial experiences of the individual (at the level of

body tissue, events of satisfaction and depletion) and of his culture (at the level of the mythological events of creation and dispersion). Generally divided into two sub-scenes as life processes or death processes are being celebrated (*zen abiale, zen awu*), and according to whether the key instrument is the soft cult harp, *ngombi,* or the intense drums, *obango.*

4. *Evangile:* ceremonies of communication of the "word" from the powers, and confirmation of the bonds of the spiritual community.

Although there may be some variation in the distribution of these scenes and in the arrangement of the more than two hundred songs and a dozen dances that appear as part of them, the general distribution shows us *minkin* and *njimba* embracing the road of the cult harp which themselves embrace the evangile as the nested and nuclear event of the evening.

Although there is considerable variation in the distribution of scenes within the total scenario, and particularly as we descend in level to the inspection of smaller and smaller segments of scenes (Pike 1967), nevertheless the distribution is not probabilistic and dependent solely upon the outcome of the accumulating series of scenes. "In acting as well as in speaking persons have an image of the pattern to be completed and make plans according" (Frake 1964:125). It is just this series of images that must be scrutinized if one is to understand the cult and have some modest foreknowledge of its necessary development. My view is that these images are contained in metaphors, which organize scene development in a fundamental way.

Let me then examine four metaphors which arise in Bwiti as members comment upon the evening's progress. We find them referring to various constellations of the ceremony as: here we are such and such, there he is such and such—*eyong dzi bi ne, eyong te e ne.* Four of the most recurrent predicates are:

> *bi ne esamba*—We are a trading team (in file through the forest).
> *bi ne ayong da*—We are of one clan.
> *me ne (e ne) emwan mot*—I am (he is) the son of man (man child).
> *bi ne nlem mvore*—We are one heart.

Although these metaphors emerge in liturgical commentary, one finds them running through cult life and providing a periodic familiarizing reinforcement, or leitmotif. Merely to identify them is not enough. We must (1) demonstrate their aptness and (2) show how, in performance, they accomplish those transformations of experience which is the prime function of religion.

First consider their aptness, for the fitness of ritual lies in the aptness of metaphor, and it should be one main object of anthropological method to indicate the contexts by which metaphoric associations become appropriate or apt. It may be asked: is not aptness a function of purpose? Is not something apt or appropriate to a certain purpose? Bwiti participants articulate several purposes that bring them together for worship. Predominant among these are the desires to obtain surcease from the sorrows of village life, to obtain some sense of vitality in that life, and at the same time to obtain effective contact with the ancestral dead and the powers of the beyond. In fact, the purposes of the cult are not dogmatically, even clearly, formulated, and it is difficult to obtain consensus about them (Fernandez 1965). One may, abstracting from the evidence before us, say more accurately that the cult ceremonial is not explicitly regarded as a technique undertaken with a practical purpose in mind but is rather valued for certain kinds of affirmation it makes and inspirations it gives. And to understand these affirmations and inspirations—we may still wish to call them "purposes"—one must examine the metaphors themselves. For a very fundamental kind of purpose is declared in the very choice of these metaphors.

The metaphor of the *esamba* appears first in the transformations I want to consider. It is the metaphor that belongs typically to the *minkin*. The metaphor connects the cult members to a cohesive trading band marching with determination through the forest. Historically the main association of this term is that of the adventurous team of young men which collected rubber and ivory at the turn of the century and took it to the coast to exchange for trade goods. This group was characterized by high solidarity, the euphoria of hunting and gathering, and a rewarding trading relation with the colonial world. It was a group characterized by values and a sense of purpose which led to significant fulfillment. The aptness of this metaphor is readily understood when the goal-less-ness, the lack of solidarity in village and kinship, and the high degree of ambivalence about the larger colonial world are grasped. For these conditions provide experience to which the metaphor was, and continues to be, a compensatory representation.

The second metaphor to emerge is that of *ayong da*, one clan. It is primarily the metaphor of the *njimba*. This may not seem like a metaphor but in fact it is, for the membership of Bwiti chapels is an association drawn from many clans and to a degree from several tribes. It is not properly described, by reference to the norms of Fang social structure, as one clan. During the *njimba* when the members sit together under the eye of the elders of the cult to hear individual prayers they say: We are one clan. Prayers are made at this time, incidentally, preceded by the reciting of genealogy, the *"pièce maitresse"* of clan identification. We must keep in mind that clan relationships are much degenerated in their claims on allegiance (this is reflected in the decline in knowledge of the genealogies). Since allegiance to the clan is virtually the same thing as allegiance to the ancestors, who are its guarantors, we understand the aptness of this metaphor. For the Bwiti cult is reacting to the kinds of individualism and opportunism which have undermined the clan and the ancestors, who symbolized its viability and the viability of all its members.

The third metaphor is *emwan mot*: child of man, or man child. In the process of the *zen ngombi* phase the members speak of themselves and particularly of their leaders as *emwan mot*. This metaphor has a complex of associations, not the least of which may be a Christian one—in particular the reference to the Savior not only as the son of God but also as the son of man. In this metaphor, it seems to me, the Bwitist expresses several notions. First of all, the satisfactory spiritual experience can only be achieved by escaping from the contaminated (*nyol abe*—bad body) condition of adulthood where, it is said, sexuality and strife with one's brothers and peers burden down the spirit and prevent it from rising over to the "other side." Efforts are made in ritual costuming and in spatial arrangements in dance patterns to avoid the expression of sexual dimorphism and the driect contact between the sexes. The cooperative attitude toward all cult activities is insisted upon. Thus is the innocence of the child achieved in preparation for the passing over to the "other side" where the spirits exist in asexual harmony. Other associations make this an apt metaphor—for example, the notion that the younger the child the closer he is to the ancestors. The metaphor also aptly expresses that state of helplessness and search for aid which the cult members desire to impress upon the ancestors and the great gods. Finally by insisting on identifying themselves with the child of man they emphasize their corporeality—the primordial facts of birth, the intermediate conditions of organismic life, and the inevitability of death—which in all its aspects they both celebrate in worship and seek to pass beyond.

This last intention of the child of man metaphor is even more aptly conveyed in the metaphor of "one heartedness"—*nlem mvore*. This metaphor is affirmed at several points in the ceremony, first at midnight when the members, candles in hand, exit from the chapel in single file and move out into the forest to make final appeals to any ancestors that may be lingering there. As the members file back into the chapel they begin to spiral more and more tightly together until they form a compact mass with candles raised above their heads in such a manner as to form one flame. Here is "one heartedness," a general object of the cult, most characteristically obtained.

Organic metaphors, the extension of the body image into secondary structures and institutions, are quite common in this cult. We see the cult house itself assimilated in its various parts to the human body (Fernandez 1970b). The various torches and pitch lamps are assimilated to the life of the body, for men, like torches, are all shells within which a vital substance burns its alloted time. Membership in a corporate religious body is variously celebrated, but this almost always seems to be done for complex reasons. First, the projection of corporeality into "objective correlatives" is part of the process of escaping the burden of that corporeality—and the Banzie (member of Bwiti), however they may wish to vitalize it, do regard it as a burden. Secondly, insofar as there is a preoccupation with corporeal well-being, ritual action, in structures and institutions that have a corporeal association, is efficacious (perhaps abreactive [Lévi-Strauss 1963b]) in respect to the body's own problems.

In respect to the particular body metaphor here—the heart—its aptness consists in the fact that (1) it is the heart which is the most alive of the bloody organs, (2) it is traditionally conceived by the Fang to be the organ of thought, and (3) in its bloodiness it is associated with the female principle. The aliveness of the heart is apt because, as we have seen, one pole of the cult's intention aims at greater vitality in this life. The fact that the heart is the organ of thought (as opposed to the brain which is the organ of will and intention) is compatible with the other objective of cult life—to escape the corporeal and thus affirm unanimity at that level at which it is most significant—the level of thought. I have elsewhere discussed the focal importance in this cult of the female principle in the universe, *Nyingwan Mebege*, the sister of God. I pointed up then how this element is celebrated in the many different liturgical references to blood and the bloody organs. For blood and the bloody organs are the female portion of the corporeal; semen, bone, and sinew are the male portion. (Fernandez 1969b, 1970b) Many meanings then are at work in this metaphor, for that bloody organ, the heart, has a congeries of useful associations. The heart has so many associations that in many contexts it carries the weight of a symbol. But we are interested here in its specific predication upon "we," the cult members. Many more metaphors than these four appear in Bwiti liturgy—a liturgy that is also laden with symbols. These four metaphors, however, provide a sufficient base for the understanding of ritual as change in motion.

RITUAL ACTUALIZATION OF A METAPHORIC PLAN

We now ask the question as to what role these metaphors play in ritual behavior. Since there is more than one metaphor in any ritual the question is really how metaphors progressively interact and how they affect the participants who suspend belief in their favor. We might best represent this by elaborating the Test-Operate-Test-Exit model of planned behavior, the so-called TOTE model, put forth by Miller, Galenter, and Pribram (1960). It is an information processing model. This model suggests that a metaphor is not only an image, it is a plan for behavior.

I will take it as axiomatic in this model that:

1. People undertake experience in religious movements because they desire to change the way they feel about themselves and the world in which they live and they want to change the way they think about these things as well. They desire to achieve more definition and better definition of their inchoate selves.

2. A metaphor is an image which when acted upon by ritual moves these feelings and object relationships in the desired direction. It provides apt definition.

3. The process by which metaphoric plans operate is one of looping and feedback of information flow in which the venerable principles of contiguity (metonymy) on the one hand and association (metaphor proper) on the other account for the ritual elaboration of the image.

A TOTE account of the dynamics in ritual tenor brought about by the operation of our four metaphoric vehicles is given in Figure 2. In respect to the Fang Bwitist I regard him as coming into the ceremonial of this religious movement suffering from the anomie, the individuation, the comparative deprivation, the status denial, etc. that have long been identified as the psychosocial consequences of rapid change in the colonial situation. I see him, in other words, as coming into the cult with some constellation of feelings of isolation, disengagement, powerlessness, enervation, disphoria, debasement, contamination, and a sense of personal transgression. I load all these disgraceful states upon our unfortunate Bwitist only for purposes of demonstrating the model. It is to be supposed that religious movements have, at one time or another, to contend with all these states though rarely at one time and in the same individual. As a consequence of ritual action, that is a consequence of the operationalizing of metaphoric images which are put forth in contention with these states, we see the Bwitist and the cult group with which he performs as being able to exit from the ritual incorporated, empowered, activated, and euphoric!

The overall predication on our inchoate, and we suppose, troubled subject is "I am a Banzie," that is, I am a member of Bwiti. While in one sense this is not a metaphor but simply an identification of the individual's membership in a class, in another sense it is clearly a

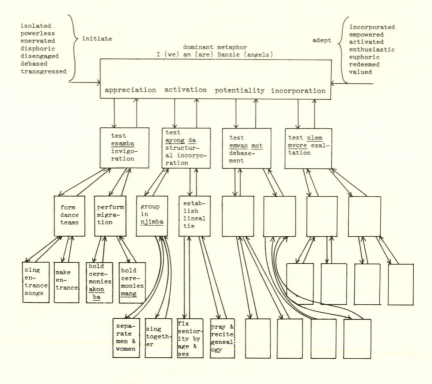

A TOTE Account of Ritual Change in Tenor

FIGURE 2

metaphor, for most members understand the name to mean angel (it is
an adaptation of the French *ange*) and hence someone who has trans-
substantiated and escaped corporeal afflictions. All other metaphors
are subordinate to this one very largely because its meaning is found
in the operationalizing of the subordinate metaphors which we have
discussed. But some of the dances of Bwiti are imitations of the flying
of spirits and hence directly a putting into action of this metaphor. One
of the main objects of the cult is, of course, to actualize or realize such
status. The subordinate metaphoric vehicles all make a contribution to
the realization of that status although their particular force may aim
at other or more specific insufficiencies in the inchoate subject. I have
labeled in Figure 2 what we consider to be the particular contribution
of each metaphor: invigoration, incorporation, debasement, exaltation.

Let us see how two of our metaphors are operated upon by a series
of ritual actions. In order to actualize the first metaphor *esamba*, the
solidarity group, a phalanx of dancers, is formed out on the far end of

the cult village. They dance repeatedly into the chapel each time singing a new song. After the completion of each entrance we suppose, in
compliance with our model, the member to test and see whether they
have realized a condition among themselves that approximates to the
image that they possess of the *esamba*. Different songs are employed
to this end. Toward the conclusion of this ceremonial scene the entrance
into the chapel is quicker and tighter as the members more and more
closely approximate the *esamba*. They will, in fact, soon be able to
exit from this phase of their activity. They will test against the overall
achievement of the quality of the Banzie and, falling short, embark
uopn a second ceremonial scene in the metaphor scenario!

Since the *ayong da* sequence is more complexly divided into sub-
routines, let me follow the operating sequences there. To establish a
quality state conforming to "*ayong da*" the members sit down together
in an open shed especially built for the *njimba*. But this alone does not
establish that group feeling which is desired. They thus commence
singing together. They sing a number of songs until a group quality is
established. Now they test for *ayong da,* but as this is not yet established a new set of sub-routines is brought into operation whose main
object is the establishment of the lineal bond between the living and
the dead. Elders are identified to represent the *ayong*. Women are
separated from men. Genealogies are recited in conjunction with
prayers. Further songs are sung, and the preparations for the separate
entrance into the chapel of men and women is made. A quality state of
ayong da is achieved by these ritual actions.

Several kinds of skepticism are in order when we subscribe in this
way to a TOTE account of ritual performance. We may be skeptical
that each participant enunciates these metaphors in responding to his
inchoate and troubled subjectivity. And of course he does not. But one
must suppose that at some point in the history of the cult these metaphors were ejaculated out of the inchoate I, we, they, etc. by the
visionaries who gave and continue to give prophetic impetus to this
religion. Metaphoric innovation like innovation of any kind rests with
the few and not with the many.

The many who are attracted to these visions and the organized routines which operationalize them need only agree on their aptness in
respect to the inchoate. They need only entertain what may be called
"social consensus" (Fernandez 1965), an agreement upon the appropriateness of the actions they are required to undertake in the cult, and
need have little concern for "cultural consensus," an agreement resting
on insight into the meaning of that action. In the end, through long
participation in action, they may inductively come to an understanding
of the metaphor that controls it. And yet there are those, the originators

and maintainers of revitalization movements who have the insight and force of character and talent for organization, to envision and "create" a new religious culture (Wallace 1956). It is their visions that rest most fundamentally upon metaphoric predications on inchoate subjects. Through force of character and talent for organization they were and are enabled to operationalize these metaphors in the manner in which we find this done in Bwiti. And as the leaders of the various cult chapels, according to their nature, constantly have new visions, new metaphors appear frequently to obtain their ritualization. Fission in this cult and in so many others like it, which often arises because of dispute over ritual (Fernandez 1965:920), may be seen, in the end, as a dispute over the aptness of metaphor.

It must also be recognized in respect to this distinction between social and cultural consensus that the participant in any highly organized activity may be paying quite variable attention to the particulars of his own activity or the activity of others while yet going through, in an acceptable way, its minimum requirements. There may be important differences in "focus." These are differences as regards the level of activity of which the participant is aware or upon which he is concentrating. In fact, the participant's attention at certain junctures may be so removed from the level of activity in the hierarchy of events which are just then qualifying a particular metaphor as to be "with" the ritual in body only. This hypostatization or removal of attention we may call daydreaming (or night dreaming, in the case of Bwiti) cannot be so complete as to prevent the participant from recognizing those cues (signals) by which scenes are changed and new metaphors put into operation. Interestingly enough, although this cult employs an alkaloid narcotic (*tabernenthes eboka*) for purposes of initiation and in very modest amounts to free the participants from the fatigue of the all night ceremony, cult leaders guard against the abuse of the drug lest it cause attention to stray and degrade the precision of the ritual.

THE TRANSFORMATION OF METAPHOR

We may be skeptical that this account of the routines and subroutines by which metaphoric predicates are realized in ritual brings us really close to the complexity of religious experience. While the nature of a phenomenological account of that complexity remains uncertain, our account may be made more apt (in relationship to the inchoate experience we ourselves have of religious behavior) by looking more closely at the problem of the transformation of metaphor. I have been presuming that in the ritual progress the transformation of the participant's attention from one metaphoric domain to another is brought about by a testing of the consequences of ritual against the desired image. The exiting to the next metaphor occurs when the pronomial image—the I image, the we image, etc.—approximates to the metaphoric predication.

But our participants are not, after all, automata. The experience of putting actions into operation to fulfill images is much thickened by the network of associations that run throughout this elementary activity and provide for differing kinds of integration and differing kinds of experience for individual participants. Here we must introduce the two laws of association: (1) the law of contiguity or cause and effect, and (2) the law of assimilation by similarity. In respect to expressive phenomena this difference as we have implied is generally attached to the distinction between metonymy and metaphor, the former being figures of speech resting on relationships of contiguity in the same domain of experience and the latter resting on perceived or felt similarities in the structure or textural quality of experiences which are not necessarily contiguous. Thse are very basic notions in anthropology, linguistics, and psychology: Jacobson and Halle (1956), Lounsbury (1959: 123–28). They were recognized very early in anthropology by Tylor (metaphor and syntax) and by Frazer (sympathetic or similarity magic and contiguous or contiguity magic). They are otherwise discussed by Plato, Locke, Hobbes, Hume, etc.

It is generally recognized in associationist theory that the contiguity principle fails to explain much of the phenomena. "We must be willing to admit the possibility that obtained associations may never have occurred together in the experience of the person who yields them—they may instead be the result of schemata which serve the function of bringing together structurally related elements from diverse experience" (Deese 1965:20). The nature of these schema have become the object of intense research in psychology and linguistics, and we will not pursue them here except to suggest that the original metaphoric insights create a framework which dictates certain associations and denies others. As Deese elsewhere (1965:159) says, "Our cognitive structures are the outcome of the operation of hypothesis upon our experience." The pronomial metaphors we have identified are surely hypothesis (predications) which are brought to bear upon experience, in particular the inchoate experience of pronomial identity.[4]

In what manner are diverse experiences brought together under the aegis of our metaphors? The two laws of association often lead to the distinction between syntagmatic and paradigmatic associations. In lan-

4. Metaphors are called by Pepper "World Hypotheses" (1942).

guage study syntagmatic associations are those which occur by reason of grammatical contiguity—the association of good with boy, kindly with neighbor, or reasonable with doubt may rest on such an association. By paradigmatic association one means associations which rest upon equivalence of function—the capacity to occupy the same slot or frame in the grammar. Thus fragmentary and rudimentary or euphoric and despicable are associated on the grounds they all can occur in the frame "this was a ——— presentation." The idea is that objects, actions, and events which occupy or can occupy the same slot in experience are associated by that fact of similarity. Slots are filled by what linguists call "form classes" (function classes) although for our purposes they constitute a very large and weak set of associations. Nevertheless, the extension of this grammatical notion to the understanding of behavior as being composed of sequences of frames each of which contains a class or set of appropriate actions or objects is fruitful. It pinpoints not only a fundamental principle of behavioral organization but also accounts for its variability (Pike 1967). For frames differ in the variety of events which will satisfactorily fill them. In most frames participants have a degree of choice. And although ritual is more compulsive in this respect, in discussing either the paradigm of metaphors which will fill the overall ritual frame or the sequence of scenes which will satisfy the metaphoric image, one must keep in mind that there are possible variations and this is always a source of creativity and complexity.

From this perspective what we have been discussing is the filling of frames and the role of metaphor in this fulfillment! In the largest sense men are framed between the remembered past and the imagined future with the need to fill the inchoate present with activity. We are, as the expression goes, "time binders" concerned to find the kind of activity that will fill this frame and bind the past and the future together. The need to bind past and future together in the present is even more pressing in rapidly transitional societies moving between tradition and modernity. In these societies, so painfully poised upon the uncertain interface of the past and the future, there are few well-proven frame-filling technical and ritual routines. Religious movements of the kind discussed here are a particularly apt way to fill ultimate frames. As we see these movements—and we see them most fundamentally as a particular paradigm of metaphors—they, in their microcosmogeny, give a futureness to the past and a pastness to the future that is fundamentally reassuring.[5]

---

5. I have elsewhere (Fernandez 1966) argued this "time binding" consequence of metaphor using Black's view of the interactive nature of these figures of speech (Black 1962).

Microcosmogeny—this filling of inchoate frames including the space framed by our own bodies at various levels of our experience—can be seen then as the product of the interplay of paradigmatic and syntagmatic association—the relationship, in other words, between metaphors and metonyms.

This is a relationship which has preoccupied Lévi-Strauss, who with frequency in his work refers to the law of mythical thought: "the transformation of metaphor is achieved in metonomy." But his thought on this matter is difficult of interpretation. The clearest exposition comes in a footnote to *The Savage Mind* (1966a:150). Here he points out the paradigmatic-syntagmatic bricolage involved in the life of Mr. Wemmick of *Great Expectations*. I interpret Lévi-Strauss's meaning here in the following way. The framework of Mr. Wemmick's life is a suburban house which may be treated metaphorically as either a villa or as a castle. What, as a bricoleur, Wemmick "undertook and realized was the establishment of paradigmatic relations between the elements of these two (syntagmatic chains) . . . he can choose between villa and castle to signify his abode, between pond and moat to signify the entrance, between salad and food reserves to signify his salad greens." By metaphoric assertion Wemmick's life as a bourgeois, a very inchoate existence we take it, is transformed into "a succession of ritual actions, the paradigmatic relations between two equally unreal syntagmatic chains. That of the castle which has never existed and that of the village which has been sacrificed."

Lévi-Strauss's difficulty comes when we are told that "the first aspect of bricolage is thus to construct a system of paradigms with the fragments of syntagmatic chains. But the reverse is equally true . . . a new syntagmatic chain results from the system of paradigmatic relations . . . metaphors take over the mission of metonyms and vice versa." I should like to rephrase these important insights in the following way. The inchoateness of certain frames of experience cause metaphors to be put forth whose effect is to incorporate into such frames other domains of experience which are more clearly understood. These frames, as Pike has made clear (1967), are hierarchally arranged and may be considered at any level of generality, from the frame that in the case of Bwiti falls between Saturday night and Sunday morning, to the most general frame we have identified above, between the past and the future. Not only does the level of generality of the frame vary but the context differs. The main point is that within any frame there is a certain and finite class of appropriate (apt) fillers. This class of functional associates is the paradigm. Hence in that frame that falls for the Fang Bwitist between tradition and modernity and between Saturday night and Sunday morning we have identified the following paradigm of apt metaphors: *esamba, ayong da, emwan mot, nlem mvore.*

The mission of metaphor is to fill inchoate frames by incorporating experience from a domain aptly included in the particular context of that frame.[6] In another current vocabulary one might say that "metaphor" is a mediating device connecting the unconnected and bridging the gaps in causality. The frame in which metaphors appear are a part of a larger syntagmatic chain just as they themselves define or at least require, at a lower level, a sequence of frames (a syntax) to fulfill themselves (as we have demonstrated). In that sense it is true to say that metaphors take over the mission of metonyms and vice versa.

In extended discussion the distinction between syntagmatic and paradigmatic relations becomes, we see, difficult to maintain. In respect to linguistic analysis Lounsbury finds the two notions of similarity relation and contiguity relation not independent: "Linguistic similarity is nothing more than shared contiguity associations" (1959:127). If we think of this in terms of a matrix, following Lounsbury, it is to be pointed out that the substitution distribution matrix $A(i,j)$ (where j is the paradigm of 1. to n frames and i is the class of 1. to no forms that may fill each of these frames) may be inverted to the substitution distribution matrix $B(j,i)$ (where i is the paradigm of 1. to n forms and j is the class of 1. to n frames in which these forms may appear). What is a distribution paradigm in one sense—the set of frames into which a class of different forms may be fitted—becomes a substitution class in another sense—the class of frames defined by their ability to entertain the same set of forms. For the fact is that the same form can appear in different frames. This is a basic kind of transformation and accounts for the difficulty of categorizing the elements of religious or any expressive experience without having these categories undergo inversions, and without having, in Lévi-Strauss's phrasing, "Metaphors take over the mission of metonyms and vice versa."

These difficulties can be illustrated in various ways. The materials we have presented, for example, suggest a cube of data (Figure 3) whose cells have the following dimensions: (1) the succeeding domains of experience framed by the metaphor (the horizontal axis, m); (2) the particular scenes performed and designed to fulfill the expectation of the metaphor (the vertical axis, s); and (3) the particular associations brought into play by each scene (the receding axis, a). This

6. The mission of metaphor, we may further add, is not only to fill inchoate frames but, by filling them with certain models, to accomplish a fundamental transformation in that subject which is being syntactically elaborated. As has been pointed out for language itself the selection of any word inevitably has a transformative effect on the entire sentence.

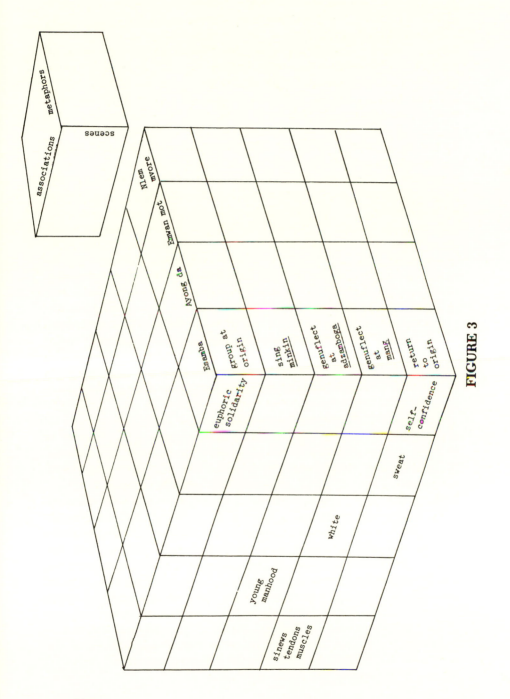

FIGURE 3

121

cube can be collapsed and inverted in various ways as we have suggested. In Figure 2 we collapsed the dimension of association so as to obtain the principal scenes of each metaphoric frame (m by s). In Figure 4 below we have collapsed the cube along the dimension of scenes so as to point up the matrix (m by a) of the principal associations for each metaphor. But insofar as there is reiteration of scenes (or associations) we can invert to obtain the principal domains or scenes characteristic of each association (a by m or a by s) as well as the principal metaphors characteristic of each scene (s by m). Although we collapse or invert this cube into various matrices to tell us about various kinds of classifications, it itself has a veridical quality in respect to the progressive transformations and reiterations characteristic of religious experience which originates somewhere and moves toward infinity.

Let me illustrate some of the particularities of our metaphoric progression by collapsing the sequence of scenes that, operating upon the metaphor, put it into effect. I would emphasize instead the chain of associations which are brought into existence by each metaphoric rephrasing of the cult situation—each metaphoric "acting out." Just as Mr. Wemmick lives in a house among other houses which he metaphorically interprets to be either a villa or a castle, so the cult member lives in a body among other bodies which he (overall) metaphorically interprets to be that of an angel (a spiritual rather than a corporeal entity). To achieve this overall corporeal transformation the members are asked through ritual to operate upon four subordinate metaphors. Examine the following chains (Figure 4) then, each associated with one or another of the images in the Bwiti metaphor paradigm. We see that all of the items in all the chains arise out of that inchoate primary experience which is that of corporeal life with the self and with others. But particular chains of that primary experience are extended into cult life according to the particular image of the body or of society or of both which has been metaphorically selected.

The basic transformation in this scheme is from a suffering corporeality (state of *emwan mot*) to an exalted spirituality (state of *banzie* —angel) and subordinately from a debilitated corporeality to a revitalized corporeality. The paradigm of metaphors aids in accomplishing this by calling into focus and scanning as it were different aspects of the primary corporeal experience. Thus the members find at various moments in their ritual celebrations the extension of various aspects of the primary experience of corporeality—that experience which is so problematic and inchoate. Each of these metaphoric images of the body and its constituents calls to mind different aspects of the body, placing it in focus in the frame so that if this aspect is not actually

Overall Basic Transformation

suffering devitalized individual	is incorporated into	worshiping body of Bwiti	which is incorporated into	spiritual body of Bwiti as Banzie (angel)

Subordinate Transformations

	Esamba	*Ayong da*	*Emwan mot*	*Nlem Mvore*
primary corporeal experience of	chain of associations	chain of associations	chain of associations	chain of associations
relatedness to others	celebration of the achievement of solidarity through the cooperation of corporeal parts!	celebration of lineal relatedness	sorrowful and beseeching celebration of helplessness and dependence, desire for relatedness!	celebration of the achievement of unity by liquification
color spectrum	white	white	black	red
body effluent	sweat	semen	cloacal exuviae	blood
sexuality	young manhood	mature manhood	childhood and latency	incorporation with the mother
body constituents	sinews tendons & muscles	skeleton & brain	flesh and skin	veins, arteries, and bloody organs
attitude or posture	energetic adventuresomeness, self-confidence, euphoria	pensive and serene reflection	inferiority and self-abnegation	self-transcendence

FIGURE 4

123

revitalized in the acting out of the metaphor (as occurs in the case with the *esamba* and *ayong da* metaphors) it is at least clearly brought to mind for functional purposes. The necessary paradigm for the over-all transformation to spiritual status must include the *emwan mot* and the *nlem mvore* metaphors.

There is a looping process in ritual by which the member's attention undergoes small transformations in associations. Different aspects of his inchoate primary corporeal experience are called out by that metaphor active at the moment and extended to different social domains of experience. The sequence of metaphors thus not only shifts attention around within the primary domain but extends that experi-ence into succeeding social domains—the domain of group adventure (*esamba*), the domain of the ancestral cult (*ayong da*), the domain of childhood experience (*emwan mot*).

A metaphor to be realized imposes certain actions upon those who would operate on it, as we have said. Our point here is that it also brings with it in association a syntax of elements (the chains in Figure 4) which are part of the experience of that metaphor.

The paradigm of metaphors which we have considered here accom-plish the following movement. The first two metaphors take the indi-vidual and include him and his body within two compensatory social structures—the first an energetic and exuberant if ephemeral solidarity group; the second a powerful and awesome and enduring kin group, the patrilineage. The third metaphor counting on the revitalization accomplished by the first two metaphors appears to move our subjects to a contemplation of the essential helplessness (if not worthlessness) of their corporeality and moves them to the final liquifaction of spiritual unification in *one heartedness*—the metaphor which represents vitaliza-tion in the most spiritual sense. Each of these metaphors picks out a part of the inchoate wholeness of corporeal existence and explores the syntax of its contiguous associations. When this exploration is fulfilled another metaphor appears in a sense trying "to return us to the whole but only succeeds in calling out another domain of primary experience for exploration." Here we note another source of the transformation of metaphor—the constant search to return to the whole, out of dissatis-faction, perhaps, with the "partness" of any of our devices of repre-sentation.[7]

In sum we may note the following shift in attention in respect to the domain of denotation, accomplished by these metaphor predicates:

7. Lévi-Strauss makes such an observation about the function of metaphor in returning to the whole. "Various forms of metonymy," he points out, "and in par-ticular synecdoche celebrate the parts of experience while the more eloquent metaphors of myth refer back to the whole for significance." (1969:342).

	Predication	*Shifts in Domain*
major metaphor	*bi ne banzie* we are angels	physiological to spiritual
subordinate metaphors	*bi ne esamba* we are an association	individuality to intense social solidarity
	bi ne ayong da we are one clan	ephemeral contemporaneity to enduring lineal allegiance
	bi ne emwan mot we are manchild	maturity to immaturity
	bi ne nlem mvore we are one heart	substance to essence, structure to content

In respect to the physiological experience which has been extended into this ritual activity and whose transformation is involved in each metaphor, we see a shift from the first two subordinate metaphors which call up the structural organs of willful activity (sinews, tendons, bones, and brain) to the organs of flux and liquifaction, in particular the heart which is, for the Fang, the organ of reflection and thought.

Several observations remain if this account is to come as close as possible to this religious experience conceived of as the actualizing of metaphor. First, although we have shown these four metaphors as appearing one time only in the process of the ritual, during the entire ceremony they actually appear several times over in thematic repetition. They appear with a rather different sequence of actions associated with them but they aim at the same kinds of objectives both in respect to the extension of primordial experience and in respect to the selection of denotative domains to which that experience can be extended.

We may secondly point out that, although we presume the study of metaphor to be primary to the study of symbolism, nevertheless symbols of various kinds are constantly appearing and being manipulated in the ritual process. In Bwiti these are numerous indeed and range from the cult harp (Fernandez 1965) to the *akon aba*, the pillar of heaven and earth, within which so many meanings are condensed (Fernandez 1970b). Other symbols are the cult dress and the chapel house itself which condenses birth and death elements, male and female sides, a spirit realm and an earth realm, a structure and a content, tranquility and activity (Fernandez 1970). Symbols of any import in ritual condense many meanings as Turner has so clearly demonstrated (Turner 1967:chap. 1). This gives them a multivocality or polysemy which makes them highly volatile in the metaphor scenario we are examining here. They are by virtue of their many meanings always likely to shift the member's attention from the metaphoric operations at hand either by hypostatizing it at another level or by shifting his attention to a meaning (say femaleness rather than maleness or bodily corruption rather than bodily exaltation) not appropriately voiced by the metaphor under which he is currently acting.

The metaphoric context in which a symbol appears tends to focus attention on a particular meaning of that symbol (by reason of its multivocality it can appear in many metaphoric contexts). Still the symbol is volatile in the sense that it is always likely to return the participants' "attention to the whole" to shift his attention away from the current metaphoric focus.[8] Symbols thus add the possibility of the experience of other levels of meaning during the basic transformations we are discussing and they fill out this universe of religious experience giving it a resonance, a thick complexity and potency, which the discussion of the paradigm of metaphors—however basic—does not fully capture.

CONCLUSION: THE IDEA OF METAPHORIC EXPRESSION

Religious metaphors recast the inchoate (and ineffable) whole of primary experience into various manageable perspectives. They do this by taking experience from more manageable domains, into which some aspects of that primary experience can be extended, to represent it. Most metaphorical images potentially imply a set of actions by which they might be realized. The utterance of metaphor itself as well as the actions undertaken to realize it is attended by a set of associations which "belong" to it by reason of contiguities in previous experience. The assertion of metaphor thus provokes a metonymous chain of elements or experiences associated with it as part to whole, cause to effect, or other contiguity in time or space. Thus for the

---

8. In a different context I have tried to assess this quality of the symbol (1965: 922). "It appears, thus, that the tension between society and culture, between causal-functional systems and logico-meaningful systems, is not only a consequence of their inevitable incongruities, but can be summed up in the tension between the symbol and the signal—the one immediate, dependent, inbedded in the existential situation of coexistence and coordinated interaction, the other autonomous with super-added meanings forever pulling the culture carrier's attention beyond his immediate situation to the larger implications of his actions—creating in him, in other words, self awareness."

metaphor *ayong da* which is the celebration of clanship and the male principle the syntax of metonyms are: the body infrastructure (skeletons and brains), for these are the sacred relics of the ancestor cult; semen, the vehicle of lineage continuity; sexual maturity, the requirement for entrance into the ancestor cult which preserves and protects the lineage.

When the frame which the metaphor is filling calls for an apposite predication upon an inchoate pronominal subject, certain kinds of associations among the great number possible to the image of the clan are selected. That is to say that the metaphor does not simply excite associations but imposes a schema upon them—a metaphor is a hypothesis which makes some things in the world relevant and all other things quite irrelevant. The associations, in short, are conceptually mediated by the metaphor. The associations thus mediated are apt to the subject's preoccupation with his (or their or our) corporeal existence and his or their social existence (status and role). In fact, the truly apt metaphors, in the religious context at least, are those that when acted upon combine in themselves some satisfactory representation of both social experience as well as primary experience. We see this combination in at least three of our four metaphors: *esamba, ayong da, emwan mot.* In these the value of primary experience is affirmed by extension into social experience, and social experience is revitalized by association with primary experience. A fundamental transformation is thus accomplished by metaphor: the socialization of primary experience on the one hand and the rendering of social experience primordially relevant on the other.

This capacity of the apt metaphor has been argued by Victor Turner to be the fundamental capacity of dominant religious symbols. In one of the most important insights of his work, he points out that the multivocality of religious symbols tends to polarize between physiological referents on the one hand and referents to the normative values of social life on the other. Ritual dramas in which these symbols are manipulated create an exchange between physiological and social experiences ennobling the former and investing the latter with emotional significance. Thus are social relationships revitalized. For the socially necessary is made desirable by having it shown that the requirements of social structure are as necessary as the primary processes themselves (Turner 1967:chap. 1). No doubt if what we are physiologically can be shown by religion to have a socially relevant manifestation, and vice versa, then religion accomplishes a fundamental transformation. Two of our metaphors aim at that goal. But religion often aims at more than that. It aims at showing that what we are physiologically and socially can be transcended. This is particularly a Christian intention, and two of the metaphors of our syncretist cult aim at that goal. In any case, this insight moves us far toward attaining that necessary level of analysis where "body, soul, society—everything merges" (Mauss quoted by Lévi-Strauss [1966*b*: 113]).

The merging of everything, the return to the whole, can only be, as far as the student of religion is concerned, the final analysis. What we have been trying to follow through here is the beginning analysis, that of metaphoric predications, and the intermediate analysis, that of the structure of associations which these bring into play in their actualization. The identification of the two basic types of association—those based on contiguity and those based on similarity—help us to understand the structure of ritual only to a degree. We should not pretend that we have solved all the problems of this analysis although we would hope to have focused our attention correctly. Although certain kinds of association can be well enough understood—how chains of association, for example, appear in relation to each metaphor—yet it is more difficult to understand how metaphors are associated within paradigms or how metaphors themselves appear!

If we look to the literature on association, we do not find much help. For this literature has tended to concentrate upon association by external contiguity or ordination within the same domain or the same tree structure. It has tended to concentrate upon superordinate (dog-animal), subordinate (animal-dog), and coordinate (dog-cat) associations. But many of the most interesting kinds of association for the student of religion are usually thrown into a wastebasket class. These are associations whose linkages seem very remote when compared to any principle of inner ordination or external contiguity.

The kinds of associations involved here would seem to be those obtained by contrast on the one hand and by mediation, synthesis, or grouping on the other.[9] Association by contrast is better studied and better understood. We need hardly discuss it. We see it in our metaphoric paradigm as *esamba* (euphoric contemporary solidarity), which provokes in some sense its opposite, *ayong da* (somber historic solidarity). Further the thought of the exaltation of the body social (in *esamba* and *ayong da*) leads by opposites to the denigration of both the body personal and the body social in *emwan mot*. This in turn

9. Deese defines two structural types (1965:160) in his discussion of the laws of association. "The manifest and particular associations we find in ordinary thought and language are derived from and can be described by fundamental structural types. These structural types are defined by contrasting relations and grouping relations." The concept of synthesis arises from the Kantian distinction between associations which are predicated on analysis and those predicated on synthesis. The distinction is similar to that between metonymy and metaphor.

leads to an exaltation and transubstantiation of the body personal and social in *nlem mvore.*

Association by mediation or synthesis is much more personal or culture-bound and not at all evident empirically. While, for example, the association between moon and white and sun and red has some easily accessible empirical base the association between moon and female and sun and males does not. These latter are based on some inner sense of relationship, customary to some individual or culture, which makes them difficult to study.

Despite the obvious difficulties it is these culture-bound synthetic associations that pose the most important problems for the study of religion. Evans-Pritchard is one anthropologist who has taken a hard look at just such associations and has been particularly concerned with the latent underlying ideas by which such linkages—such groupings or synthesis—are mediated. He was led to his observations by a problem similar to that which lies behind our discussion here: the existence of various metaphoric predications on an inchoate religious subject, in his case spirit (*kwoth*). What indeed is spirit? The Nuer say, "*Kwoth* is a crocodile." "*Kwoth* is rain." But knowing how to correctly interpret the synthesis accomplished by the copula is another matter. "What meaning are we to attach to Nuer statements that such and such a thing is *Kwoth*, spirit?" (1956:123)

In his search for the source of these associations Evans-Pritchard finds that some rest on explicit analogies but most rest on culture-bound analogies which it is the anthropologist's province to divulge. Often, he points out, there is this latent factor involved and we must understand that this consists of either (1) an indirect and usually gratuitous association or (2) a triadic relationship. In the first case snake is linked with well-being by virtue of its association with honey, which, beside its intrinsic attractiveness, is again associated with the season of fine weather. In the second case, the triadic relationship, birds are twins (Nuer) and twins are salmon (Nootka) by virtue of their common relation to a third higher order entity, spirit, of which they are both specific manifestations. If the context in which the association is to take place is a spiritual one then either birds or twins, twins or salmon may appear in that context to stand for spirit. The latent generic characteristic they have in common and which associates them is spirit.

The triadic relationship—association by a latent third principle—stands to reason but is helpful only to a point! The mind after all is one entity bound to realize the unity of its experiences at some level of abstraction. If we return to Figure 1 we realize that, although George and muffin are bizarre associations between two quite distinct domains of everyday experience, nevertheless at a high level of abstraction—organic matter—they both belong to the same domain. To a sufficiently religious mentality practically everything in the world can be brought into association as a manifestation of spirit. Certain kinds of metaphysical endeavor search precisely for those general integrating principles by which the diversity of experience—the product of categorization—can be compiled.[10] To put this caution in another way: we must be as specific about the latent factor as possible to avoid the true but not very helpful suggestion that the latent principle by which religious associations are brought into being is the inchoate itself.

Ethnography is obliged to trace as specifically as it can both the accidental chains of association that may be at work in any imaginative cultural product as well as the higher order concepts or controlling ideas that may be present in mediating between associates bringing about their synthesis. Beside progress by opposites what are the mediating concepts by which cultural performances are synthesized bringing together gods and men, heaven and earth, body and soul, man and woman, past and present, self and society? We have seen well enough how metaphors start up the syntactic machinery focusing our intentions by their predication, but whence the metaphor itself? What intention lies behind it? Does it not owe its own existence to a latent third principle or controlling idea? Are not the controlling ideas of these successive metaphors the following: corporeal solidarity should be affirmed, structural solidarity should be affirmed, social and corporeal inadequacy should be pleaded, and finally social and corporeal distinctions should be abolished.

From our experience with this cult can we suggest a set of controlling ideas or preoccupying themes which mediate between inchoate subjects and the metaphors predicated upon them? These themes or ideas have to do with transformations in either structural or primary experience. For social structural experience we have the elementary need to put forth metaphorically:

> the idea of status well-being,
> the idea of status insufficiency,
> the idea of transcendence or exaltation with respect
> to structure.

10. In an extended discussion with one of the Bwiti leaders, Ekang Engone of Kougouleu (Kango), on his use of "likenesses" (*efonan*) in his sermons, remarked that such analogies make clear that all the world was one thing. By using them he was trying to teach his members that fact, and thus defeat witchcraft. For witchcraft tries to break the world down and isolate men in order to eat them (Fernandez 1965:911).

For primary corporeal experience we have the need to put forth metaphorically:

> the idea of corporeal well-being,
> the idea of corporeal insufficiency,
> the idea of exaltation or transubstantiation with respect
>   to structure.

Simply on the evidence of the cult we have before us we can say¹ that there are three basic controlling ideas which mediate in religious celebration: ideas of adequacy, ideas of inadequacy, and ideas of exaltation. Of course, cults will differ as to the kinds of frames that the culture history of the people involved calls upon them to fill and the kinds of controlling ideas with which they are preoccupied and find socially useful to put into effect. Hence metaphoric statements which can function to fill these frames and express these ideas will differ. Thus the statement of any set of elementary and controlling ideas does not eliminate the need, in any case, for the study of the metaphoric structures by which the inchoate is given palpable form and by which these ideas, pale abstractions at best, are given substance.

Only if we do this with careful attention to detail are we entitled to state the controlling ideas. And since we have done this for Bwiti we may even state here the overall controlling idea which mediates for all metaphors. It is not anything given to us by our informants. But is it not the idea that the primordial self can first be incorporated into some body social and that these together can be surpassed to the quite insubstantial spiritual? Among the Banzie is not the progression of metaphors controlled by the idea that men grounded in blood, bowels, muscle, and sweat, in sinew bone and of peurile origin, can yet shrug all that off and fly?

Chapter
5

Carrying the Village:
Cuna Political Metaphors

JAMES HOWE

Anthropology may have given the culture concept to social science, but the notions of political culture and political socialization have developed outside of anthropology for the most part, and with a few notable exceptions (e.g., Levine 1960, 1963), anthropologists have not made much of them. Despite this neglect, the voluminous political socialization literature (see e.g., Almond and Verba 1963; Dawson and Prewitt 1969; Hyman 1959; Jaros 1973; Langton 1969; Sigel 1970), though derived largely from a few Western, industrialized nations, demonstrates clearly that any political system depends not only on a set of shared understandings about such concrete matters as what political roles are to be filled and who may fill them, but also on common attitudes toward political life and the powers-that-be, and even on broad assumptions about the nature of politics and government on the level of generality of "All men are created equal—or unequal." It is clear, moreover, that most societies devote considerable time and effort enculturating their members into these ideas and attitudes.

Although ethnographers studying this topic in nonliterate societies lack some of the sources of data open to political scientists, such as school textbooks, newspapers, and other mass media, they can often assimilate some of the dominant themes of a political culture fairly readily if these themes are expressed in some concise and stylized verbal form, such as proverbs. The San Blas Cuna of Panama, who are the subject of this essay, can hardly be said to have proverbs at all, but they do spend an extraordinary amount of time promulgating the official Cuna line on such matters as morality, cosmology, and politics, through the didactic use of a distinctive kind of metaphor.

The Cuna of San Blas, agriculturalists and fishermen inhabiting some fifty villages along the northeastern coast of Panama, most of them located on small islets within a few hundred yards of the mainland, have become well known among anthropologists through the work of Nordenskiold, Stout, Holmer, and Wassén.[1] Stout has detailed some of the changes in Cuna culture that result from several centuries of contact with Europeans and blacks, but given that contact, the continuity and persistence of Cuna culture are at least as striking as are the changes in it. Metaphors play an important part in the political and religious meetings that more than anything else maintain that continuity.

THE PLACE OF METAPHORS

The Cuna are great talkers, orators, and singers (see Sherzer 1972, 1975; Kramer 1970). Apart from the conventions of public speaking, the colloquial language contains many word games (Sherzer 1970, n.d.), riddles (Nordenskiold et al. 1938:379), and other special speech forms, while the numerous ritual genres have their own traditions, secrets, epic songs, and special vocabulary, that take from several months to many years to learn. The metaphors that appear in almost all speech varieties have attracted the attention of several writers (e.g., Nordenskiold et al. 1938:373–81; Kramer 1970:58–64; Sherzer 1975), although to date the examples and analysis of these metaphors available in the literature have been fragmentary, and in some cases misleading.

The metaphors I examine here belong to the repertoire of Cuna chiefs, a repertoire that also includes Cuna history-cum-mythology—there are no emic grounds for distinguishing the two—conventional wisdom and morality, singing techniques, and the proper things to say at particular events. The degree to which a chief has mastered this material and the skill with which he uses it determine as much as anything else his reputation among his peers and followers.

The primary context for the chiefly metaphors is the nightly meeting

1. See for instance Nordenskiold et al. (1938), Stout (1947), Wassén (1938, 1949), Holmer (1951), and Holmer and Wassén (1958, 1963). For more recent work on the Cuna see Holloman (1969), Howe (1974), Sherzer (1970, 1975), Sherzer and Sherzer (1972).

(*onmakket*), often called congress or *congreso* in the literature, and which I shall refer to here as the gathering, its literal meaning (see Sherzer 1975:264–71; Howe 1974:81–138). Although arrangements vary slightly from island to island, gatherings in the community I studied fall into two classes: talking meetings usually limited to the men (*macherkampi*), in which they adjudicate disputes and handle other community business; and singing meetings that include the women (*omekan pela*). In the latter, one of several village chiefs sings to the assembled community for an hour or two, seated in his hammock, while another chief in the hammock next to him sings short ritualized replies at the end of each phrase. Policemen (*sualipkana*) patrol the hall, occasionally calling out to the audience to stay awake and listen, and after the singing, an interpreter (*arkala*) stands and explains the chief's chant.

The ordinary singing meetings alternate nights with the talking meetings on a fairly regular basis, and if one chief visits another's island, as frequently happens, the singing goes on each night until the visitor leaves. Every two weeks or so, chiefs from regional groupings of about fifteen or so islands gather in one of their communities to sing twice or three times a day for several days. Thus both adults and children are constantly exposed to great amounts of singing and spoken interpretation.

This material imparts a knowledge of Cuna traditions combined with moral teachings. Many of the stories themselves that the chiefs sing contain inherent moral messages as do episodes in the Christian Bible, although they are considered historically real events, unlike, say, the parables of Jesus. The series of disasters that God inflicted on the world, and the sins which aroused his wrath, are particularly relevant to the present, since traditional Cuna expect another disaster soon. The following brief excerpt from the interpretation of a chant illustrates the topical use of histories. Delivered a few days before a convocation of chiefs was expected on the singer's island, it concerns one episode in the life of *Mako*, an early culture hero, as he went from village to village teaching proper behavior to semihuman animal-people:

Then he went to another village. . . .at *Takkekuntiwar* lived *Olokupyakiner*, the chicken people. . . .They slept in the midst of bad things. They threw bones just anywhere around the house. The chicken people were like that. Mako counseled them like the others: "God did not say you should act this way, that you should act just any old way like this, he didn't say that at all.". . .

Now young women, the chief is counseling *us* about this subject, he is counseling us in anticipation of the visitors' arrival, on the chance that you might take care of the visitors for us in the same way. In case you might feed the visitors in the midst of trash; in case you might feed them in an unswept dirty house with bones lying around. The chief said this to you in anticipation of the visitors' arrival. . . .

In singing the traditions, chiefs use narrative forms, grammatical constructions, and vocabulary different from those of everyday speech (see Sherzer 1975:267–69). The vocabulary includes affixes and non-metaphorical lexical substitutes for everyday words, as well as metaphors, which may or may not convey immediate and direct messages. Thus calling the clouds "the clothing above" (*mola pillipa*) (Chapin 1970*b*:1.21) can be considered merely a poetic convention, but singing that some men in early times wore white clothes and others wore spotted means that some were moral and others were not, and a competent interpreter would make sure his audience caught this meaning.

Alternately a chief may sing directly about recent events or even his dreams, although if he does this too often he reveals an ignorance of tradition or lack of respect for it. Better, he can sing about the landscape of heaven and the journey the soul makes there after death, or he can sing metaphors—elaborate, self-contained conceits set apart from the history-mythology, each of which conveys a message.[2] Most often the chief sings about only one part of the metaphor, what the editors of this volume call the vehicle or discontinuous term (p. 7 above) without mentioning the tenor or continuous term, and then afterward the interpreter relates the two and sets forth their meaning. To give a simple example, a chief may sing that he is giving a grain of corn to everyone in the audience, which they should not discard or feed to the chickens after the meeting but instead take home to show their children next morning. The interpreter explains that the corn represents the chief's teachings, which people should heed and pass on to their children. Skillful interpreters play with the metaphors, presenting the discontinuous term a second term and interjecting rhetorical questions before revealing the metaphor's meaning: "What does the chief mean when he says a grain of corn?" or "Why is it said thusly? He says it this way because. . . .

Chiefs and interpreters use the same metaphors in public, spoken

---

2. It will be noted that various aspects of Cuna cosmology enter into the metaphors presented further on in the essay. However, in the chants alluded to here concerning heaven and the way to reach it, the relationship with everyday life is metonymical (before and after, cause and effect) rather than metaphorical.

admonishments (*unaet, uanaet*) which it is their job to give from time to time to particular classes of people, such as medicine men, midwives, adolescent girls, wrongdoers, and newlyweds; and on special occasions such as the opening of puberty ceremonies (Howe 1974:123–26, n.d.). The puberty ceremony admonishments are delivered in the puberty ceremony house, but most *unaets* occur as events within the gatherings. The political metaphors I examine here appear frequently but not exclusively in the installation ceremonies for chiefs and interpreters.

In its most restrictive sense, the term *unaet* refers to counseling a specific person or class of people, whether it is a chief publicly counseling newlyweds or a father counseling his children in private, but in a looser sense the chief counsels (*unae*) the total audience whenever he sings to them, since he is informing them and advising them, and he may moreover direct his chant at a specific class of people such as adolescent girls. If no one is available to sing the ritualized replies, or if a recent death makes singing forbidden, then a chief may speak his chant to the audience rather than sing it. As in the spoken admonishments, he may either set out each metaphor completely and then interpret it himself, or he can interrupt the flow every so often to explain it bit by bit. Clearly then, although singing can be taken as the classical mode of presentation, chiefs and interpreters deliver metaphors in a number of different forms and settings that differ among themselves in minor ways.

The flexibility of the chiefs' material sets it apart from medicine songs and other genres. A curer learns a particular named song, often memorizing it line for line, and although he may perform the song in different ways from one cure to the next, he cannot stray too far from its basic outline. Chiefs, on the other hand, learn a body of knowledge that they can adapt as they wish to the particular task at hand. One may sing about a single episode in elaborate detail or give a broad overview of Cuna history. With metaphors, one may string together a group of them sequentially, or alternate them with historical episodes that make the same point. Similarly, in spoken admonishments, one can adapt a given metaphor to bring out a single theme more clearly than others.

Whether spoken or sung, each metaphor can take whatever length seems appropriate to a given presentation. On different occasions the same metaphor might appear briefly in rough outline, or stretch out in elaborate detail for fifteen or twenty minutes, or return several times in successive fragments. One speaker can extend or reuse the metaphor introduced by a previous speaker, or with extreme brevity, he may allude to it in a single sentence or phrase.

METAPHOR

In Cuna, "to sing in metaphors" is *purpar namakke* and "to speak metaphorically" is *purpar sunmakke,* while a noun "metaphor" can be constructed only by nominalizing the verbs with the suffix *-t(i),* for example, *purpar namakket* "metaphorical singing or song." The modifier *purpale* (short form *purpar*) and the less common alternative *purpakkwa* derive from *purpa,* "soul, shadow." *Purpa* refers in an extended but literal sense to a great many things other than actual human souls, in addition to taking a number of euphemistic and general metaphorical meanings.

Purpale means in part "covertly, invisibly, incorporeally": thus the invisible animals which perch on the roof beams during puberty ceremonies are present *purpale,* and *purpar sunmakke* in some contexts refers to speaking in euphemisms or other indirect speech forms, rather than using the didactic metaphors examined here. Both chiefly metaphor and euphemism share the quality of being hidden, at one remove. The *purpa* of a medicine chant is its secret key meaning or *essence,* and perhaps the best gloss of *purpale* in the context of chiefly metaphors is "in the hidden essence of things."

Since the discontinuous term of a metaphor is delivered first in a deliberately obscure manner and only afterward elucidated, the character of *covertness* noted in the definition of *purpale* does inform the presentation of chiefly metaphors, most notably when a chief sings rather than speaks them. The formal logic of the event suggests that the audience cannot fully understand either history or metaphor until an interpreter makes them intelligible, no matter how many times they have heard them previously, and the leaders do in fact seem to doubt the ability of ordinary people, especially women, to remember much from one session to the next.

This does not mean, however, that an interpreter ever explains every detail of a metaphor, or that the images that appear in it lack any previous significance for the average person. The metaphors draw for their vehicles on such things as hammocks, arrows, plants, canoes, and rivers—objects and beings that have numerous and significant associations for ordinary laymen as well as for specialists in other ritual traditions. Almost always the speaker assumes that some connections between continuous and discontinous terms require no special mention, and he may at his discretion neglect to give more than the general gist of the metaphor's significance or even omit any explanation at all, if he decides that previous metaphors have made the identity of the discontinous term obvious.

Considerable ambiguity sometimes results from such vague or incomplete interpretation. Used intentionally the ambiguity can reinforce that reticence, the quality of *being at one remove,* inherent in the metaphors. Just as everyday euphemisms allow the Cuna to discuss such touchy subjects as snakebite, childbirth, and sex with delicacy and reserve, so chiefly metaphors allow leaders to make their opinions known on an issue and exert the force of traditional norms on its resolution without naming names, referring to it directly, or even perhaps committing themselves to a clear-cut stand. These qualities of metaphor make it appropriate to the role of a chief, since ideally chiefs should keep their distance from the problems and disputes of village politics. As representatives of tradition and moderation, they should wait to sum up and guide consensus, rather than leaping into the thick of debate, and they should avoid harshly contradicting others, to the point of not answering criticisms aimed at themselves. Metaphors provide one tool with which to approximate this difficult ideal of distance and impersonality and at the same time retain some measure of influence over events in the gatherings.

Typologically I find it convenient to distinguish three varieties of metaphor here. The grain-of-corn metaphor makes a good example of the first type. Here the vehicle is clearly fictitious, since everyone can see that the corn does not literally exist. The second type suggests correspondences between things and relationships in the natural world and things and relationships in the Cuna social world, and the singer presents both sides as literally true. He sets up a kind of quasi-totemic parallel, in which flowers, stones, and animals correspond not to particular groups of people, such as moieties or clans, but to classes of people, such as quarrelsome women or stingy chiefs. Some of these animals, plants, and objects that are taken as vehicles for metaphors about people were themselves human or semihuman in earliest times and only later became differentiated from humanity; that is, from a Cuna point of view, some natural and social things which are now separate but equivalent were once unified and undifferentiated.

In practice, since the question of what people *really* believe in their minds usually eludes the anthropologist's grasp, it is difficult to determine whether the singer takes as literally true what he is singing, and similarly whether he intends those listening to accept it as such. Nordenskiold discusses this problem (Nordenskiold et al. 1938:xviii), but his general picture of chiefs handing out notions to credulous audiences that the chiefs themselves find childish oversimplifies the ambiguities in the belief of both singer and audience.

The third type consists of polysemic terms that unite disparate domains and thus create a simple metaphor just by joining the domains. When these single-term metaphors appear within elaborate metaphorical conceits and tableaux, they reinforce the connection between the domains of the larger metaphor or add further complications to it. Many such metaphors lie dormant in the colloquial language, just as they do in other languages, waiting for a clever speaker to wake them up and use them in the gathering house. In one case, a chief was able to save a young woman accused of having had sexual relations with a black sailor by pointing out that one does not blame the hen when the rooster chases after her, an elaboration of the everyday use of chicken (*kannira*) in Cuna to mean "woman" (Chapin 1971: personal communication).

This essay concerns itself only with metaphors about politics, first because that choice gives a manageable selection of metaphors with which to work, second because it seemed a natural set to the chief who provided most of them, and third because I came upon the metaphors during research into Cuna social and political organization. Further, I suggest that these metaphors do convey some of the most general assumptions Cuna hold about politics and government, although only a much longer essay including more metaphors as well as the political material in the mythology could give a really balanced outline of these assumptions (see Howe 1974).

Most of the metaphors examined here derive from tape-recorded texts spoken as if they were part of an admonishment or interpretation, while one or two come from recordings of actual songs and admonishments in the gathering house, and a few I have only in note form from interviews in Spanish and Cuna. The text excerpts I have borrowed from my colleague Joel Sherzer derive from his recording of admonishments given to a newly installed chief.[3]

ANIMALS HAVE CHIEFS

The first text begins as a rationale for chiefs:

God put us into this world having leaders. . . . If there is no leader, the village cannot be maintained. The members would go just anywhere [i.e., do

3. Fieldwork ran from February 1970 to February 1971, supported by a predoctoral fellowship (MH46502-01) and field training grant from the National Institute of Mental Health, whose assistance I gratefully acknowledge. In further fieldwork from September to November 1971, following the writing of the first draft of this essay, I was able to go over the manuscript with an informant and gather some additional material. I owe special thanks to Mac Chapin, Gonzalo Salcedo, and Joel Sherzer for their generosity with information, suggestions, and metaphors. Both Sherzer and Chapin checked some statements from the first draft in the field and supplied new data, although this does not of course commit them to the interpretations offered here.

wrong]. The place would be full of fights, everything would be wrong, if there were no chief, the maintainer of the place. All the animals have leaders, and we that much more. . . . In the morning when the sun has risen, the minnows (*unus*) will come around here. . . . You won't see just three or four minnows. The minnows come in one big group. They have a leader it's said. Their leader carries all his followers . . . at sunset, the minnows will go out of our waters and back into their whirlpools. Not one minnow will stay behind. They'll go back in following their leader's word. That's the way the world is.

A description follows of the *Kiplu* bird, which is either the Broadwinged Hawk (*Buteo platypterus*) or Swainson's Hawk (*Buteo swainsoni*) (Wetmore 1965:210). Both species migrate through Cuna territory in October. In the text the *Kiplu* fly around in lines one after another and then land on a large tree for the night: "At that place their leader will say to them: 'We'll rest here and tomorrow we'll go again.' " The text then turns to *yannu*, the wild pig or White-lipped Peccary (*Tayassu pecari, Dictoyles labiatus.* Méndez 1970:239–46).[4]

One day you might also see animals, you might see forest animals, you'll see wild pig. The wild pig has a leader. Since the wild pig has a leader, you'll see one line, two lines, three lines of wild pigs, the followers can't stay behind. When night comes, the followers will stop all together and rest. No one can stay behind. When day comes, at dawn, they'll move off again. When their leader calls, right away they're off in a line with him. He is their leader, their leader carries his own. . . . Tarpon (*mila*) are the same. One day you might see tarpon, many great tarpon rising out of the water. You can't see just two or three, but a group of them. They'll group together in a bay, they'll come together following their leader's direction. Then they're off again. And again, its all of them. No one can stay behind.

Finally the text describes the Jack (*Kelu*), a small but conspicuous and exciting silvery fish that moves around in schools thrashing the water as it chases minnows. Like the minnows, the Jack spend the night in whirlpools under the sea.

The equation, human chiefs are to human followers as animal chiefs are to animal followers, is clear enough, and so is the affirmation that group living is natural and God's will. "The elders-predecessors say, 'All the animals have leaders, we are that much more that way, we are people. We are people, so how could we do away with our leaders, those who maintain the place?' " For non-Cuna, the significance

4. Nordenskiold identifies *yannu* as *Dicotyles torquatus*, the collared peccary, but Chapin, Méndez, and my own notes are in agreement that the species the Cuna call *wetar* is *torquatus* (Méndez 1970:239–46; Chapin 1971: personal communication; Nordenskiold et al. 1938:287; cf. Lévi-Strauss 1969:74).

of the single-file progressions in which some animals travel needs clarification: among the Cuna, funeral participants, policemen announcing gatherings, visiting chiefs going to meals, puberty-ceremony participants, and other classes of people in special events, all go in single-file progressions. Apparently in the recent past family work parties traveled in strict order of seniority, both on mainland trails and in canoes (see Stout 1947:25), and today the Cuna I saw are taking with gusto to the borrowed custom of parades.

The text then switches from the daily movements of animals to the daily movements of humans: As the day begins, the personified Sun, *Machi Olowaipippiler* ascends into the sky with his consort *Nan Olowaili.* She sets the women to work sweeping, while he sends the men out of the village to the mainland. "He is the one who sets us to work . . . one will go fishing, another will go clean out his coconut groves, another will go cut bananas, another will go hunting in the forest. They'll go forth to do any number of things. They'll go out from inside the 'corral' [*kalu,* a key word to be examined below]."

Later the workers return, the sun goes down, and *Nan Kapsus,* the personified darkness, comes to "take care of us." "*Nan* sits there as the chief of our 'corral' (*kalu*), she comes to open the door, she puts us all back in the corral, we will come together in the corral." She treats the people as a Cuna mother does her children, stroking them, fanning them, taking them out to urinate, and finally she leaves them at dawn: " 'Boys, get up,' she says, 'all my children, get up.' "

Digressions follow on the theory of dreams and on the beneficial effects of bathing, and then the text concludes: ". . . as chickens are kept in a coop (*kalu*), so *Nan Tummat* ('Great Mother,' God's wife) puts us in our corral (*kalu*). That's how Great Father and Great Mother care for us. Great Mother and Great Father, in the way that we would keep a pig in a pen, take care of us. Therefore, how could we be afraid?" *Nan Kapsus* swings a net over the village that protects it from *ponis,* a kind of dangerous spirit, unless bad behavior lifts the invisible net and lets the spirits in.

A variety of peripheral metaphor appears in the text, since Cuna speakers digress frequently, and some of the elements in it could be recombined to send different messages. A chant recorded by Chapin for instance (Chapin 1970b) uses the material on *Nan Kapsus, Machi Olowaipippiler,* and the progression of the day combined with other elements to criticize women for their readiness to quarrel among themselves. In this text on the other hand, a concern with groups, communities, and their leaders clearly dominates the text, and a single set of parallels unites the first section on animals with the second on humans.

Since these parallels do not however replicate themselves perfectly on each level of the comparison, the structure of the metaphor will reveal itself best if the explication begins where the parallels are clearest, in the comparison between minnows and jackfish on the one hand, and humans on the other. As the text suggests, these fish sleep in whirlpools (*pirya*), special fish homes under the sea, from which they venture out during the day in search of food, returning again each night. In the same way the text describes people venturing forth from their island villages—which also sit out in the sea—and retreating back inside as the day ends.[5]

Cuna: Village
Fish: Whirlpool

The trees and resting places where birds, mammals, and the other fish stop for the night make less convincing counterparts for villages than do whirlpools, since the animals do not shut themselves in them or return to the same spot every night. This discrepancy at first appears particularly acute, because the Cuna believe that each class of fish has its own whirlpool home, and that birds and land mammals (as well as monsters and spirits) come from special animal strongholds in the mountains, (a very common belief in South America, cf. Zerries 1961:258ff.). Why then does the text not mention the strongholds?

The answer lies in the empirical observation of nature. Although the Cuna do for the most part stick within their villages at night as the text says, they occasionally go hunting or fishing in the dark, so they know that during those hours most kinds of animals can be found in the forest or out in the sea. But they seldom or never see minnows or jackfish after sunset, and in the early morning these two classes of fish begin to come in close by the islands and the mainland only after the sun has risen, giving the impression (to me as much as to the Cuna) that they are indeed arriving from somewhere else. The Cuna say of this that Jack and minnows go back to their whirlpools every night, but that other animals, once they have escaped or been let out of their whirlpools and strongholds, return only after long stays out in the world.

Although these strongholds thus lack some of the similarities which hold between villages and whirlpools, the text does indicate indirectly but unmistakably through their name (*kalu*) that they have a position analogous to villages in the domain of animals and birds. The word *kalu* refers in essence to an enclosure of cane, slats, or poles, such as

5. The word *pirya* appears in many chants (though not here) as the metaphoric term for the gathering house.

a garden fence of cane. In the elevated language of the gatherings, chiefs substitute *kalu* for the more ordinary terms for village, *kwepur* and *nekkwepur*, and this text in particular not only uses that terminology but also explicitly describes the village as an enclosure into which *Nan Kapsus* puts its inhabitants at the end of the day (p. 141). The text further compares the village to a chicken coop or hog pen, both of which also take the designation *kalu*. My principal informant sometimes spoke of the animal strongholds themselves as if they were *corrales*, and the name does suggest this image, but when pressed, he described them as invisible houses within mountain caves. However the strongholds are conceptualized, the common term *kalu* clearly identifies them with villages, and equates both of them with a number of other things as well.[6] Thus:

Cuna	Village (*kalu*)
Birds	Stronghold (*kalu*) trees
Animals	Stronghold (*kalu*) resting places
Fish	Whirlpool (*pirya*) resting places
Pigs and Chickens	Coop, Pen (*kalu*)

The parallels between the domains include the various beings—animal, human, and spiritual—mentioned in the metaphor. According

6. Strongholds and whirlpools appear frequently in Cuna ethnographic literature, especially in the texts edited by Nordenskiold, Holmer, and Wassén. Judging from these works, my own brief notes on the subject, and Chapin's unpublished findings (personal communications), I find that variant traditions place the *kalus* in the mountains on earth and/or on another level of the cosmos, and different versions also ascribe diverse physical characteristics to them as well. For strongholds with ferocious animals and dangerous spirits, see Wassén 1938:124ff.; Chapin 1970a: 18, 24, and for animal *kalus* in general see Wassén 1938:127–29; Chapin 1970a:68; Nordenskiold et al. 1938:285–89. On the meaning of the word *kalu* see the following word lists and dictionary: Nordenskiold et al. 1938:664; Peñaherrera and Costales 1968:162; and Holmer 1952:42. On the various forms of strongholds see Wassén 1938:129; Chapin 1970a:24; and Holmer 1951:29.

In a further parallel to Cuna villages, not mentioned in the metaphor, the strongholds are said to unite under the leadership of the senior stronghold, *Kalu Ipakki*, through which God sends messages to the spirits (see Wassén 1938:129, 130).

The Zinacanteco Mayan belief in corrals in the mountains that hold "animal spirit companions" of humans (Vogt 1969:80) resembles the Cuna conception of strongholds in several respects. On a more general level, *kalus*, the net thrown over the village, and the use of enclosures in Cuna ritual have some connection with the importance of fences and enclosures in the mythology and ritual of other South American groups (Lévi-Strauss 1969:83–108; Reichel-Dolmatoff 1971:index "fence").

to the text, the spirit guardians watch over the people as human owners care for their domestic animals, and more important, they act in ways that are unambiguously parental: *Nan Olowaili,* the sun's companion, puts the girls to sweeping as a Cuna mother does, and *Nan Kapsus* lulls the people to sleep at night. The title *Nan* in both their names means "mother." Similarly the sun acts as a Cuna father or father-in-law does to the junior males in his household by putting them to work (*oarpae*). As other, less poetic texts make clear, he does this as representative of the strongly paternal high god, *Pap Tummat* "Great Father," while *Nan Kapsus* is nothing more than one manifestation of *Nan Tummat* "Great Mother," the wife of God.

Similarly the first section of the metaphor straightforwardly ties animal chiefs together with human chiefs. However, these leaders do not correspond in this metaphor to the spiritual guardians of the second half of the text. The animals, in addition to beastly leaders, have spiritual guardians or owners, who manage the strongholds and whirlpools, and at least in the case of the wild pig *yannu,* they shepherd them invisibly through the forest, occasionally allowing humans to hunt a few. The text ignores these game owners (although all Cuna know of them), probably because their mention would weaken the argument that herd behavior proves the existence of animal leaders. One informant statement stressed at length that the spirits own their animals in the way that Cuna own domestic animals, and that they herd *yannu* as Panamanian herdsmen move livestock in and out of corrals. So, to complete the set of correspondences alluded to in the text, two classes of being must be distinguished, which can conveniently be called "leaders" and "overlords" or "guardians" (cf. Wassén 1938:130).[7]

The structure and intent of the metaphor should by now be clear. It should be pointed out that in playing up the importance of village life and group movement, the speaker is not celebrating some secondary aspect of Cuna life. Without exaggerating too much, the village might be seen as *the* primary unit in social organization. The Cuna handle most of the problems that arise within the community through village organization, and villages engage in a staggering number of projects

7. The equivalence of villages, whirlpools, and strongholds is a fixed feature of Cuna cosmology, but the various "leaders" and "overlords" correspond to each other in a looser way that varies slightly from metaphor to metaphor. Another (not included here) compares the chief with the sun, since both work all day in God's name at maintaining people and the world, while another, one of the most important political metaphors, equates the chief with a father (see below). Further, the spirit owners act in a number of ways that are clearly chiefly (cf. Wassén 1938), and other metaphors may reverse the emphasis in this one, playing up the game owners and neglecting the animal leaders.

	Locale	Leader	Overlord
Cuna	Village (*kalu*)	Chief	God and God's wife the sun, his companion, darkness
Family	House? (walls=*kalu*)	—	father and mother father-in-law
Birds	Stronghold (*kalu*) trees	Chief	spirit owner
Animals	Stronghold (*kalu*) resting places	Chief	spirit owner
Fish	Whirlpool (*pirya*) resting places	Chief	spirit owner
Pigs, Chickens	Coop, Pen (*kalu*)	—	Cuna owner
Livestock	Corral (*kalu*)	—	Panamanian herdsman

and enterprises—building wharfs, schools, and airports; clearing trails; netting fish; running lotteries and raffles; selling bread, rum, and meals; raising coconuts; even running passenger and cargo boats up and down the coast. Indeed, most San Blas villages put the wild pig and jackfish to shame. Keeping up such a high level of activity requires constant exhortation and encouragement, most of it direct and obvious, but some, like this metaphor, more elevated and indirect.[8]

THE CHIEF IS A TREE

Trees and their woods play a central role in medicine, ritual, and mythology among the Cuna. Several mythological episodes concern

8. In contrast to the Cuna, their nearest neighbors the Chocó, who receive no mention in this metaphor, lack both chiefs and villages. They also retain a great many anomalous traits that the Cuna say they themselves discarded long ago when they became fully differentiated from animals. In the domain of animals, the text states repeatedly that "all animals" have leaders, and the proof of this lies in the group movements described by the text, but the Cuna know that only a few species display herd behavior. In the original draft of this paper I speculated that the unmentioned animals who lack herd behavior, an anomaly within the limits of the metaphor, form a counterpart for the also unmentioned and anomalous Chocó.

When I presented this idea to the chief who spoke the metaphor, he said that it was a legitimate twist on it (an indication of the openness and flexibility of the metaphors), but one that he hadn't intended. He added that *all* animals have leaders, though nongregarious animals leave them behind in the strongholds. In dream interpretation at least, the white-lipped peccary (*yannu*) corresponds to Americans, and others like the collared peccary (*wetar*) to Panamanians. Panamanians, although they have leaders, generally pass through Cuna territory singly or in small bunches, while the Americans that the Cuna know best, the soldiers in the Canal Zone, march around directed by trumpet calls, just like *yannu*.

animals or people associated with trees or interacting with trees, and in daily life, the Cuna often hunt animals that have gathered to feed at fruit trees. Chiefs lend themselves to metaphorization as trees, since the numeral classifier for trees, *sakla* (short form *sar-*), also means "chief," and each tree has a *sakla*, its "base."[9] The next metaphor compares two kinds of trees, both ritually important in other contexts, to two kinds of chief. In the distant past, the Cuna say, these trees were human or semihuman and were themselves chiefs.

Both types of tree bear fruit which animals come to eat, suggesting via the metaphor that chiefs are in general basically nurturant figures. But one tree feeds more animals than the other. The *Ikwa* tree (*Dipteryx panamensis,* "Tonka Bean Tree") bears an oval fruit one or two inches in length. The fruit's hard brown shell, which takes the same general bivalve form as a clam or a walnut, protects the meat within (Duke 1968:48, Chapin 1971: personal communication). At the beginning of the tableau, the *Ikwa* announces: "I am a good chief. I care for all the animals," but its actions belie its claims. Parrots of several species feed on its fruit, as do a variety of mammals, most of them like the tapir "large important animals" (*ipitar tummat*), and all of whom "have teeth" (*nukar nikka*). But other forest birds which arrive with their children can only peck ineffectually at the tough-skinned fruit without eating their fill.

"This means that some chiefs carry the spirit of the Ikwa." Chiefs who resemble the *Ikwa* tree offer personal hospitality to medicine men, chiefs, and other "big people" (*tummakan*), but unimportant people, those "without names" (*nuy suli*) who come to the chief's house get nothing and "leave without drinking." Such chiefs are also unfair as representatives of their villages' collective hospitality, where they must handle requests for items in short supply on other islands. The chief like an *Ikwa* has his village fill requests from visiting chiefs, but otherwise, "We don't collect things for those without names," not even for a poor woman who requests a little vine with which to rebuild her falling-down house.

The other tree, the *Isper* or *Esper* (*Manilkara zapota,* "Nispero"), says, "As for me, I take care of *all* my children." When the *Isper* first gives out its small orange fruits, hummingbirds, butterflies, and flies drink the whitish fluid that the fruits exude. (Notice that the *Ikwa* tree only gave solid food. In day-to-day intra-village hospitality, drinks of

9. In the picture-writing book of a death-chanter (*masartuleti*), Chapin came upon pictures of trees with faces. Whatever significance the trees may have in the death chant, the placement of the faces, at the bases of the trunks, relates to *saklas* and trees (Chapin 1971: personal communication).

various sorts are as important as food, so the *Isper* is thus more metaphorically complete in its provision of both liquid and solid.) Then the parrots and the mammals come to eat the fruit itself, along with a number of small animals not mentioned in connection with the *Ikwa.* When the *Isper* fruit rots on the ground, rats and the forest birds that the *Ikwa* frustrated eat too. One bird arrives with its children and drinks water (liquid again) caught in the crook of a branch, literally the "lap" (*nukku*) of its branch, a parental touch.

The metaphor continues by describing the generous acts of the *Isper*-like chief, but only briefly, since it has already communicated clearly the obligation on chiefs to be outstandingly generous and even-handed in their hospitality and gifts, as well as the expectation that many chiefs will fall short in these duties.

A common term, *tula,* for animals and village members strengthens their equivalence in the metaphor. As an adjective *tula* means "alive," while as a noun designating a class of people it means "member" or "inhabitants." *Tula* is regularly suffixed to animal names, and although it cannot be used by itself in everyday language to mean "animals," this text repeatedly refers to the animals as the *tula* of the tree, that is, as its "followers" or "members." A related verb, *otuloe,* describes both the hospitality to humans and the offering of fruit to the animals. Applied to dead or dying people, *otuloe* means "revive," but its more general sense is "give life to," so it suggests that both tree and chief are life-givers, those who make their *tula tula.*[10]

Within the two groups of *tula,* the animals without teeth clearly correspond to the humans "without a name," an equivalence reinforced by the similarity of the two words, *nukar* "teeth" and *nuka* "name." Moreover it is generally the large animals who eat well at the *Ikwa* and the small animals like rats and insects who are mentioned exclusively in connection with the *Isper,* just as only "big people" (*tummakan*) succeed with the *Ikwa*-like chief.

The particular text analyzed here ends with a coda about all the uses that the Cuna make of the excellent heartwood of the *Isper,* women for household items, men for axes and house construction; in this way metaphorizing the popularity and respect which will come to the fair and generous chief, as well as the people's dependence on their leaders. An admonishment collected by Sherzer plays on the ease with which an *Isper* can be cut down—despite the durability of its wood—and the

10. Two words, *tola* "native" and *tule* "person," come close to *tula* both in sound and meaning. Some of the animals that once were *immar tule* "animal people" are now *immar tula* "animals," although speakers occasionally slip and call them *tule.* Nordenskiold's gloss of *tula* as "life," an abstract principle, seems to be in error (cf. Holmer 1952:165).

fertility of the ground where it stood, while the *Ikwa* resists all but the most determined efforts to fell it (Sherzer 1970: field notes).[11]

The same situation, animals coming to feed at the base of a tree, can also metaphorize other aspects of relations between chiefs and followers. In the following verses excerpted from a chant, *Isper* and *Ikwa* are equally good: the contrast is not between two kinds of contemporary chief but rather between the great chiefs of the past and the lesser leaders of today. Underneath each verse I include a paraphrase of its hidden meaning, as given by the chief who sang the chant.

Truly kinsmen, in the East stood the *Isper* trees.
(The old traditional chiefs lived in the East.)

Truly therefore, on the top of a great hill stood an *Isper* tree.
(In a large village used to live a famous chief.)

Truly the good *Isper* tree that stood there before our time really gave good fruit in the bright season.
(The chief was very knowledgeable and attracted students.)

Truly, those who eat *Isper* fruit, the white-lipped peccary, came to the tree.
(Other chiefs came to study with the famous chief.)

Truly therefore, in the branches of an *Ikwa* tree, perched on a cotton thread, a parrot sang.
(In the gathering house of another distinguished chief, a visiting chief sang, seated in a hammock.)

Truly the fathers kept a flower garden by the base of the *Isper* tree.
(In the gathering, the women sat near the chief who was singing.)

Truly, from time to time the fathers swept around the flowers.
(The ancestors often admonished the women.)

Truly friend, the *Isper* trees that gave such fruit have begun to be rotten in parts.
(The great old chiefs are getting old and feeble.)

Truly, after the fall of the *Isper* tree, the flowers dry up.

11. The *Ikwa* and *Isper* appear differently in various versions. Sherzer's text describes the *Ikwa* as out-and-out bad (although an informant dictated another metaphor to him with a good *Ikwa*), while different versions of the metaphor I collected describe the tree as not-bad-but-not-very-good or slightly-bad. The *Ikwa* wood's toughness—it is in fact so hard the Cuna seldom try to fell them—sometimes stands for the virtues firmness and strength, and sometimes, as in Sherzer's version, stupid obstinacy and meanness. Finally, some metaphors expand the arboreal dyad into a triad, one *Isper* and two *Ikwas*.

Isper	Ikwa no. 1	Ikwa no. 2
Good	Pretty Good	Bad
Sweet Fruit	Sweet Fruit	Sour Fruit
Soft-skinned	Hard-shelled	Hard-shelled

(After the knowledgeable old chiefs die, the women no longer come
often to the gatherings.)

Truly therefore, the parrots gathered in our time sing only once in a while.
(Modern chiefs sing less well and less often.)

Truly, the Isper trees that we still have today are all saplings, without
heartwood.
(The chiefs of today are ignorant.)

Tree metaphors in general seem especially open to topical elaboration and change. The admonishments collected by Sherzer repeatedly
use the planting of a tree to describe the installation of a new chief,
and the discovery of a valuable tree at a distance in the forest to
describe the process of choosing a new chief. Chiefs that last only a
few years are trees which become uprooted soon after planting, and the
toppling of a tree by an earthquake described a recent case in which a
chief was removed from office for particularly scandalous bad behavior.
The late high chief Nele Kantule elaborated on these images in a chant
rendered into English by Nordenskiold and his collaborators (1938:
376–78), which deals with the Cuna revolution of 1925, the chiefs
deposed during it, and the process of reestablishing order:

A severe storm has passed over this land of ours and the trees were overturned by it. By reason of the tempest, the animals that had made their
abodes in the trees were thus dispersed. Now we shall build up again all
that the tempest has torn down. According to my way of thinking, we should
plant a tree that will last many years, a tree possessing great resistance, and
when we have planted it, we also ought to plant others about every village.
I think that when our tree bears fruit, to its branches there will come grouse,
parrots, and birds from all directions to eat the fruits of the tree. For this
reason the tree should be of a kind that bears much fruit. Then we ought to
keep the ground about it very clean so that the vultures (Panamanians,
Blacks) may not come and besmirch our tree. We should securely fence in
the flowers (women) that we are going to plant about our tree. We should
plant cocoa trees. . . . (Nordenskiold et al. 1938:376)

Interestingly enough, my informants claimed that after the revolution,
Nele Kantule urged the Cuna to plant (literally) for cash-cropping the
same tree, cacao, that in this speech he urged them to plant (metaphorically).

THE CHIEF IS A LIGHT: MORALITY METAPHORS

The *Ikwa-Isper* comparison, no matter how strongly it urges chiefs
to be generous, cannot by itself convey the extremes to which the Cuna

go in insisting on good behavior from their chiefs, or the general extent
to which morality, both public and personal, is intermixed with politics.
If in actual *practice* the Cuna lack the puritanical rigidity attributed to
them in various ethnographies, it is hardly surprising that their constant public worrying about morality deceived the ethnographers. The
gatherings interfere to an amazing degree in disputes and misdeeds
that other cultures would consider private matters or at most sanction
informally, and speakers repeatedly link up individual failings with the
collective moral state of the village and the Cuna as a whole—we have
already seen this connection implied in the notion of the net over the
village that a little sinning during the night can lift, letting in dangerous spirits.

Just as the great historical leaders of the Cuna came to lead the
wicked away from sin and teach proper behavior to the brutish, so
Cuna chiefs today have a mandate from God to maintain by counsel
and intervention the morality of their villages, in the same way that a
father admonishes and looks over his children (Howe 1974:102–3,
107–11, 165–66). Several metaphors touch on the chief as moral
guardian—although the histories have more to say on this subject—
while other metaphors assert the importance of admonishments in the
preservation of morality.[12]

One such metaphor about admonishments describes an imaginary
table in the gathering house. Each verse in the chant excerpt below
describes a different object on or under the table which represents the
good effects of admonishing.

> Truly, Great Father, on top of the golden table, put a
>   medicine-trough.
>
> Truly, Great Father, on top of the golden table, put a
>   medicine rock.
>
> Truly, Great Father, underneath the table, put water-aunt
>   juice (*tiamma nis,* a cold medicine).
>
> Truly, Great Father, on top of the golden table, put
>   good soaps.
>
> Truly, Great Father, on top of the golden table, put
>   good scouring stones.
>
> Truly, Great Father, on top of the golden table, put good
>   white cloth.

12. In another paper (Howe n.d.) I describe in greater detail the place of admonishments in Cuna cosmology.

> Truly, Great Father, on top of the golden table, put
>   cold-cloth.

The medicines, scouring stones, and soaps can do away with any ill-
nesses or stains—that is, immorality and social problems—that the people may bring with them to the gathering, while cold-cloth and cold
medicines cool off heated, angry situations.

A related but nonfictional metaphor of the same type as the animals-
have-chiefs example supports admonishments by arguing that the
inhabitants of whirlpools, strongholds, and the various levels of the
other world all receive counsel or moral admonition. Just as God sets
men to work for him, so he counseled all the elements of the natural
world as he set them to work. "Thus since Great Father put his sons
into the world, when he was ready to give them work, he admonished
them. 'Boy, you will work at this, you will do such and such work for
me'; thus God gave the way to his sons. Thus the elders-predecessors
say that God put his sons into the world counseling them."

"All the trees receive counsel. The river is counseled. The rocks are
counseled." Thus no human can resist counseling either. "A chief can
be counseled. An interpreter can be counseled. A medicine man can
be counseled. . . .Thus when Great Father sent us to this earth, he sent
us to a world of counseling."

The chiefs themselves "are obligated to observe irreproachable conduct in their public and private acts," as the written constitution of the
San Blas reserve expresses it (Holloman 1969:493), on pain of removal
from office. Morality metaphors for both leaders and ordinary people
usually take their vehicle from simple images of the physical manifestation of good and bad conduct, such as a piece of paper blotted by the
stains of one's misdeeds, good and rotten fruit, or the image mentioned
above of the soiled and unsoiled garments. Objects already associated
with chiefs such as trees of course make the most appropriate vehicles
for metaphors of chiefly morality:

I don't know how well we will plant this tree. Elders you sit here, those who
know medicines are sitting here, you policemen sit here, the interpreters are
sitting here, and the chiefs are lying in their hammocks. We don't know
whether we have gotten ourselves a good *Ina Kalewar* (another variety of
tree) without splits, whether we prunned and cared for a smooth trunk without holes. If we grow a tree on the edge of a farm, sometimes within a year
it rots and we pull it out, which is making work several times for your
brothers-in-law. But if in the distant fallow fields we carefully plant and
look after a tree which is all heartwood without holes or splits, it will last
for many years. Why do I say this to you? We ourselves do not know our
future conduct. The Great Father who lives above, he alone gives a good
spirit to someone. . . . (Scherzer 1970: field notes, my translation)

One recurrent metaphor, the notion that chiefs and other dignitaries live in a bright light, describes their fame as well as the special moral obligations and lack of privacy inherent in that fame. The following comes from an admonishment of an *inatulet* "medicine man."

You live in brightness. The elders-predecessors say of this that medicine men live in a bright light. A medicine man lives in a bright light, a great light, they say, one with a glass lens. Every day he is with a bright-shining light, and from pretty far away, since the medicine man is coming in the midst of light, people recognize him from a distance. "Elder medicine man is coming." Why is it said thusly? The elder has a name, Elder Medicine Man. Should he be coming through the streets, right away the children recognize him. "That elder, that's the medicine man coming," they say. The young girls recognize you, the medicine man. The young men of the village all recognize you. Should you travel afar, should you go to another village, your name has spread pretty far away, and you are recognized there too, those brothers recognize you. "A medicine man is coming." You have a name. That's why the elders-predecessors say, "Elder medicine man lives in a bright-shining light." He is recognized. Thereafter, medicine men, good conduct is wanted from you, the elders-predecessors say.

A nonmetaphorical passage (which however contains some everyday metaphors) taken from the admonishment of a newly installed chief puts the matter more crudely:

Working in God's way (inspires) great jealousy, strong jealousy. All of the members are watching us chiefs, us leaders, with their eyes wide open; all of the girls are watching us like that. I have a name, and if a flower (i.e., a young woman) and I are talking in a dark spot, right away they think badly of me. Right away they spread rumors about my misdeeds (Sherzer 1970: field notes).

The Cuna also say the chief is himself a light and the village members are shadows, a phrase that seems to mean that he is the embodiment and source of the village's moral state and reputation.

As with other metaphors, these can be recombined and changed for particular occasions: in one piece appropriate to visiting another chief's island and commenting on his morals, the singer describes himself being blown by the wind in his canoe toward a place on the coast. There he sees a tall tree on a hill set back from the shore, in whose branches a light shines out into the distance. He describes himself landing and setting out to find the tree, not knowing whether it will be sound or full of rot and holes.

I consider it crucial that the metaphors imply at least some immorality at the same time that they condemn it. They suggest that, inevitably, some people will wear spotted garments, some chiefs will always be

Ikwas and not *Ispers*, and some trees will be rotten. The histories are equally pessimistic: many leaders in the distant past could not stem the tide of immorality, while others were themselves corrupted by their office and actively drew their followers into evil ways. Thus the Cuna have a kind of mythological and metaphorical charter for the inevitability of human evil and political corruption, a charter which perhaps signals the degree to which they eventually forgive and forget the wrongdoings of both chief and commoner, no matter how strongly they initially condemn them.

HOUSES, RIVERS, BODIES: METAPHORS OF COMMUNITY

We have seen that the metaphors argue for the necessity of both group action and individual leadership, and that they convey expectations about how leaders and ordinary people ought to act. The metaphors in this next section (and in the one after it) also do these things, but they do something else as well: they provide models for conceptualizing the nature of the primary political unit, the village, both in terms of its constituent elements and as a whole. They suggest the village as the body in which decisions should be made and problems resolved, and they build an image of the village, not merely as a residential agglomeration, but as a corporate group and a community.

One of these builds on the highly polysemic word *sakla,* which we have already seen means "chief" and "tree base." As a suffix on adjectives, *-sakla* indicates extremity; *akkarsakla* for instance means "as different as it could be." *Sakla ki,* with the addition *ki* "in, on" means 'in the beginning'. The one most relevent meaning here is "head," which by itself makes a simple and almost universal metaphor about political leaders. After the chiefs in rank come the interpreters or speakers, often called *voceros* in Spanish, whose Cuna name, *arkar* or *arkala,* extends the metaphor begun by *sakla,* since it means "rib(s)" in reference to the body. The chief as "head" suggests intelligence, direction, primarity, and uniqueness, (although, in point of fact, several secondary chiefs back up each first chief). Since *kala* "bone" means "strength" in Cuna, ribs connote strength, as well as support and multiplicity.

As policemen are *sualipkana* "masters of the staves" (of office), and secretaries are *sikkwi* "birds," the terms for other village officials clearly do not carry forward this metaphor of the body politic. Nor did I hear anyone pick it up and revitalize it during my fieldwork, but happily, Nordenskiold's informants did, in a speech by the late high chief Masta Coleman:

You gentlemen know that our body has two hands which help each other when something is too heavy for one hand. We also have a heart and a liver, a stomach, lungs, and intestines. Throughout our lives these things help our body to function well. Thus each village has various men who help the community, such as those who know the medicine (chants) *sia ikar* and *kurkin ikar*, the interpreters, and the various other officials we have. We do not want anyone to speak against another, so that even those who lack all ritual knowledge will help the community when it is threatened. (Nordenskiold et al. 1938:95, 99)

A house metaphor reiterates the same points by comparing each official to a structural member of the building. (Remember the popularity of *Isper* wood as a building material.) The main vertical posts (*puara*), which are in general symbols of endurance and permanence, represent the chiefs, the secondary vertical posts (*usola*) the *arkars*, and the roof support poles (*makket*) are ritually knowledgeable men who are not chiefs or *arkars*.[13] These major timbers embody important qualities of the "big people" of the village: the timbers are firmly placed and enduring; each has a name, just as each big man "has a name"; and they all work hard at holding the building up. The ordinary people in contrast, correspond to the walls (*kalu*) of the building, thin lengths of cane that require frequent replacing. The police are the *kalupupa*, stout poles which hold the cane walls in line, just as the police keep the people in order. The speaker or singer can link up various other officers or ritually knowledgeable men to other parts of the building, the choice of which correspondences and how many he wishes to make depending on context.

However the detailed correspondences work themselves out, houses make especially good metaphors of a corporate—or perhaps edificate—unity that is organic and yet manufactured at the same time. The gathering itself most clearly manifests the community solidarity represented by the house, and as the speaker or singer unfolds the metaphor, the vehicle surrounds the audience. Interpreters explicitly state that the shelter which the gathering house gives the assembled community metaphorizes the political and spiritual shelter that its officials and its general unity provide the village. They emphasize that even the smallest parts of the building are essential, and although the main post bears the most weight, it cannot hold up the building by itself.

The house as a vehicle lends itself to elaboration of the sort already encountered with trees, and the following, which discusses bad chiefs

13. In a ritual now no longer used, when a divorced man returned to his wife, her father would knock his head against the *puar*, in this way both punishing him and magically imparting the permanence and stability of the post.

and the problems they cause, resembles the metaphor that treats chiefly morality in terms of a tree—which of course the house posts once were.

We are about to plant a pole. If we plant it badly, if we plant one with holes and knots, in a year you will hear an *ulis* (a kind of insect) singing in the hole. You'll hear a spider singing, you'll hear a cockroach singing. You'll hear a big granddaddy of a scorpion singing in his hole. The women will all be afraid, and you'll have to pull it out again. Therefore the elders- predecessors say, "plant a smooth pole without any holes or splits."[14]

Sherzer collected a further extension of the house metaphor on the occasion of the reinstallation of a chief who had earlier been thrown out for misconduct, (a fairly common occurrence). The speaker noted that sometimes after they set up the center post of a house, the builders find that it is rotten, so they pull it out and trim away the rotten parts before setting it up again.

This set of messages about communities conveyed by the house and body metaphors reappears in still a third metaphor, suggesting that they touch on concerns vital to the Cuna. The third metaphor takes for its vehicle rivers, which are in general very important and positive symbols and are themselves often metaphorized in highly flattering clichés as "a canoe full of medicine" and "the breast milk of God's wife."

In the dry season, the river rocks are "covered with slime" and "slippery," "the water is stagnant," and the river is in general fouled and "ugly." Things get worse if someone cuts trees along the river, because their trunks lie in the water clogging it further.

If it rains just a little, so that only the main river rises up a bit, things do not improve significantly. With a little more rain, the major tributaries feed into the river, which swells considerably, but the big snags still block the stream. Only when all the tributaries of the river feed into it, including the little rivulets and the source streams at its headwaters, does the river rise right out of its banks and clear away the tree trunks. Then the flood scours the rocks clean, sweeps bare the river bottom, and deposits sandy beaches in several places. "The place looks good."

It should come as no surprise that "a chief is like a river." When the

---

14. This passage illustrates nicely the point that speakers can interpret metaphors in varying degrees of thoroughness. In this version (collected by Sherzer), the speaker assumes that the audience will understand that the pole stands for the chief, and that the insects represent various unspecified problems. In a version I collected, each fault, knot, weakness, and termite corresponds to a different problem. A bug making noise in a hole for instance metaphorizes a person of bad character whispering suggestions in the chief's ear.

chief adjudicates a major problem disrupting the village by himself, if the other "big people" will not help him, then he will fail. But if the *arkars*, the other officers, other important older men, and the rising young men who are not yet officers, all speak and help adjudicate disputes, then even the greatest problem cannot help but resolve itself. The fallen trees represent problems, or especially difficult problems, of a general nature, a representation that derives its aptness from local riverine conditions without implying any connection to other metaphors where trees stand for chiefs.

Nordenskiold has recorded the outlines of a related metaphor that describes the process of solving problems caused by outsiders in terms of letting the rivers flood to wash away the pelican dung which dirties them (1938:201–2).

The emphasis on the *stillness* of the river suggests that motion, or the lack of it, is as metaphorically important as filth and obstruction. The Cuna often call a chief the *ney seet* "the one who maintains the place." In this context they usually translate the verb *see* into Spanish as *mantener* "maintain," but it literally means "carry." In general, *see* describes the action of rivers in carrying objects downstream, and in this passage in particular, both successful river and successful chief are said to "carry the place." The animal chiefs listed in the very first text have the same job: they direct their followers' *movement* from place to place. Here one puts something in order by setting it in motion.[15]

According to the text, the problems metaphorized by the tree trunks foul up the collective life of the village, not the personal affairs of the chief, so the river is obviously a dual metaphor for the whole village as well as for the chief, as the following sentence suggests: "In the same way that the main river rose up, the village is put in order." This makes sense, given that villages are invariably associated with a mainland river from which they draw their fresh water, many villages take their names from their rivers, and the chiefs frequently allude metonymically to villages as rivers or river mouths in admonishments.

Clearly the messages conveyed by these three metaphors are similar but not identical. The first two lack some of the concern with disputes and problem-solving characterizing the last one, as well as the note of direct exhortation on which it ends: "Therefore . . . , if you hear in the gathering house that a problem exists, you work too. You speak along with the chief. . . .The gathering house is there to work for God. So why should you not want to work there?"

15. In a text I collected on the creation of the world, one of the most important of God's acts was setting the rivers in motion. The histories of at least two San Blas villages recount how great Cuna leaders made them inhabitable by clearing away obstructions at the mouths of their rivers (Nordenskiold et al. 1938:19, 124).

One important constant in all three metaphors is the theme of limits on the chief's power, which contrasts with but does not contradict the emphasis in other metaphors on the importance of the chief as ritual, moral, and consensus-managing leader of the community (Howe 1974: 177–94). Beyond his inability to go against the expressed will of the majority, each Cuna chief finds himself hedged in by situation-specific checks, particularly outside the meeting hall. If for instance, the village men work on its wharf or clear trails through the forest, all the chiefs and interpreters must subordinate themselves to the officer in charge of that type of communal labor, and if a chief still resides matrilocally after becoming chief, as two did in the village I studied, he must follow his father-in-law's directions within the household. If a politically important man wants to learn some ritual specialty, he must defer to his teacher as his superior while he is learning, no matter how unimportant the teacher's position in the gathering house.

Most constraining perhaps is the fact that while at large in the village the chief cannot directly enforce those rules which he urges on his followers in the gathering house, especially if his enforcement would bring him into contact with quarrelers, who in the heat of the moment might forget the respect due to a chief. This restriction showed itself vividly when two women began a particularly nasty quarrel only a few yards from a chief's house. They screamed and yelled at each other and used obscenities in the presence of children—both very bad form in themselves and doubly bad near the chief's house—and the chief's wife talked about going over and shutting them up. He himself however merely listened for a minute or two and then hurried off to the meeting house to confer with the first interpreter on how they would adjudicate the matter the following evening. The metaphor most relevant to this case urges chiefs to pick up whatever things they might find out in the village and store them away in a trunk until another day. More generally and more directly, the Cuna say, "The chief is chief only while in his hammock in the meeting house."

Although all three community metaphors present the chief in much the same way, the depiction of village members or "big people" changes in one important respect. In the river metaphor, the elements vary only in size—all are tributary streams—but the parts of the body and the house differ in kind as well as importance, in this way representing the role differentiation for which the Cuna strive in political and ritual office. A multiplicity of lesser *saklas*, secretaries, and treasurers supervise community activities such as wharf-building and trail-clearing, and it is hard to avoid the conclusion that here the Cuna are to a certain extent interested in creating positions for their own sake, since the offices have multiplied beyond the demands of the tasks themselves.

This same multiplicity of roles characterizes ritual. Most ethnographers of the Cuna have harped on the four most prestigious ritual positions—*inatuleti* (medicine man), *nele* (seer, shaman), *apsoketi* (exorciser), and *kantule* (puberty ceremony chanter)—but a host of other chants for curing, hunting, mourning, and handling dangerous animals occur as well. Traditionally, most men elect to learn several of these in their lifetimes: any one chant is known by only some men of the village, and even fewer men learn an identical combination of chants.

The Cuna talk a lot about jealousy and competition, and it is a constant theme in the mythology; they expect it most often between those who know the same things or occupy the same offices. Thus for instance, in the puberty ceremonies, which provide the major occasion for men to sing and show off their ritual knowledge, they fear status challenges in which one man casts doubt on another's knowledge (*penkueti*). The admonishments urge that instead each man alternately sing and listen respectfully to what his neighbor is singing, and indeed in most of the little knots of singing men to which I listened, not only did each man sing something that the others in the group had not learned, but they made a point of stressing the uniqueness of the singer's knowledge. The high chief Masta Colman made the same point in an admonishment of village chiefs collected by Nordenskiold's informants:

I do not want those who are living in and governing their respective communities to be jealous of each other. I want you to be counselling your men and women and not be saying, "I am greater than the other chiefs." Gentlemen, you know very well that *each person has learned some things different from other people.* . . . (my italics, Nordenskiold et al. 1938:92).

I suggest, although I cannot prove it here, that the interest in the variety of house and body parts, each with its separate function, metaphorizes a sought-after Durkheimian organic solidarity of sorts, a solidarity which avoids by diversification the evils that the Cuna find inherent in uniformity (Howe 1974:222–74).

WE ARE A FAMILY

Metaphors based on kinship and parentage, as was the family level of the animals-have-chiefs metaphor, seem to occur in most cultures. For the Cuna, perhaps, the most central and important political metaphor is the community-as-family, an identification that, like the chief-as-head, shows itself more often in terminology and usage than in chiefly singing. Speakers in the gathering house address each other as *kwennatkan* "siblings, cousins, relatives," and they often refer to a member as a "child" (*mimmi*) of the village. (The *Isper* and *Ikwa* trees call the animals that feed on their fruit their children.) The chief is of course the father of the village, and though his "children" never address him as *Papa* "father," the metaphor makes its way even into the written constitution of the reserve: "The authority of the chiefs is paternal" (Holloman 1969:493). As previously noted, the parent-child metaphor informs the manner in which chiefs interfere in their followers' morals, while to indicate the special degree of sexual restraint required of the chief himself, the Cuna say that if he has affairs with women of his village, he is committing a kind of father-daughter incest. Rounding out the metaphor, his wife becomes the village's mother:

. . . .His wife sits listening too. She grew in stature, first you were the wife of an *arkar*. Today you have been elevated, to be a chief's wife, chief X's wife. You have become a great mother. You are about to become the mother of the young girls [of the village], about to become the mother of the young men. You are about to become the mother of all the girls sitting here, which makes me happy. (Sherzer 1970: field notes; my translation).

The people of the island where I worked frequently used *kwennatkan* to refer to Cuna from other villages, thus projecting the family metaphor onto a larger field. In this case, the father, if he enters into the metaphor, is most often God himself, *Pap Tummat* "Great Father."

Interestingly enough, another ethnographer of the Cuna reached similar conclusions starting with her identification of Cuna villages as demes (Holloman 1969:136–58), following Murdock's exposition of this construct (Murdock 1949:63). Holloman argues from the degree of interrelatedness inherent in endogamous villages, and from the use of the term *kwennatkan*, that village members conceive of the community as a real kin group, in the way that deme members should according to Murdock's theory (Holloman 1969:141; Murdock 1949:159).

Leaving aside the difficulties involved in using the ethnographer's perception of interrelatedness to analyze the native point of view, this argument brings us back to the knotty problem of how literally native users interpret metaphors. I found nothing to suggest that the Cuna conceptualized the essential nature of their villages as large endogamous kin groups, or that they considered the relations between communities in terms of interaction between families, lineages, or demes. Both village and Cuna people as a whole, as much as they are families, are nuclear families writ large.

All the same, the family idiom is *not* just a manner of speaking, any more than God-the-father is just a manner of speaking to either Cuna or European. The metaphor has become real enough to transcend merely expressing the structure of the village by actively molding it. The reality lies I think in the complete acceptance of the family *model* and of the roles inherent in the family, not in biological interrelatedness. Even if the Cuna do not view their village as some kind of large kin group, it still seems a family to them, in sentiment if not in genealogy.

A variant version of the village-as-family, the village-as-matrilocal-household, deemphasizes the primacy of the first chief. The in-married brothers-in-law of the household, the *ampesukan,* metaphorize the chiefs of the village as a cooperating group. Such brothers-in-law usually split up into separate households after the death of their father-in-law, but occasionally they get along well enough to continue under one roof, graded by seniority (as chiefs are), and led by the eldest brother-in-law (the first chief). Each task that such brothers-in-law might carry out together for their household metaphorizes something the chiefs do for the village: they plant trees (install new chiefs) for instance, or they spread sand over slippery spots in the street (warn the people of possible future problems). Usually the brothers-in-law of the metaphor work hardest at cutting down weeds around various kinds of plants, thus portraying the admonishment of various classes of people: flowers or cacao (young women), cotton (albinos), cane (men), and so forth to the limits of the singer's imagination and interest.[16] As the inclusion of the tree metaphor shows, the brothers-in-law in fact provide a framework into which the speaker or singer can fit any number of other metaphors.

Finally, like the village-as-family and the *Ikwa-Isper* metaphor, the brothers-in-law vehicle can be transposed onto the larger political arena to represent the assembled chiefs of many islands, in which case the metaphor describes a still-living father-in-law (a regional chief of several islands) directing the efforts of his sons-in-law.

CONCLUDING REMARKS

Most previous sources on the Cuna that have touched on the gathering metaphors treat them as if they consisted of little more than a

---

16. Cotton represents albinos in a straightforward way. A young girl, *sia*, resembles cacao, *sia*, in her name as well as her desirability. The cane that is like the village men, stands in the *kalu* "wall" of a house, which in the house metaphor also metaphorized in the village men (p. 153).

special vocabulary for singing the histories and talking about current events (e.g., Nordenskiold et al. 1938:373–81; Kramer 1970:58–62). It has, I hope, become clear that they also include extended metaphorical conceits and tableaux conveying messages that the user may apply to particular issues and events, but that in their generality transcend mere topical comment. In addition to moral exhortations such as "chiefs should be generous and leave the women alone," they suggest ways of conceptualizing Cuna political organization, that is, they teach an official native model of politics, a constitution of sorts in metaphors.

If this essay has pointed out only a few basic features of the constitution, it is because I and the other ethnographers of the Cuna concerned with their use of metaphor have just begun to come to grips with the subject. Conclusions in the strict sense of the word would be inappropriate so early in an ethnographic enterprise, but a few final generalizations, for the most part on the place of political metaphors in the wider fields of tradition and special speech forms, may tie together a little more neatly the bundle of metaphors presented here.

I have had to exclude the chiefly histories from more than passing mention, but the chiefs themselves treat history and metaphors as two variant aspects of metaphor taken in a wider sense—and they see this more general phenomenon as a key attribute of the role of the chief. From their viewpoint, ordinary people handle matters in the gatherings in terms of the immediate issues at hand; they deal with them "just superficially" (*ukkaskimpi*). Chiefs, on the other hand, attack problems "thoroughly, in depth" (*akkapaysale*), by anticipating the future of an issue, pointing out parallels from past history, and drawing analogies from nature and nonpolitical parts of the cultural world such as the family. In recent years they have also begun to point out similarities observed in the cultures of Panama and the Canal Zone. Each of these several types of metaphor establishes the nonuniqueness of particular events by showing how they recur at various times in Cuna history and various domains of the present day.

Although chiefs may occasionally take trivial or fictional vehicles for their metaphors, ultimately they can talk about things in depth only because God made the world with fundamental underlying attributes that hold in all times and places. Above all, he set everyone and everything to work for him at maintaining his creation. To an outside observer it may seem that the Cuna project features of the political realm out onto other domains and other times, but to them, the metaphors and histories merely point out parallels, not create them.

The reader should not, however, take the emphasis of this paper on similarities between domains to mean that dissimilarities and distinctions—anti-metaphor—are nonexistent or irrelevant in Cuna tradition.

Things and relations in different domains may be alike in fundamental ways, but the domains are still separate, and in some cases, such as animals or foreigners vis-à-vis themselves, the Cuna take great pains to keep the domains separate. Even in combination with histories, the metaphors examined here make up only part of the picture:

	Similarities	*Differences*
THROUGH TIME	Historical Constants E.g., We repeat past mistakes of the animal people.	Historical Changes Animals and people have become differentiated.
TIMELESS OR PRESENT	Metaphors Animals have chiefs like ours.	Anti-Metaphor We are *not* animals. Animals do many things differently.

Some of the metaphors here have incorporated a few aspects of differentiation, as when the animals-have-leaders text says, "But we are that much more that way, we are people" (p. 12). And when comparing Cuna and foreign institutions, the tone of the comparison often seems to be, "Even those crazy foreigners do it, so it must be universal."

If then the Cuna consider that the metaphors do more than provide a convenient means of talking about one thing in terms of another, how do they explain the many seeming inconsistencies between metaphors? Village members represented as a river system appear essentially uniform, but comparison with body parts suggests diversity. The father chief toils alone, while the brother-in-law chief works with others. The river chief moves himself and is a mover of others, although the house post stands as the very acme of immovability.[17]

The answer to the contradictions at the conceptual level that I infer from hints in the texts and informants' remarks lies in the centrality of the Cuna in God's scheme of things. The attributes that separate out in every other domain come together in Cuna institutions. For every positive attribute that an animal or tree has, the Cuna say they are that much more that way, and although house posts stay in place when rivers move, the chief incorporates the essence of both.

Ultimately of course the resolution must be contextual—the appropriate metaphor for the occasion at hand. A chief standing firm in the winds of opinion suggests a house post, while the chief leading his

17. The river/post opposition may not be so strong as it seems at first, since the river and its branches are "in place" (*yoyoi*) just as much as the house parts are, and both river and animals move in ways that are orderly and directed; they do not go just anywhere. Still, the opposition is only partly resolved.

followers toward the resolution of a conflict resembles the animal leaders or the river. If a speaker wants unanimity, he makes the village a river system, but when he asks his listeners not to cast doubt on each other's ritual skills, they become house or body parts.

Almost all the metaphors examined here deal with the chiefs and their relations with the village, hardly a surprise given that chiefs and interpreters all but monopolize access to the use of the metaphors. (Indeed, after taking in the chiefly self-flattery that permeates some of the metaphors, the reader may need assurance that ordinary people subscribe to most of the sentiments expressed in them. They do.) At the same time, although we might expect that the metaphors, largely used and controlled by the chiefs and their interpreters, would most constrain others, actually many of them work as a check on the leaders themselves. Each chief and interpreter, although he may want to glorify his position, has as much interest as any ordinary person in reminding the other leaders through metaphor of their duties and the proper limits on their powers.

This criterion of access to the metaphors has two aspects, the one just mentioned of access to their use, and another of access to their meaning. The hidden or secret quality of metaphor that came out in the examination of the word *purpale,* when combined with the distinction of access, can neatly separate chiefly metaphors out from other Cuna indirect speech forms, according to when and to whom the meaning of a metaphor is hidden or revealed.

According to at least the formal logic of the gathering, the chief's audience cannot understand the underlying meaning of his singing until after he finishes, even if *he* can. Users of ordinary figures of speech, on the other hand, assume that their audience catches their meaning at once without special explanations, while those who speak in euphemisms hope that some of those listening (adults) will follow what they are saying and others (children) will be puzzled. Singers of medicine chants intend that familiar spirits should understand the chant's secret meaning, but that the uninitiated should not. In one case, everyone listening understands, and in the other two, only some understand. Although the ignorant can learn (children become adults, laymen learn chants), the situation is in essence static and synchronic.

Only in the gathering house does the presentation of secret meanings entail their immediate explanation to the audience. Each time the chief sings, he sets out an opaque mystery, and then afterward the interpreter renders the mystery into a transparent lesson for the assembled people. The two thus carry forward a process of continuing and repetitive revelation, in which they make the hidden essence of things intelligible by unraveling secrets, over and over again.

Chapter 6

My Brother the Parrot

J. CHRISTOPHER CROCKER*

This essay investigates the social nature of cosmological metaphor through an extended discussion of a single ethnographic case. The problem, which has been the subject of academic debate for over sixty years, is just what the Bororo of Central Brazil mean when they say, "We are red macaws." I intend to discuss first the classic analysis offered by Levy-Bruhl when he originally brought the issue to general attention, and then to argue that the aphorism is not so much an example of "totemic participation" implying identity, but rather must be interpreted as a metaphor of similarity. To substantiate this view, it will be necessary to explore various Bororo concepts and practices concerning macaws, as well as their several definitions of "we." My conclusion shall be that neither a totemic framework nor one reflecting metaphysical beliefs nor yet one based on Bororo taxonomic classificatory principles is sufficient grounds for understanding the postulated identity between a certain animal species and human kind. Rather, it is an example of paradigmatic association in terms of the structural equivalence of men and macaws in several distinct relational contexts. Its meaning and logical character cannot be understood without an appreciation of the particular social situation in which it is utilized, as a strategy for expressing the ambiguous charac-

* This article has profited from the analytical systems of T. O. Beidelman, James Fernandez, and Claude Lévi-Strauss. For their careful editing and many valuable insights I wish to thank David Sapir, Marc Schloss, Peter Stone, and Joseph R. Crocker, Jr.

ter of the actors in that context. Through this analysis I also hope to show that an understanding of the distinguishing characters of various tropes in figurative language is essential to any analysis of a society's cosmological system.

In his first work addressed to the nature of mystical participation (*Les fonctions mentales dans les sociétés inférieures,* 1910), Levy-Bruhl utilizes a Bororo datum to document some of his most crucial points about the characteristics of this phenomenon. While the importance of a single illustrative example to his total argument should not be overemphasized, its early and recurrent appearance in that book raises it above the level of the casual, anecdotal aside. Further, the apparent lack of ambiguity in the statement, as Levy-Bruhl reports it, is likely to impress even the sophisticated reader (Van der Leeuw 1928:8; Lowie 1937:218; Percy 1961; Vygotsky 1962:71–72; Geertz 1966:37–38). He took this and other Bororo material from Steinen, whose work on the Indians of Central Brazil had appeared in 1894.[1] The critical passages in Levy-Bruhl are the following:

"The Bororo . . . boast that they are red araras (parakeets)." This does not merely signify that after their death they become araras, nor that araras are metamorphosed Bororos, and must be treated as such. It is something entirely different. "The Bororos," says Von den Steinen, whose affirmations, "give one rigidly to understand that they are araras *at the present time,* just as if a catepillar declared itself to be a butterfly." It is not a name they give themselves, nor a relationship [parenté] that they claim. What they desire to express by it is actual identity. That they can be both the human beings they are and the birds of scarlet plumage at the same time, Von den Steinen regards as inconceivable, but to the mentality that is governed by the law of participation there is no difficulty in the matter. All communities which are totemic in form admit of collective representations of this kind, implying similar identity of the individual members of a totemic group and their totem. (1966:62)

Primitive mentality sees no difficulty in the belief that such life and properties exist in the original and in its reproduction at one and the same time. By virtue of the mystic bond between them a bond represented by the law of participation, the reproduction *is* the original, as the Bororo *are* the araras. (1966:64)

[He goes on to specify that this bond is above all a totemic one]. The very existence of the social groups. . .is most frequently represented. . . as a participation, a communion, or rather a number of participations and communions. . . .The collective representation in this case is exactly like

1. I am indebted to Van Baaren's perceptive article on this same topic (1969:9) for the references to Van der Leeuw, and to James Fox for drawing my attention to this material. I also wish to thank Rodney Needham for the Vygotsky reference.

that which so astonished Von den Steinen when the Bororos "rigidly" maintained that they were araras. . .Every individual is both such and such a man or woman, alive at present, a certain ancestral individual, who may be human or semi-human. . .and at the same time he *is* his totem, that is, he partakes in some mystic Fashion of the essence of the animal or vegetable species whose name he bears. (1966:75)

It is worth examining these statements, and other aspects of Levy-Bruhl's argument, in some detail.[2] He quite explicitly raises some of the most vexing issues in the analysis of figurative language and belief systems, and the various interpretations which he rejects form the ethnographic substance of this essay. First, Levy-Bruhl says that the Bororo claim to be macaws does not reflect any belief in particular transformations of the individual soul. Actually, this was the conclusion Steinen reached, in spite of the ultimate acceptance of the "literal" truth of the native's own position with which Levy-Bruhl credits him. Steinen finally decides that the declaration "We are macaws" is to be understood, neither as reflecting the supposed metamorphoses of the soul after death, nor as deriving from totemic aspects of the clan system, but strictly in reference to the physical appearance of the soul when it leaves the body at any time (Steinen 1894:512–13). He reports that the Bororo believe the soul assumes the form of a bird, usually a red macaw, when it departs the corporeal self, regardless of whether this occurs during dreams or at death (1894:510–11). Steinen's own evidence on this point is internally contradictory, and I found no confirmation of such a belief during field work seventy years after his. But Levy-Bruhl rejects it out of hand in favor of his dominant totemic emphasis.

Just what was Levy-Bruhl after here? It should be made clear that the Bororo do indeed compare themselves to macaws, although only in certain social contexts that shall be described below. While there are some problems with Steinen's description of the native exegesis, in comparison to the ones I obtained, the basic facts are as he reported them. Given that Levy-Bruhl had apprehended a true ethnographic problem, what significance does his interpretation have for the general topic of this volume, and for the recent work on animal symbolism (Firth 1966; Leach 1964; Tambiah 1969; Bulmer 1967; Douglas 1972)? More particularly, what are we to make out of his contention that the Bororo statement, and others like it, reflects the "actual identity" between clansmen and their totems which is the logical essence of any

2. As Van Baaren notes, Levy-Bruhl probably used the second edition (1897) of *Unter den Naturvolken Zentralbrasiliens.* He cites one critical passage as occurring between pages 305 and 306, whereas in the 1894 edition the same passage is found on pp. 352–53 (Van Baaren 1969:10). Unfortunately I have not been able to secure a copy of the second edition to confirm this point.

totemic system, in view of Lévi-Strauss's analysis of such systems in terms of symbolic, figurative meanings (1963*a*:passim)? For Levy-Bruhl makes it very clear that in his view the Indians mean literally what they say. He explicitly denounces the view that a Bororo=macaw equation might be a label or emblem, a "name." This we would now understand as a case of synecdoche, a part-whole relationship. No more, he says, is a historical relationship of descent from some original macaw involved; in our terms, such an association would be an instance of metonymy, in that cause (ancestor) would stand for effect (descendents). Likewise, Levy-Bruhl denies Steinen's synecdochic interpretation that the soul (part) appears as a macaw when it leaves the body (whole). The "law of mystical participation" does not rest either on syntagmatic contiguity or on paradigmatic association, for both imply a logical distinction of some type between the conjoined entities. Levy-Bruhl claims that totemic systems make no distinctions of any type between clan members and their totems; consequently such analytical niceties as symbols and tropes are simply irrelevant to the understanding of these systems.

In sharp contrast, Lévi-Strauss's conception of totemism emphasizes the conceptual separateness of the animal–human domains. Comparisons between these domains can therefore only be metaphorical in logical nature. Metaphor, by definition, involves intuitive leaps which connect aspects of two distinct semantic realms. But metaphor can occur only where these realms overlap in some fashion. "The metaphor in a word lives when the word brings to mind more than a single reference and the several references are seen to have something in common . . . the name of one subordinate is extended to the other and this, as we shall see, has the effect of calling both references to mind with their differences as well as their similarities" (Brown 1958: 140). This feature—the way metaphor establishes connotative similarities through a recognition of denotative contrast—is crucial to Lévi-Strauss's approach. But if "a metaphor is a device of representation by which a new *meaning* is learned" (Van Steenburgn 1965:678), Levy-Bruhl would argue that, as Bororo dogma, "we are parrots" is a self-evident truth and far from anything "new"; as readers will attest, Lévi-Strauss's treatment of such dictums involves novel revelations indeed.

Clearly the issue cannot be resolved on a priori grounds, and must rest on a complete ethnographic account of the logical connections between man and animal, culture and nature, perceived by the society. It is necessary to examine all the various connotations and denotations of the Bororo senses of "man" and "macaw" to determine which of the meanings are actually operative in the statement "we are macaws." For other situations are theoretically possible here beyond the two envisaged by Lévi-Strauss and Levy-Bruhl. We might discover that red macaws and the Bororo are characterized by the same set of criterial dimensions, that the two species are identified as one or another aspect of a single whole (e.g., the clan or some "universal spiritual substance"). As long as some kind of indigenous distinction is made between such aspects, such that a macaw totem might represent the clan but is as partial an expression of that whole as any single member, then synecdoche rather than "mystical participation" would be operative.

Indeed, there are general difficulties with Lévi-Strauss's absolute division between the natural and cultural realms. As Tambiah points out, his categorical rejection of the Radcliffe-Brownian notion that rules of ethical conduct toward animals reflect man's sense of affinity and even identity with them renders his answer to the problem of why societies have a "ritual attitude" toward animals much less than satisfactory (Tambiah 1969:453–54). Lévi-Strauss stresses that such normative considerations as dietary regulations, sacrifices, and clan names demonstrate that the totemic system is much more than a linguistic code, and is far from being an abstract metaphorical series having the most distant intellectual relation with the concerns of daily life. But his analyses beg the issue of why this should be so (1963:15–32).[3] I contend that certain Bororo ritual attitudes toward macaws involve synecdoche, in that various attributes of macaws are considered aspects of clanship, and vice versa; other Bororo comparisons between men and macaws will be held to rest on more purely syntagmatic contiguities, and reflect metynomy. In these totemic and cosmological terms per se, the conclusion must be that Levy-Bruhl is more correct than Lévi-Strauss even though the former's argument rests on a faulty premise. But I also argue that neither the totemic nor the related cosmological realms of discourse are at all relevant to the case in question, which instead deals with the problem of man's nature rather than the clan's culture.

THE CASE FOR TOTEMS: CLANS AND SPECIES

The contemporary villages of the Eastern Bororo[4] are scattered along the São Lourenço River and its tributaries in north central Mato

3. This issue is most obscure and slippery; Lévi-Strauss does certainly not affirm that the four logical types of totemism he distinguishes (1963a:16–18), of which the last three may well involve our connections of metonymy and synecdoche, are logically water-tight compartments.
4. The Western Bororo are extinct and have been so for at least two generations. However, I shall follow current usage in referring only to the Eastern Bororo (Albisetti and Venturelli 1962:passim).

Grosso, Brazil, to the east and southeast of Cuiaba. The language may be distantly related to Ĝe (Kietzman 1967:34), and certainly the Bororo manifest such Ĝe characteristics as a hunting-gathering ecology, dyadic social structure,[5] uxorilocal residence, and great complexity of ritual and cosmology. Although the society has suffered severe population loss in recent years and been intensively exposed to Brazilian influences, certain communities manage to preserve much of their traditional organization and ceremonial practices.[6] Normatively, all Bororo villages are divided into exogamous moieties in which post-marital residence tends to be uxorilocal. Each moiety is composed of four clans, and membership in these corporate groups derives from possession of personal names taken from a stock of such names owned by the mother's social unit. Each clan is divided into two "sub-clans"[7] which are in turn differentiated into three to six matrilineages each.

Although the characteristics of these last units are somewhat ambiguous, even in the orthodox Bororo view, they are here assumed to be the locus of rights over the usage and disposal of a variety of cultural "goods," or scare values. These include the personal names mentioned above, without which a person is not a member of Bororo society; various decorative styles used for utilitarian objects (baskets, pots, clubs, sleeping mats, and so forth) and for ceremonial objects (ornamental bows, headdresses, rattles, armbands, musical instruments, necklaces, and somatic paintings); and specific ceremonies which purport to represent various species of animals, fish, birds, and marvelous spirits. These last are part of an extensive though supposedly fixed set of natural and supernatural entities intimately associated with the clan.

I frankly hesitate to label these entities "totems." While their relationship to the corporate group is characterized by many elements which an earlier generation of ethnographers would have deemed properly totemic, Lévi-Strauss (1963a) has thoroughly demonstrated the logical and empirical fallacies of their criteria. He himself, I think,

---

5. I understand this phrase in Maybury-Lewis's sense, "A theoretical society in which every aspect of the social life of its members is ordered according to a single antithetical formula" (1967:298).

6. I have worked mainly in two of the four or five such self-preserving communities, during 1964–65 and again in 1967. By "preserve" I mean that a quite self-conscious and thorough effort was made to maintain ancient customs, so that, for example, communal rituals occurred nearly every week.

7. In earlier publications both I and the Salesians have described the clan as divided into three sub-clans. While these statements reflect the views of the most traditionally learned informants, it must be admitted that neither they nor other Bororo place much importance on the "middle" (Boedadawu) sub-clan. It seems to be utilized as a residual category when it is mentioned at all. I am obliged to Zarko Levak, who has recently done extensive field work with the Bororo, for sufficiently emphasizing the importance of this point.

would label the Bororo case "totemic" since it seems to reflect that postulation of a homology between two systems of differences, the one natural and the other cultural, that he has cited as basic to "totemism" (Lévi-Strauss 1963a:passim; 1966:152, 153–55). It is true, for example, that in certain contexts, the entities associated with the clans serve to differentiate them and appear to be utilized as a metaphorical code for human relationships. Yet thus far I have not been able to demonstrate to my own satisfaction any consistent, systematic, logical homology between the systems that must, in Lévi-Strauss's theory, exist in any totemic system. Further, as the next section of this chapter will describe, certain aspects of the clan members' relationship with their totems have a logical and social character than can hardly be described as purely metaphorical. For the sake of convenience, and until a separate publication can examine the problem in detail, I shall provisionally refer to the species linked to each Bororo clan as its totem, and let the reader draw his own conclusions as to the appropriateness of Lévi-Strauss's definition of the term for this case.

It might be mentioned here that all modern Bororo communities generally agree on the details of the "totemic" system, including which of the more than three hundred entities is associated with what clan; such consensus also obtains for nearly all of the other distinctive rights of each social unit. That is, the Bororo share the same complex and systematic structural, ritual, and cosmological systems wherever they are found. This is perhaps all the more remarkable since the Bororo have apparently never had a supra-village political organization. While maintaining a strong sense of its tribal identity, the community is the largest autonomous unit. This is relevant to the present issue because, for the Bororo, dogmas such as "we are macaws" are something more than local poetic intuitions; they are political manifestoes of the cosmological implications of tribal membership.

Now, as to Levy-Bruhl's hypothesis: is it the case that the man = macaw equation derives from the totemic system? The matter is very complex, and involves Bororo conceptions of the totemic entities themselves, of the relation between them and the clan, and of the connection between individuals and totems in various contexts. The Bororo say that all totems are *aroe*, which I translate as "spirit." This category is also applied to a number of other mystical beings and conditions, and the logical connections between the synonymous types of *aroe* are crucial to a comprehension of the principles linking Bororo cosmology with their social organization. One of the most important referents of *aroe* is to the immortal, incorporeal, and individuated spirit possessed by all creatures, especially man. It is this personal spirit which leaves the body at night during dreams and which departs permanently at death.

Consistently *aroe* is also applied to the collectivity of souls of deceased Bororo, that is, to the ancestors. These spirits are thought to follow traditional Bororo customs in an afterlife very much like that of the living, although with certain differences, some of which, by no means coincidentally, involve parrots and other birds. The ancestors are irrelevant to nearly all daily concerns of modern Bororo, and with some exceptions, ritual does not involve them to any notable extent. Informants often give the Portuguese *alma* ("soul") as a gloss for *aroe* used in reference to individual spirit or to the ancestors.

Another use of the term *aroe* initially seems quite distinct from this first set of meanings. The Bororo speak of a class of spiritual being in a manner that appears to express a concept of an animated form unique to certain natural species, somewhat in the manner of a Platonic ideal. Thus they refer to *Bokodori Aroe*, "Armadillo Spirit"; *Adugo Aroe*, "Jaguar Spirit"; and *Nabure Aroe*, "Red Macaw Spirit." Each of these is said to consist of a single male and female which have the general form and attributes of the species, but with transcendental differences. They are described as much larger than normal, with odd bands of color, unique growths around the head and other unusual morphological features which make them at once very beautiful and "awful," in the archaic sense. Normally these *aroe* forms dwell in the other world inhabited by the souls of the ancestors, but they sometimes venture into this life where they may be seen by mortals, usually with dire results.

It is this pure being rather than the species itself which the Bororo say are associated with the clans in that variety of manners I have characterized as "totemic." The relation is cosmological. Thus, just as each clan occupies a specific segment of the compass in the east-west oriented village, so too in the other world the *aroe* totems of each clan are said to live together in the corresponding region. The Bokodori Exerae clan is localized, for example, in the northeast segment of the village. The *aroe* totems of that clan, including Bokodori Aroe, live in the homologous geographical area in the world of the dead. In the Bororo view, all living beings, things, and space itself are ordered through the same eightfold division.

Now, particular members of the species and the clan itself stand to the spirit version much as, in Platonic philosophy, a given chair stands to the Ideal Chair. In this sense the spirit form can be said to be at once the very essence of the species, its ideal form and the emblem of the clan's uniqueness and perpetuity. Moreover, all the clan's property—ceremonial artefacts, decorative styles for utilitarian objects, songs, and ceremonial representations—stand in the same logical relationship to the totemic spirit as members of the species do. Six of the eight Bororo clans are eponymous in being called after one of their totemic *aroe*, and the stock of personal names from which an individual's title is taken again derives from the same source. Therefore the totem *Bokodori Aroe*, Armadillo Spirit, can be expressed through the proper name *Bokodori Paradu* ("the armadillo which balances"), a somatic painting consisting of red and black patterns, by a bow with such markings, by a ceremonial rattle decorated in the same way, by a necklace made from its claws, and by the total ensemble of these aspects of the Bokodori Exerae clan as well as by individual armadillos of the species *Priodontes giganteus*. But I believe the point made by Evans-Pritchard concerning the nature of Nuer totems (1956a:77–79) also applies here. The Armadillo Spirit itself transcends these concrete reflections of its being, which are only the modes through which man apprehends its reality.

THE CASE FOR TOTEMS: RELATIONSHIPS

The Bororo characterize their individual and corporate relationship to the *aroe* totems of their own clan by calling them "*aroe i-edaga, aroe i-maruga*," relationship terms which are otherwise applied respectively to senior men of the clan (e.g., the mother's brother) and to senior women of the father's clan. This usage does not reflect any belief in the derivation of the individual soul from maternal and/or paternal sources, but is instead a very literal consequence of contemporary ritual practice. Bororo infants are given names by a senior matrilineally related male, preferably the mother's uterine brother or *i-edaga*, and by the woman who assisted the mother at birth, whom the child terms *i-maruga* regardless of whatever genealogical bond might exist between them.[8] As mentioned above, it is this naming which endows the child with corporate membership and with all the rights and obligations encumbent upon it. It should be stressed that all the clan's *aroe* totems, from twenty to fifty of them, are *i-edaga* and *i-maruga* to the clan member, not just the one from which his or her personal name is taken. Now the clan property, also derived from the totems, is usually given to persons and segments of other groups through a complex system of ritual presentations which symbolize all facets of intergroup transactions. The *aroe* totems thus provide the material content as well as the categorical form of all interclan relationships, and are not without their

8. Generally, informants state that the prototypical *i-maruga* is a female member of the father's clan, e.g., a FZ. But in this case, the midwife should normatively be a female member of the infant's father's father's clan (i.e., a member of ego's own moiety). She is regarded as a putative patrilineal relative even though she usually is the MM or MZ.

relevance to behavior within the clan. In providing names they are the ground of every Bororo's social personality, and through their refractions in property and ritual permit him to express vital elements of that social being.

But the closeness of this relation to the totems should not be exaggerated. The Bororo do not believe themselves to be even mystical descendents of their clan *aroe* totems, nor do they claim that what happens to the species they represent has any impact on them. With one or two exceptions, there are no normative injunctions to particular behavior with respect to any species qua totem; members of the Bokodori Exerae ("the Armadillos") kill and eat armadillos with as much relish as any other Bororo. Does any of this material demonstrate Levy-Bruhl's contention that clan members mystically identify with their totemic *aroe*? The situation with macaws may be utilized to resolve this issue.

The Bororo distinguish three kinds of macaw, contrasting them on the explicit basis of color and habitat: *xibae* ("blue" macaw, *araracanga* or *Ara cholroptera*); *kuido* (yellow-breasted macaw, *arara* or *Psittace caerulea*); and *nabure* (red-breasted macaw, *ararapiranga* or *Psittace cholroptera*). They claim that *kuido* inhabit gallery forests while *nabure* and *xibae* nest only in the cliffs and rock pillars found along the upper São Lourenço. The *kuido* is one of the totemic *aroe* of the Paiwoe clan, while the *nabure* is associated with the Arore clan and the *xibae* with the Bokodori Exerae (the last in a less systematic way than the first two). Thus an Aroredu can and does refer to a particular *nabure* as *i-edaga aroe* and it is possible, although I have never heard such a usage, that he might say to an outsider, "I am a *nabure*," or "*ipie*" (otter) or "*bakorororeu*" (coral snake), or similarly identify himself with any of the other totemic *aroe* of the Arore clan. The sense of any such utterance might be phrased as "I, my mother's brother, my sister's sons, and all other members of the Arore clan share a unique cosmological and social status which is reflected in the uniqueness of the *nabure*'s pure form" (or otter's or coral snake's). The Paiwoe, of course, stand in an analogous manner to the *kuido*, and members of the two clans are thus potentially able to express various nuances of their clan's relationship through a "parrot code." Lévi-Strauss would phrase this as Paiwoe:Arore::*kuido aroe*:*nabure aroe*. But the aptness of this formula does not in itself demonstrate that the parrot-clan connection is necessarily a metaphorical one. Surely the analogy rich:poor::satin:rags rests on synecdoche, on contiguity. Some kind of contiguous part-whole relation between man and totem, or even Levy-Bruhl's postulation of "total identity" could underlie the Bororo case just as well as Lévi-Strauss's insistence on semantically equivalent paradigmatic resemblance. It is necessary to examine another aspect of the relation between *aroe* totem and Bororo clan to arrive at a conclusion as to whether this relation is one of metaphor, metonymy, synecdoche, or mystical participation.

One of the most esteemed components of the clan's jural character is its rights over the symbolic representations of certain of the clan's totemic spirits. The representations themselves involve body paintings, ornaments, dance steps, and songs through which aspects of the spirit entity, the "Ideal Form" of Jaguar, Armadillo, or whatever, can be embodied by men. By far the greatest part of Bororo collective ritual involves the performance of such representations. The members of the clan owning the costumes and other paraphernalia seldom perform as representatives of their *aroe*. Instead, they apply the appropriate paintings and ornaments to the personnel of specified lineages or clans in the other moiety. These persons then dance and otherwise perform as the *aroe* entity, while the actual owners watch and sing. Thus, one of the representations of the Arore clan is that of "Nabure Aroe." Two members of the Kie clan are selected to perform this representation of red macaw "essence." The Arore clansmen decorate them with a certain facial painting, coat their bodies with red juice from the urucu bush, and provide them with specific types of headdresses, armbands, and other ornaments owned by the Arore clan, all of which are made with feathers from all three types of macaws. The two Kie then imitate the movements of macaws in a short dance.

Performing as *aroe* representatives is regarded as conferring great honor on the performers.[9] The paintings, ornaments, and the act of representation are indeed considered a gift from the owning clan to the performing clan. As with all prestations of scarce values, it entails considerable obligations on the latter group, and the owners of the representations must be compensated with various ritual services, including the counter-prestation of performing as representatives of one of the debtor clan's *aroe*, and with certain goods, including women. That is, the *aroe* representations are expressions and instruments of the prescriptive alliance between the moieties. Thus persons can and do address those members of the other moiety who perform as their totem as husband (*i-toredu*) or wife (*i-torududje*), even though there may be no current marriages between the groups involved. One reason for such extreme importance of the representations is that, in Bororo opinion, the performers actually *become* the *aroe* entity represented. The address terminology sometimes embodies reference to this belief.

9. Such a situation should not strike American readers as particularly strange, since the Hopi appear to have had a strikingly analogous custom (Titiev 1944:109–16).

For example, on this general normative and categorical level, an Aroredu might correctly term a Kiedu as either "my wife the red macaw," or "my brother-in-law the parrot."

In point of fact I never heard Arore use these or comparable statements as far as *nabure* were concerned. The representation of red macaw essence is considered a very minor prestation, and *nabure aroe* a rather trivial totem; only two of my informants remembered its actual performance. The Arore, though, have a number of highly regarded entities among their totemic *aroe* such as the *aije* (loosely, water spirits). These are represented in major ceremonies which bring great honor both to the sponsoring Arore clan and to the performers' group. Indeed, on formal occasions I have heard an Aroredu address the members of the other moiety who represent specific *aije* with the titles of those spirits, coupled with the appropriate sex-and-age alliance category. As minor as macaws might be in this system, then, we might conclude that there is more epistemological grounds for a given Kiedu in the midst of the ceremony in which he performs as *nabure aroe* to state in an entirely literal way, in Levy-Bruhl's sense, "I am a red macaw," than there ever is for any Aroredu to make the same claim, even though his clan "owns" the totemic essence of *nabure*. The direct Arore relationship to *nabure* is bound up with quite specific refractions of the "Idea of Red Parrot," such as certain personal names and particular artifacts. But this is far from claiming identity or even affinity with the species as a whole. Just as the Arore are not equivalent to or substitutable for red macaws, neither are the Paiwoe for *kuido*, nor the Bokodori Exerae for *xibae*. The latter two clans even lack complete representations of the *aroe* version of the parrot species associated with them.[10]

THE CASE FOR TOTEMS: NAMES

At this point we might recall that the Bororo characterized the *aroe* totems as "name-givers," and this would seem to imply that they realize the distinction between definer and thing defined. In terms of the material already examined, it can be said that along with all the other entities singled out as totemic, macaws might be utilized in certain

10. I assume Lévi-Strauss had in mind comporable situations when he insisted on a sharp distinction between the totem species and the attributes of the clan members. However, at least for the Bororo case, this logical breach between category of nature and social category exists only at the most abstracted level of relationship. As far as individuals and clan elements are concerned, their bond with totem involves extremely personalized aspects of totem, which is to say, cases of synecdoche and metonymy.

ritual contexts as an extended synecdoche to express the relations among corporate groups, of belonging and not belonging. This does not exclude the possibility that in other contexts the relationship with the totem might have metonymic elements. A limited number of each clan's totems, usually those regarded as its principle ones, can be differentiated into levels of specificity in an hierarchic order that corresponds to varying levels of inclusiveness within the clan. As a unique, idealized form-of-being, the totemic entity is associated with the clan; two sub-forms (male and female, black and red, large and small, and so on) are connected with the two sub-clans; yet more particularized forms, differentiated on the basis of size again, specific markings, or yet other morphological or behavioral attributes, correspond with the lineages; finally, the precise attributes of the most specific form supply the individual name. I was able to obtain only a few instances of perfect symmetry between all totemic forms and each level of inclusiveness within the clan, but informants were convinced that all totems were capable of such social segmentation, although the details had been "forgotten" in most cases.

It is thus hypothetically possible that an Arore might refer to an older brother in the other sub-clan as "my brother the red-banded male *nabure*," contrasting him to a senior brother in his own sub-clan who was "my brother the black-banded male *nabure*." In fact I have heard this done in quite formal contexts with respect to jaguars, armadillos, *dourados* (a large species of fish, *Salminu cuvieri*) and other important clan totems. In this sense, in the intraclan context an individual's or lineage's relation to the totem might well be characterized as a case of metonymy, since the derivation of proper names follows a syntagmatic rather than paradigmatic pattern.[11] (Cf. Lévi-Strauss on this same point, 1966:166–90, 200–209, but especially 212–15). As intriguing as these considerations might be, and as important as they are to the comprehension of the semantic logic of Bororo totemism, they have little bearing on the specific issue of macaws. In my experience, at least, proper names derived from any of the macaw species are never utilized to differentiate clan members and segments from one another. Informants gave examples of highly specific personal names derived from macaw attributes, and were confident that these could be arranged hierarchically in terms of clan organization, but they were unable to give any account of this conceptual order.

In short, whether as generative devices for differentiated personal/

---

11. This is a bit more than a formal argument, since the named statuses are loosely associated with the right to various artifacts and to occupy ceremonial roles (all of which are seen as deriving from the totem). Such privileges are an important aspect of the Bororo political process.

group statuses, as empirical referents for corporate property, or as the subject of ceremonial representations, macaws are simply not important within the context of the Bororo totemic system. Such creatures as armadillos, crows, monkeys, jaguars, and many others are exceedingly crucial to that system, and the Bororo do use a code based on it to express many aspects of social relationships. The semantics of this code must be analyzed in a later publication, but it is apparent from the preceding information that metonymy, synecdoche, and metaphor are all involved. Even Levy-Bruhl's mystical participation is quite relevant. But obviously the meaning of the particular assertion "we are red macaws" is not to be found in additional consideration of the nature of the totemic system. Such a conclusion is enhanced by two further points. There is absolutely no reason to assume that Steinen's interlocutor was in fact an Aroredu. And even if he were, I trust the material presented above has demonstrated that the variety of subtle associations between an Aroredu and the red macaw species could never be summarized in such a gross overstatement of total identity. Steinen was quite capable of distinguishing between statements about totemic relationships and other assertions concerning the character of man's connections with animals. As we shall see, when Bororo use the phrase they have in mind human kind, not clan kind.

TAXONOMY, ANOMALY, AND THE NATURE OF MACAWS

The task now is to account for the logical connection between the two terms, "man" and "macaw," as it is perceived by the Bororo. This can only be accomplished by examining the total range of meaning of each term, and then determining which portion of that range is actually operative in our key statement. A logical starting point for such examination is avian taxonomy: what criterial attributes do the Bororo use to differentiate macaws from other bird and animal species? But any account of such classificatory activity must include the social contexts in which men interact with macaws, and the ethical rules which govern these transactions. That is, I feel an interpretation of the symbolic importance of macaws in Bororo thought which is based exclusively on their taxonomic status would be woefully incomplete. As Tambiah puts it so well, "Simple intellectual deductions from a society's formalized scheme of animal categories will not take us far unless we can first unravel the core principles according to which people order their world and the valuations they give to the categories (see also Bulmer 1967)" (1969:452). These "principles" and "valuation" ought to be manifest in the details of Bororo interaction with macaws. In this particular case, we have seen that the "core principles," whatever they might be, have little connection with the totemic system in any of its ramifications. To anticipate, they will be found in the area of male-female relations but only as these transcend the arena of corporate, exogamous social bonds—just those partially expressed in the totemic code. The importance of examining this aspect of the problem does not, of course, deny the equal analytical relevance of the empirical attributes of the species as they are perceived by the society. Clearly it is necessary to investigate how the Bororo view macaws as part of the natural order: the emic interpretation of macaw morphology, habitat, diet, plumage, and so forth is critical. In the following sections I shall try to show first how each of these perspectives, the taxonomic and the transactional, relate to one another, and second, how they might express aspects of Bororo identity.

In most contexts, Bororo classify together under the term *kiege akiri* ("white-feathered birds") macaws and other members of *Psitacideos,* most of the other families of the order *Coraciformes* (tucans, king-fishers, mutums, woodpeckers, etc.), and nearly all water birds. This category is contrasted to that of "carnivorous birds" (*kwagere poiwe kiege,* exact meaning obscure) and a somewhat residual category of "birds" (*aribe*).[12] (It is perhaps worth noting that the Salesians derive the generic designation for bird, *kiege,* from *kuido,* commenting that the macaw is the very essence of bird (Albisetti and Venturelli 1962: 725–26). Informants specify that nearly all members of the first category share the attribute of beauty (*matureu*), although they admit that a sub-set (*kiege mori-xe*) in the second group (birds of prey such as hawks and owls) also has this quality. There is some aversion to eating the majority of birds in the first two categories, and in the case of certain species (hawks, flamingos, cormorants, and tucans) this almost amounts to a specific prohibition. But in no case are they regarded as inconceivable as food, nor are they included among those species regarded as highly polluted and dangerous (*bope ure*). Rather, they are held in low repute as foodstuffs; the crippled, maladroit, or very young demonstrate their inability to secure better food by consuming water fowl and parrots publicly. These views may reflect the somewhat

---

12. As far as my data goes, Bororo animal taxonomies do not have many inclusive generalizing categories; they utilize descriptive phrases rather than distinct lexemes to differentiate large sets. Such taxonomies are not uncommon and are said to relie on "covert categories" (Berlin, Breedlove, and Raven 1968:296–97). However, my material on these points is unclear; certanily the terms used here are not mutually exclusive or exhaustive of Bororo terms for this topic. For example, certain species of hawks are included in the category *kiege akiri* as well as that of *kwagere poiwe kiege* and *kiege mori-xe.*

liminal attributes perceived as common to both classes. Within the first category distinctions are made between birds of running water, birds of still water, and land birds. Each of these classes is further broken down on the basis of contrasts in diet, habitat, and plumage. These considerations are mentioned here only to demonstrate that macaws are hardly anomalous in terms of Bororo taxonomic principles.

Together with beauty, perhaps the most emphasized common element in the first category, is that all species included in it are said to be manifestations of spirit (*aroe*) in the generic sense. The empirical elements cited as evidence of this association have a somewhat ad hoc quality. In the case of most water birds, their habitat itself, white plumage (*akiri*) and fish diet are perceived as isomorphic with eminent characteristics of the spirits. (Perhaps one might regard this as a case of metonymous association, since water birds and spirits are different semantic domains of a single natural zone.) The bones of deceased Bororo are immersed in lakes, although in some parts of Bororoland they are usually deposited in caves. All nonhuman types of spirit are said to live in rivers and lakes. The most terrible of this kind of spirit, the *aije*, are ceremonially represented by somatic paintings done with a special kind of white mud (*noa*) which is found only on the banks of a few streams and lakes. The bullroarers which imitate the *aije*'s roar are made from certain species of soft wood trees which grow only near water. The spirits of the dead themselves are usually pale or actually white, according to the shamans who alone among mortals may actually see the spirits. Indeed the spiritual element in all living men, that same soul (*aroe*) which survives after life, is compared to smoke or fog, and the Bororo do recognize the "wetness" of fog. Finally, all types of spirit are very fond of eating small fish.

But while indigenous explanations for the association between water birds and spirit are numerous, the situation in the case of parrots and related species is a bit more obscure. Informants give essentially five kinds of justification for linking parrots with spirit.

MACAWS AND SPIRITS: CATEGORIES
AND CONDITIONS

1. Although *aroe* (here, spirits generically) enjoy eating fish, the major component of their diet is thought to be vegetable products such as nuts, fruits, palm shoots, corn, and the post-contact domesticants rice and beans. These substances are contrasted to all kinds of meat, above all those which have a strong "gamey" taste; these are considered the regular diet of the other variety of supernatural entity, the *bope*. The

type of shaman who dealt with the *aroe* traditionally limited his diet to vegetable products, fish, and the immature young of mammals in order not to offend the *aroe*. Parrots are strongly associated with a vegetable diet, especially one featuring nuts and fruits.

2. The Bororo seem to infer that the strongly variegated and dramatic coloring of parrots in general, and macaws most of all, is clearly a manifestation of spirit. Although whiteness, or absence of color, is treated as the most usual condition of spirit, it is also expressed through presence of all colors. I have heard it said that such creatures as the harpy eagle and the jaguar reveal spirit in their mottled coloring; although the observation came from an unusually perceptive and learned informant, it could not be termed a conscious element in the collective representation of these species. Of more general validity is the frequent metaphorical comparison of the extended chants describing the elements and activities of spirits to a multicolored cloth which stretches "just as a trail" along which the singers and the song progress. Soon after contact, the shaman of the souls (*aroe etaware are*) forbade the indiscriminate use of variegated cloth on the grounds that such color combinations, especially red and black, were restricted to matters connected with spirit (Albisetti and Venturelli 1962:174). Finally, rainbows are regarded as a direct manifestation of one particular category of *aroe*.

This identification of spirit with mottled hues should not be that exotic to us, for it is not unknown in our own cultural tradition. Hopkins in "Pied Beauty" proclaims, "Glory be to God for dappled things—/ For skies of couple-color as a brindled cow;/ For rose-moles all in stipple upon trout that swim;/ Fresh-firecoal chestnut-falls; finches' wings; . . ." (Hopkins 1956:30). One mgiht even suppose that such iridescence is often found characteristic of liminal conditions or entities, a possibility which finds confirmation in at least one other culture (Kaguru; cf. Beidelman 1968:119–23) beside the Bororo and our own Catholic one.

3. Macaws are connected with spirit in the dogmatic context of the soul's metamorphoses after death. During the rites that accompany the final interment of the body, the soul (*aroe*) is instructed to enter in turn jaguar, macaw, otter, and hawk. (Ocelot is sometimes given as the terminal species in the sequence.) The diet of this species is thought to include those particular types of mammals, fish, and plants which are considered polluted, and which Bororo cannot eat before shamanistic intervention has made them pure and safe. Such polluted species (*bope ure*) include deer, tapir, rhea, capybara, corn, wild honey, and some others. In the indigenous view, that class of mystical beings dialectically

opposed to the *aroe*, the *bope*, has certain rights over these species which are manifested in their dangerous quality for men (Crocker 1975:passim). The improper consumption of these restricted foods and related polluting acts are usually considered by the Bororo to be the effective cause of death. Through the sequence of metamorphoses, in the emic view, the deceased's soul is able to secure revenge on those things and powers (i.e., the *bope*) which destroyed his corporeal self. That is, as a macaw or jaguar the soul may consume at will and in perfect safety those substances which previously were restricted, and thus commit with impunity those same transgressions which led to the death of his body.

With the exception of Van Baaren, earlier analyses of the macaw = self metaphor have considered but finally rejected this aspect of Bororo cosmology as underlying the metaphor. Van Baaren argues that the caterpillar-butterfly analogy Steinen used to clarify the belief probably came from the Bororo themselves, and therefore, "The comparison of caterpillar and butterfly leads us to conclude that the arara is a form in which man manifests himself after a transformation, after death" (1969: 12). But Steinen himself states at one point that the belief in metamorphoses has nothing to do with the declaration of identity with red macaws since he understood the informant to mean that the identification obtained now, at the present moment. Not only did my informants agree with this, they also asserted that caterpillars and butterflies were two entirely different species. Finally, the macaw is only one of the forms temporarily assumed by the soul, and the Bororo deny they are jaguars or otters or hawks in the same sense they are macaws. It might be added that they do not believe in reincarnation; there is no presumed "cycling" of souls back into this life. Nor, for that matter, did I ever hear any Bororo aver that the soul during dreams often or ever assumed the form of a macaw.

4. Macaws are associated with the *aroe* on the basis of purely syntagmatic contiguity. As mentioned above, *nabure* are said to live in rocks and cliffs, and *koido* in buriti palms (*marido*). The leaves of this palm are staple items in the construction of Bororo ritual paraphernalia; the tender shoots of the buriti are one of the souls' and the Bororo's most preferred foods. Indeed, one might say that in terms of providing raw material for the representation of spirit, buriti palms are in the plant domain what macaws and jaguars are in the bird and mammalian domains. Moreover, these palms are often found in low, marshy places, such as the borders of those small lakes in which the decorated baskets of ornamented bones are deposited in the secondary interment. Traditionally these baskets were also placed in caves in the same rocky

prominences where *nabure* nest.[13] Furthermore, those same caves are regarded as leading directly to the other world where dwell *aroe* in all their variety.

These associations between *aroe* and macaw provide the ground for many varieties of tropes, which are employed in songs, myths, and other traditional lore. The shared attributes of diet, habitat, and variegated coloring are the bases for synecdoches and for metaphors derived from these, while the macaw as agent for the soul's revenge after death is itself metonymy. However, none of these rhetorical figures provides any clues as to possible connections between macaws and man. For these it is necessary to turn the last of the modes in which macaws are linked with spirit.

5. The last aspect of this connection involves exactly that dimension of interaction between macaws and human society which I maintained earlier was basic to any investigation of the collective representation of natural entities. The entire argument of this essay hinges on the fact that macaws, and to a lesser degree other parrots, are the only kind of domestic pet now found among the Bororo. Recent analyses of various cases of this topic (Leach 1964; Lévi-Strauss 1966; Beidelman 1966; Tambiah 1969) have stressed that domesticated animals, and especially those living in intimate commensality with man, are likely to be the vehicles of a complex symbolism. They are structurally anomalous in occupying a position neither wholly animal nor completely human, and hence they may be utilized with great rhetorical effect to affirm, deny, modify, or otherwise express various nuances of man's nature. It seems crucial to me to make a sharp distinction between commensal association per se and those fosterings of creatures which have a marked nonutilitarian character, such as that expressed in our category "pet." Thus, the Bororo indigenously had domesticated dogs and still continue to raise them; and since contact they have adopted chickens and pigs from the Brazilians. Although these animals live in conditions of great intimacy with their masters and other members of the nurturing household, they are practically never the object of any affectionate regard. The last two species are raised as cash crops for sale to Brazilians and other Indians, and the dogs for their utility in hunting. Dogs do have certain qualities of pets in that they are given names and are never eaten. But their names compare with human nicknames, and even are marginal to these in that most are derived from Brazilian language and usages. For example, one dog was called "Preguicoso," the Portuguese

13. Red macaws (*nabure*) are perhaps more intimately associated with the essence of liminal force precisely due to their coloring. Although white is the color of the *aroe* under most conditions, just as the *bope* are consistently associated with black, red is always utilized in ritual contexts stressing vitality and transcendent beauty.

term for "lazy." Their owners take minimal interest in them, so that they are nearly all emaciated, half-wild, and vicious. A good hunting dog is sometimes given more care than is usual, but even these are so unimportant as not to be included in the disposal of property following the owner's death. Most often only the owner knows or cares which of the dozens of dogs lying about the general precincts of the village are actually his.

In contrast, everyone from the very young to the aged knows who owns which tame macaw. These birds are one of the few items of personal property aside from certain ritual items (e.g., jaguar teeth necklaces) which an heir receives. Inquiries into the possibility of eating domesticated macaws (and other parrots) occasioned expressions of intense repugnance, whereas the same suggestion concerning dogs was regarded as bizarre but not unconsiderable. Many pet macaws receive proper names, or dimunitives thereof, taken from the owner's matrilineage. To be sure, practically no one outside the family and not even all its members know a particular macaw's proper name, but everyone is aware it might have one. Further, a macaw, and to a lesser extent other parrots, is included among the property and persons which are considered to be extensions of the owner's social personality. Infractions of the rights over such property are considered a serious matter indeed. If a pet macaw is stolen or accidentally injured or killed its owner may legitimately demand compensation over and above simple restitution. In the single case of this in my field experience a dog severely mauled a macaw. The dog was immediately killed by its owner, who then made a number of minor ceremonial prestations to the damaged party. For these reasons macaws and other varieties of parrot wander around the community with as much impunity, and with the same effect, as a cow in a Hindu village.

In one village in which I worked, about one hut in every three had pet macaws, smaller parrots, or parakeets as co-residents.[14] These pets receive excellent care; they are given food at least once a day, their flight feathers are trimmed regularly, and shelter is given them in inclement weather. Women and especially children play with them by the hour. The birds are taken from the nest as fledglings and fed premasticated food directly from the mouths of their owners, with the result that they become extremely tame. Unlike dogs and other domestic animals, macaws always accompany their owners on journeys away

14. As a general rule, all the considerations involving domesticated macaws apply to lesser parrots and parakeets, but with much less symbolic and social force. Just as it would be a desperate man indeed who resorted to parakeet feathers for his clan's ornamentation, so too few Bororo would deign to bestow a name on such a pet or to bequeath one.

from the village, riding on top of the women's loads (Albisetti and Venturelli 1962:809).

Indeed, ownership of macaws is almost entirely limited to women. The stereotyped Bororo explanation of why certain households maintained domestic parrots to the extent of invariably replacing ones which died was, "Women who have lost many children now have *kagere.*"[15] While very few Bororo are reluctant to sell items of traditional property, no matter how great its symbolic value, adult macaws, parrots, or even parakeets are practically never willingly sold by their owners. Finally, and I hope this clinches my argument, the death of such a pet is sometimes formally mourned (*oragudu*) by its female owner, admittedly briefly and cursorily. Only humans are otherwise mourned, and Bororo men regard such behavior for a defunct macaw as perhaps a little ridiculous but by no means illegitimate.

In response to the query "Why do you keep pet macaws?" Bororo usually say that they are convenient sources for the raw materials used in ritual, and because the spirits like them to do so. (The Salesians, who often cite verbatim glosses of informants' comments, give the same two reasons [Albisetti and Venturelli 1962:809].) The first of these motives involves the fact that nearly all the highly diverse items in the Bororo ritual catalogue must utilize macaw feathers to conform to traditional standards, which are taken very seriously. The blue, yellow, and red macaw breast feathers, for example, are painstakingly glued together to form mosaics which are applied to gourd whistles, rattles, and dolls, and to the head or skull of those undergoing such rites of passage as name-giving and funerals. The long tail feathers are used to make the spectacular headdresses (*pariko*) of which every clan owns four or five distinctive forms. Hence macaw feathers are essential to Bororo ritual, and the social relationships it mediates, and yet are quite scarce, especially those of red macaw (*nabure*). These figure in virtually all ornaments perhaps because, as noted in an earlier footnote (14), red is the medial color.

While tame red macaws are prized above all other varieties of parrot, all domesticated macaws are living banks of rare and critical ritual material. Following a major ceremonial cycle nearly all the birds in the village are pathetic denuded bundles of flesh and bone. A frequent

15. Although the Bororo clearly recognize the implied psychological identification between children and pets, they also have in mind the symbolic consequences of such associations. Such women have certain ritual items (such as gourd whistles by which the "soul's breath" is reproduced), heavily decorated with macaw feathers and kept in special baskets filled with white down. The lost child's soul enters these items for short periods, as it may possess the birds kept by the grieving mother.

excuse for delaying a ritual is that the individuals responsible for making the ornaments have not been able to acquire the requisite feathers. Wild macaws are killed whenever possible and *all* their feathers carefully removed. The long tail feathers are so rare that after a headdress or similar item becomes ruined through long usage, the less bedraggled feathers are removed, cleaned with oil, and stored against employment in a new ornament. Nearly every adult male and some females have cylindrical boxes (*maregwa*) made from the trunk sections of the buriti palm (once again, cf. item 4 above, the Bororo being farily systematic in their symbolism) which are used exclusively for the storage of macaw feathers.

Although the items made from these feathers are never sold but given away in formal exchange for ritual services, the feathers themselves are sometimes sold to nonkinsmen. However, even this action is fairly rare since a stock of feathers whether boxed or alive virtually guarantees ability to carry out ritual obligations, and such ability is a potent factor in political prestige. It is almost axiomatic that every man of status has either a full box of macaw feathers, or is related by consanguinity or alliance to a woman with a tame macaw, or both. I would not argue that macaw feathers are the equivalent of noncommercial money for the Bororo, for they participate only in a very limited cycle of transactions in which the other equivalent items are animal skins, teeth, and claws, and certain ritual services (Bohannan 1955, 1959; Dalton 1967:276–77). But they are perhaps the most important instance of a scarce nonconsumable resource in the Bororo system.

The other indigenous justification for domesticating macaws, that the spirits approve of the practice, rests on somewhat obscure grounds. Entirely aside from the momentary and singular transformations of the soul during the post mortem cycle of metamorphoses, *aroe* generally are believed to enter or to transform themselves into both wild and tame macaws rather frequently. The Bororo postulate three motives for this habit. First, "the *aroe* wish to be beautiful (*matureu*) like the macaw." Second, the *aroe* are wont to eat the nuts and other plant substances which are the staple in both macaw and spirit diet. (Both these reasons draw on the syntagmatic or synecdochic association between these forms of being.) Informants said these facts were part of the justification for providing plentiful food for pet macaws, since a deceased relative might benefit from such largesse. I find this rationalization of dubious worth for the analysis. There is absolutely no way to distinguish those moments when a pet macaw is actually harboring the soul of a dead parent or child or other Bororo, nor are there, as far as I could discover, any other "empirical" consequences to this belief. In any case the souls of the ancestors as well as other forms of spirit, are only marginally involved in Bororo social life. They are rarely credited with causing illness, accident, or misfortune either to individuals or to groups; they are never propitiated and their assistance in crisis situations is seldom implored. To be sure, the *aroe* are invited to participate in communal rituals, and most Bororo appear to believe that they do so; yet even in those circumstances they are characterized as having the manner of aloof and distinguished visitors. It is, one might say, the deceaseds' absence rather than their presence which is the focus of Bororo ritual concern.[16] The pet macaw, then, can in no way be interpreted as any sort of "domestic shrine." It is not in itself a direct mode of communication between this world and that of the spirits. To employ an illustrative metaphor, it is a window rather than a door between these worlds and a somewhat clouded window at that.

The belief in the *aroe*'s frequent assumption of macaw form might be regarded as simply a logical deduction from the whole set of associations between *aroe* and macaw, rather than significant in itself.[17] But there is the third factor mentioned above but yet unconsidered, another attraction besides preferred food and desirable appearance that motivates *aroe* to become macaws. The Bororo believe that the ancestral souls and most other forms of spirit never copulate in their "natural" condition, supposing them indifferent to all such bodily appetites. On the rare occasions when desire overcomes them, they instead enter or transform themselves into living entities for intercourse, and prefer the vehicle of macaws to any other creature. Informants cited as evidence of this practice the shamanistically revealed fact that the legs of spirits bend backward rather than forward at the knee, "so that they must copulate from behind, like macaws." They also specified that the spirits have intercourse in this manner only with other spirits, never with actual macaws. It is very tempting to speculate on the possible symbolic status of the offspring of such hypothetical spirit-macaw unions; the Bororo regarded my queries on this topic as too obscene to warrant a response.

16. Much of Bororo ceremonial hinges on the institution of the *aroe maiwu*, the "new soul." Every Bororo decendent, except for infants who die before receiving a name, has a ritual replacement drawn from the members of its father's clan, in the opposite moiety. To a limited degree, this replacement, the *aroe maiwu*, assumes the deceased's social status, including certain obligations to matrilineal kinsmen (Crocker 1975). Without such a custom, informants claim, dead persons would be very quickly forgotten.

17. It may be appropriate to note, at this point, that the Bororo do not attribute any symbolic or other importance to the parrot's ability to replicate human speech. While they are aware of this potential, they very seldom act upon it and never cite it as a reason for the intimate connection between macaws and human beings.

But these points are crucial. Red macaws are clearly thought distinct from the *aroe,* for otherwise the *aroe* would not have to become macaws for the unspiritlike activities of eating and fornicating. The Bororo regard other bird species, such as the heron, as much "purer" total refractions of the essence of spirit. Their attitude toward the raucous flocks of parrots and macaws, for all the birds' utility as the source of ritual material and frequent vehicle of spirit, is one of indulgent respect rather than reverence. At the same time, for all the intimacy of their domestic association with human beings, macaws are far from being the objects of anthropomorphic sentiments. The men typically regard the women's occasional demonstrations of feeling toward their pets with tolerant amusement for such inability to discriminate between radically different states of being. They still scorn any of their fellows so shameless as to eat a wild parrot, and sharply reprimand a child who teases a domesticated macaw rather than a sibling. In short, the Bororo view macaws as thoroughly bird, albeit as having natural attributes which render them attractive to the profoundly different spirits and valuable to man. Therefore we have answered one of the initial problems, in that the distinction between the domains of spirit, man and macaw, has been established. I must conclude that macaws can be treated as liminal mediators precisely because they are neither pure spirit nor totally human, while sharing both some esteemed and some gross qualities of each. The postulation that "we are macaws" is thus not founded on metonymy nor on synecdoche; it remains to be seen how it is metaphorical.

THE HUMAN CONDITION: BIRDS AND MEN

The important point now is just how the macaw's status as domestic pet and as the vehicle of spirit connotes adornment when mankind is compared to it. A response to this requires an examination of the other term of the equation, the cosmological and social characteristics of man within the Bororo system. I can only sketch in the rough outline of these dimensions here. They are typically perceived as ambiguously dyadic, in that human beings are often said to be a compound of "spirit" (*aroe*) and "force" (*bope*). The *bope* are an inclusive category of spiritual being dialectically and dramatically opposed to the *aroe.* In their most typical, or most essential manifestations, the *bope* are associated with all processes of growth and decay, specifically with fertility and death. They are the dynamic force which manifests itself in day and night, and in the oscillation between rainy season and dry; the sun and moon, and rain itself, are actually specific ramifications of *bope. Bope* cause all living things to reproduce, and to die.[18] That dimension of man which is represented through the *bope* is precisely his "natural" self, including his appetites for food, sexuality, and deviance from normatively enjoined conduct. An individual's personal idiosyncracies and particularly those physical transformations through time which we would characterize as aging (white hair, wrinkles, feebleness, and the like) are ascribed to this particular history of interaction with the *bope*. Since these spirits control all transformations, they respond to human infractions of their rights over the natural order by causing various types of anomalous disasters, such as eclipses, epidemics, floods, and early deaths.

It is important to stress that, in the Bororo view, not only men but the entire natural world in its varied aspects is a compound reflection of both principles, *bope* and *aroe*. Therefore the dichotomy between two forms of spirit, and the logical principles they represent, cannot be expressed in terms of a simple opposition between nature and culture, since all things have characteristics of both principles. For example, the Bororo are not so consistent as to maintain that an infant derives his *aroe* from his mother and his *bope* from his father, as a cursory examination of their social organization might lead one to expect. They believe each parent contributes the same physical and mystical substances to the fetus, and differentiate the sexual roles on a nonsociological basis. In arguing the appropriateness of this view to the logic of Bororo collective life, informants point out that a child, as a member of the opposite moiety, can embody the *aroe* totems of his father's clan, and is otherwise intimately connected with them.[19] At the same time, they stress, the uxorilocal household is the locus of consumption both of food and of women, and the site of all death and birth, all of which are very much matters connected with the *bope*.

As I shall now try to demonstrate, the metaphor "we are red macaws" attempts to express through a single convincing image the inchoate sense in which Bororo find themselves to be the fusion of antithetical cosmological principles.

These principles have their correlates in manifold aspects of Bororo social life, but the ones most relevant to the present issue involve the dichotomous relations between men and women both within and out-

18. With the crucial exception of fish and certain other water creatures, which are controlled by the *aroe*.

19. Thus, a decedent's ritual replacement (*aroe maiwu*) should be a member of his father's clan. In payment for his various services undertaken in discharge of this role's duties, the replacement may utilize certain of the ceremonial privileges of the dead person's clan. This is the only way other than matrilineal descent that such categorical rights may be legitimately gained.

side the context of the domestic group. This is because informants strongly implied that it is only Bororo *males* who are said to be macaws. This opinion emerged only during direct inquiry into the assertion. Although when the formula was mentioned informants recognized it as a traditional expression, I have never heard it uttered spontaneously.[20] Typically, I believe, it is perceived as characterizing various situations in which Bororo men have direct contact with the *aroe*, such as the sacred hunts (*aroe e-meru* or *aroe e-kodu*), funerals (*itaga*), or any totemic representation (*aroe etawuje*). During such moments there is a sharp symbolic antithesis between men and women: the latter are not allowed to witness various portions of the rituals, under pain of angering the spirits, while the men (excluding noninitiated boys) are secluded in the men's house or off in the jungle. During a few rituals, notably the *aije aroe etawuje* (intrinsic to funerals and initiations), this ritual separation develops into formalized aggression against the cloistered women. The actors portraying the *aije* spirits throw balls of white mud against the houses and boast among themselves how terrified the women are of these supernatural entities. They maintain with some glee that if a female should chance to see one of these actors or the bull-roarers they manipulate, the *aroe* spirits would cause her belly to swell up until she dies (Albisetti and Venturelli 1962:19). Many discrete beliefs reflect a view of femininity as inherently dangerous to men. Since during the sexual act a woman robs her partner of his vigor (*rakare*), men should avoid intercourse as much as possible; a menstruating woman contaminates food and masculine weapons; women are inherently dissentious and lacking in a sense of shame; and so forth.

All these attitudes reflect the more general social fact that Bororo males are in a sense caught between matrilineal origins and uxorilocal residences. Each man is an intruder into the female-dominated households of the other moiety, in which he resides, ingests food and enjoys sexuality, procreates and exists on a daily basis. This residence is not without its more sublime attractions. The Bororo prize conjugal happiness even while admitting it is all too rare. They emphasize the unique value and joys of patrifilial bonds, and the genuine solidarity of the father-son bond is given considerable jural and ritual weight (Crocker 1969a:passim). On the other hand, a man is responsible for the affairs of his mother, his sisters, their children, and all others living within that house, which is his legal domicile. He possesses status and controls

---

20. The usual phrase such explicit questioning elicited was "*pa-edo nabure*." *Edo* designates present conditions of existence rather than permanent states of being. This, of course, does nothing in itself to resolve the problem of meaning since it could apply to presumed metamorphoses of the soul, or, indeed, to all the previous hypotheses.

scarce resources, such as rights over spirit representations, only to the extent that he fulfills his matrilineal obligations. Caught between the demands of his uterine and affinal bonds,[21] he spends a great deal of time in the men's house, where the *aroe* also congregate during rituals. There he may share his existential dilemma with all other Bororo men. These are, to be sure, categorically divided into "brothers" and "brothers-in-law" (*i-mana* and *in-odowu*), "fathers" and "sons" (*i-ogwa* and *i-medu*), or "mothers' brothers" and "sisters' sons" (*i-edaga* and *i-wagedu*). Yet they all share the status of ambiguous creatures whose obligations of uterine domicile are in some ways opposed to their affinal residential duties. As Lévi-Strauss noted so perceptively a number of years ago (1963*d*), the concentric dualism of the village is one concrete expression of this masculine solidarity gathered together at the center in the face of the female-derived conflicts of the periphery. The opposition, though, transcends even the village structure, since the men frequently go off together on ritualized collective hunting and fishing expeditions. These are under the aegis of the spirits, and therefore are rigidly interdicted to women, just as is the men's house (except under certain conditions, Crocker 1969*b*). When in ritual, the *aije* "attack" the women in their huts, the spirits come from the river, through the forest and to the men's house, and then back again; the "exterior" is as much opposed to the periphery as the "interior."

The men's society, wherever it might be found, is generally tranquil and relaxed. Yet ties through women order relationships within it and disturb its harmony. Uterine brotherhood is one of the most basic models for masculine solidarity, yet in the Bororo view brothers are notorious for their inability to get along with one another. The shared jural status of common matrilineal descent that binds them normatively also entails their bitter competition for the scarce resources to which they share title. A "zero-sum" situation is assumed to hold in that one brother's loss is taken to be another's gain. This is obviously true for wives, and since jural authority in the clan is ordered hierarchically, brothers can only be "superior" or "inferior" to one another. (Much the same is true for sisters, of course.) The arbitrators in intraclan disputes between siblings are supposed to be their affines, especially the fathers of those quarreling. I sometimes feel that the Bororo ritual and normative emphasis on patrifiliation represents one vast convulsive

---

21. I should stress most emphatically that the Bororo version of this typically matrilineal problem has various dimensions which render it somewhat less acute than the thoroughgoing classifier might suspect. The most general ameliorating factor is that obligations toward uterine and affinal kin are quite different and involve nonoverlapping sets of scarce resources. Thus, one is obliged to instruct one's sister's son in the niceties of clan lore, while one's son deserves material assistance in the form of weapons and instruction in the arts of hunting.

effort to escape the almost total dominion of women. But, as in all thoroughly matrilineal societies, agnatic bonds cannot endure through time. Although relations through males and through the *aroe* may order transactions within the men's society, no one can live permanently in the men's house. Thus, all enduring social relationships among the Bororo are initiated and defined by reference to women. Through their procreation and nourishment of men, they bind masculine loyalties and check their freedom of action just as surely as they domesticate macaws. Male symbolic protest in ritual notwithstanding, there is ample justification for the feminine view that it is they who are exchanging men, rather than the reverse.

These considerations, aside from the odd and uniquely Bororo twist of the "inverted" representation of totemic spirits, are obviously common to many matrilineal societies. I believe it would falsify and impoverish the Bororo case to let the matter rest on this sociological level, without consideration of the more idiosyncratic cosmological elements. Certainly the Bororo appear to realize that it is in the social nature of things for wives to draw men away from their clans, and divide brothers. Some may even apprehend that the clan itself is internally differentiated by contrasting uterine descent. Yet none of this is the crux of the matter for the men themselves. Rather, they appear to respond to the way in which, on the conceptual level, the matrilineal totemic system is a "terministic screen," in Burke's sense (1966:45–47). This "system-screen" exhaustively defines reality through a single terminology and thus, due to its very nature as a classificatory system, is a deflection of reality. The Bororo, I think, share with other men some resentment of such arbitrary constraints. Even death itself does not transcend the limits of matrilineal self, for even after dying a man's identity continues to be defined by his corporate group's categorical attributes, through their projection into the domain of spirit. In a very real sense, a Bororo can never leave home. Like a macaw, he is perpetually a child of collective mothers.[22]

The single mode through which a Bororo can escape the female dominion of definition is within the context of the ceremonial representations of the totemic spirits and the souls of opposite moiety persons. It is then that a man can become not-self, and moreover, the very essence of pure being and form, as he performs as the representation of a totemic being or as the personification of another's soul. Yet even here there are limitations, which are summarized quite neatly in the

---

22. Thus, every Bororo decedent's soul, save for those of the newly born, is assigned to the responsibility of some woman of his or her clan. This woman, preferably the mother, is obliged to nourish the soul, and its representative, who is, as noted earlier, invariably a member of the opposite moiety.

comparison of men to macaws. Both transmutations of defined form occur only for limited periods during specific rituals. Both entities, men and macaws, are only partially and temporary vehicles for the *aroe*. The spirits utilize these means for quite utilitarian ends of their own, manifesting little concern in the process for the consequences to either birds or humanity. To put it another way, the feathers of macaws and the bodies of men are the raw material for social transactions. The feathers are the common material element in all the clan's ceremonial wealth which men exchange, as well as the vital portion of the costumes with which men enable other men to represent the *aroe*. But even in the midst of the ceremony a man is just as limited an aspect of spirit and of transcendence as a macaw. For all these transactions under the feathered aegis of the *aroe* involve prestations of food and of sexuality, and do not the *aroe* eat and copulate in the form of macaws? In metaphorically identifying themselves with red macaws, then, the Bororo do not seek either to disparage or to adorn themselves; but to express the irony of their masculine condition.[23]

23. Sapir's initial response to this conclusion was the perceptive inquiry: "If men are macaws, what does that make women?" He was asking, in other words, if it was possible to discover a metaphor for the feminine conditions that paralleled the masculine one, thus moving from an internal (men = macaws) to an external metaphor (cf. above pp. 25–27). My response had to be no, not to my knowledge. The Bororo utilize a great many tropes, including several complex analogic systems to express aspects of sexuality, but of the figures utilized to describe women none has the same logic and the same quality of dogma as the macaw = men metaphor. One possible figure would be "women are buriti," since this plant is intimately associated with macaws, the *aroe*, social transactions, etc. But men do not "own" buriti palms nor are there the ambiguous associations linking them with the *bope*. And, besides, I never heard the Bororo use such an expression.

Chapter 7

The Fabricated Child

J. DAVID SAPIR*

The folktale to be examined in this chapter provides in narrative form
a number of comments on Kujamaat notions of legitimacy.[1] Briefly, it
is about the ambiguous resolution of a woman's problem which raises
an irresovable child's problem. For the Kujamaat, a woman to be considered a fully "legitimate" wife must have children. Similarly, to be
"legitimate" a child must have recognizable consanguines. If a woman
has a child, as she does in this tale, by extraordinary and magical means
and not in the "natural" way, the social position of the child is placed
in complete and irremediable jeopardy. This follows because such a
child will have no real kin.

I consider the tale as an instructive example of what Kenneth Burke
(1945:430–40) calls the "temporalizing of essence" where basic ideas,

* T. O. Beidelman, J. C. Crocker, Marie-Paule Ferry, and Tzvetan Todorov each
read the original version of this chapter, and their comments were of great value
in preparing the revision. During the rewriting I was associated with the Laboratoire d'Ethnologie et de Sociologie Comparative, Université de Paris-X (Nanterre).
At that time my colleague Dan Sperber offered a number of pertinent suggestions
that have been incorporated into the text. An earlier and somewhat longer version
of this paper appears in *Poetics* 5 (June 1976) : 157–84.

1. The Kujamaat number about eighty thousand and make up the northern most
sub-group of the Diola, a congeries of ethnically and linguistically similar groups
located in the lower Casamance region of Senegal, West Africa. Elsewhere I have
referred to the Kujamaat as the Fogny or Diola-Fogny (1965, 1969, 1970). Fogny
is the term used by the Senegalese administration and by the Kujamaat's neighbors. However, Kujamaat is the term they themselves use and I accept, if belatedly,
their own correct name.

usually key values and beliefs, are dramatically acted out. In this case, however, it is not so much the temporalizing of essence, but instead the "temporalizing of essence*s* brought into conflict." Basic beliefs and conditions are dramatically evoked, then tampered with. The resulting disarrangement evokes a second set of beliefs which in turn question the possibility, or at least the advisability, of the original tampering.

If the tale's normative essense relates to Kujamaat notions of legitimacy, then the tale's basic content and action develop from a central metaphor that equates the womb to a beehive. I take as my present task an extended discussion of these two aspects of the tale and proceed as follows: First, two versions of the tale are given, one told by a man (AK), the other by a woman (FJ).* Since the woman's is rather odd, even surrealistic, I allow myself a brief digression about its actual performance. This should explain some of its peculiarities. I continue with comments on Kujamaat notions of legitimacy as they apply to the tale. This leads to a brief discussion of the tale's linear structure, and finally to an elaboration of the womb-beehive metaphor and its variants.

AK's [the man's] Version

1. Sit, sit; I sit as if there were many travelers (*quoi*).[2] 2. Bon. The woman married the man. There were four wives. Those had children, this one did not. Bon. The man was there for a long time. 3. He said, "I am going on a trip and when I return whosoever has not had a child I shall cut her throat!" Bon. Those who had a child, each of them had a baby with only one eye. The other one did not have a child and she said, "I am going to run away and get lost."

4. She ran and ran for a great distance. Finally she arrived in a large forest where she met a bush spirit. The bush spirit said to her, "Woman, where are you going?" 5. She said, "My husband went on a trip and he said that when he returned whoever had not had a child he would cut her throat. And, I have no child. My co-wives have children. Each has a one-eyed baby." 6. Bon. "Now I haven't any, so I ran away and got lost before he returns to cut my throat. That's why I'm running." And he said to her, "So that's all?" "Yes," she replied. He said to her, "Come here." And she came, the woman she came and arrived right there. 7. He said to her, "About the baby, it is only because of this that you have run away to get lost?" "Yes," she replied. He said to her, "Wait, and I

---

* The original transcriptions appear in an appendix at the end of this chapter.
2. A standard opening, ignored in FJ's version, to a Kujamaat folktale.

will fix it so that you will have a baby." She said to him, "Don't lie to me." "It's the truth," he replied. 8. He went off; he went and cut a small stick, and he told her, "This small stick that I'll give to you, go and on arriving take it and put it in a beehive. When you cook rice take some and put it inside [the hive]. Each time you cook rice take some and put it inside. 9. Then one day when you are pounding [rice] you will hear the baby crying from inside the beehive. When it cries from inside the beehive, run to carry it, then go and place it in a room."

10. And she did just that. She carried hither the baby. . .what do you call it. . .the small stick and on arriving put it in the beehive. It was in there for a long time. And then one day while she was pounding she heard the stick crying from within as if it were a baby. 11. She ran right there: it was a baby. She carried it. She carried it and on arriving she placed it in the room. She then cooked rice and placed it inside, she cooked rice and placed it inside so that it could eat.

12. And then when her co-wives threaded beads, so would she. And when they went to look for chickens, so would she. Her co-wives said, "What's this? Wait and we'll see. She who has no child and she threads a string of beads. She looks for a chicken in order to kill it for our husband. We'll see." 13. When the very day of the man's return arrived those who had children, each one brought her chicken to show it to her husband. She also brought her chicken and gave it to him. And they (the others) scratched their heads saying, "Look! This one without a child, she goes and does as we do, wait and we'll see if it is her throat they will cut!" 14. Now when they had finished cooking the rice, they gave it to their children to bring; this one gave it to her child to bring, this other one gave it to her child to bring, and this other one also gave it to her child to bring. And she was inside making her baby very pretty. She brought the rice and gave it to the baby. 15. And there it was coming with little bells: tingling tingling, tangling tangling, tingling tangling. When the man saw the baby, he just saw it and said, "Those one-eyed ones get up, get up, get up; you one-eyed ones go back there to your mothers, go back there to your mothers!"

16. Bon. Now when they were eating their rice, you see, those you know, who had had from before the one-eyed children, were angry. It didn't please them at all how the other one had brought out the baby. You see they knew that she had not given birth to the baby. 17. Bon. Now there he was, there he was and then one time when the woman went to draw water they said to the baby, "You, who were fabricated, you, we know, that your mother did not give birth to you. You who were fabricated. That's why Papa when he saw you he discarded ours saying that they are no good, they with one eye." 18. Now after awhile he said to his mother:

[Song]   Mother, mother your co-wives say,
              I'm fabricated, fabricated.
              I'm going home.
              Father, father your wives say
              I'm fabricated, fabricated.
              I'm going home.

                              [repeats song]

19. And there he was losing himself in the ground, there he was getting lost, and he entered under ground. Yes, there he was losing himself in the ground. Now there was his mother crying. There was his father crying. His father was there taking his gun to kill himself, but they stopped him. His mother ran to fall down a well, but they stopped her. 20. And he was saying:

[Song]   Father, father your wives say
              I'm fabricated, fabricated.
              I'm going home.
              Mother, mother your co-wives say
              I'm fabricated, fabricated.
              I'm going home.

                              [repeats song]

21. He did just this till he was lost. And when he was lost the woman ran off, the woman whose child it was, she ran. She ran and lost herself in the bush, not to return. His father also ran off to lose himself. 22. Now, My story my story. . .PEKES.[3]

FJ's [the woman's] Version

1. The man went away, saying, "I'm going up into the sky." He went and arrived up there. [Before leaving] he said to his wives, "I'm going thus and when I return whoever I find who has given birth to a girl, I will cut her throat." 2. Well then he passed on and went up into the sky. The wives got hold of another wife who had no child. One of them said to her, "Come, and I will cook rice and you will put it here and we'll listen for the man." 3. Well now, there they were being vain and proud, very vain and proud. And the man was up there in the sky, well he was up there until he came and arrived back. He called together the children's kin, all of their uterine and agnatic kin. All of them. 4. He said, "I place here the mat on the courtyard. Whoever has not had

3. A standard closing; PEKES refers to the noise of breaking pottery.

a child, she, today, I am going to cut her throat." Well then the wife remained quiet, she remained there for a long time. She said, "God hasn't given me a child."

5. Now off she went in search. She went to the bush spirit. It saw her and said to her, "Woman, you come now into the bush, why?" She replied, "I am going like this because I'm crazy, I'm one who has nothing, I am barren. 6. Our husband went off into the sky saying that when he returned whoever had nothing, he was going to cut her throat. Now it is for this that I have come." It said, "Whew! knock it down for me with a stick." She asked, "What should I knock down for you? I shall be the one to go off in search of it." 7. Well now, off she went, she went a long ways until she met up with another little old woman who said, "Child, right here, knock it down for me here!" And she replied, "And what should I knock down for you? I am going now, it is I who have nothing, that is why I am going now." 8. She said to her, "Come and shave me." She replied, "I am unable to shave! If I shave you I'll ruin it." She said to her, "Come and shave me." So she said, "Ok, give it to me and I'll try, but you will make me late." Now she gave her the knife and she began to shave, and shave, and shave, and shave. After a while it went, "Pe!" 9. "What's inside?" she asked. She replied, "Eggs are inside. One is crossed, another straight, and a third is soft." She said to her, "Leave the soft one inside, leave the soft one inside, but take out the crossed one." 10. And she took the crossed one and went. She said to her, "As you go now, when you get to the forest, bring back a. . .what do you call it?. . .a little whistle." She said, "If I have the little whistle for which I'm going, what am I then to do?" She replied, "Go and get the whistle and you'll see. 11. When you get the whistle I'll tell what it is you must do so as to have [what you want]." She went on till she got to the forest from where she brought back the little whistle. Now she asked her, "You have the whistle?" And she replied, "Yes." She said, "Go and climb up, then I'll tell you." 12. She went and she climbed up, up, and up. Then she saw Hare come running her way. He came and arrived and asked, "Woman, why are you clinging up there?" And she said, "I am an unhappy person, for this reason I'm way up here listening for God." Now he told her, "Whistle!" And she whistled and whistled and whistled. 13. A cow came out and mooed, "Maah." And she whistled and whistled and whistled. Bajending [cow's name] came and lowed, "Maah, nyaah." And he said, "Come down and climb up [on the cow]." She came down and climbed up. She whistled, and whistled:

14. [Song]   Dinondin, dinondin.
                 Dinondin, dinondin.

Papa, father, open so Bajending can enter.
Dinondin, dinondin.

15.   She climbed up, and she came and she came and arrived.

[Song]   Oee, climb up on me.
              Dinondin, dinondin.
              Papa, father, open so Bajending can enter.
              Dinondin, dinondin.

16. Now she came and hither she arrived, and they broke open the fence, woooo, and Bajending entered. In she came and sat in the courtyard. Then the man said to her, "Even if you have cows, no matter how many, it is a child I want!" 17. She said, "Whew, father's sister, what shall I do?" She replied, "Now you serve out and put it in the beehive. Serve into the beehive and then we'll all see what God will do." 18. She served and pushed it in, she served and she pushed it in, she served and pushed it in, and she saw shins. She served and pushed it in, she served and pushed it in, and she saw the underknee. 19. She served and pushed it in, served and pushed it in, and she saw the belly. She served and pushed it in, served and pushed it in, and she saw what was underneath [genitals]. She served and pushed it in, served and pushed it in, and she saw everything there. 20. She served and pushed it in, served and pushed it in, and she saw there the string of beads. She served and pushed it in, served and pushed it in, and then she saw now a head there.

21. Well now. He said, "Now it is you who are my wife, now I take your way. But now all these whose children are one-eyed, each must go her own way. Whoever doesn't go her way, I shall cut her throat!" Now he finished and went off.

22. Now then they went and said to the woman that they were going to look at the child. "You today are a fabricated child, you are a fabricated child." Each time they passed, "You today are a fabricated child." 23. Well. The child said, "Mother because of what you did so as to have me, call all your kin so I can tell them what your co-wives have told me." 24. She called them, she called all of them. They came and arrived. He went and stood in the courtyard. There he was doing Bajending's song.

25.   [Song]   Oee, climb up on me.
                    Today you say, "What am I to do if I come?"
                    To me, my mother's co-wives say
                    I'm fabricated, fabricated.
                    I'm going home.

26. There he was disappearing!

> Oee, climb up on me.
> My mother's co-wives say
> I'm fabricated, fabricated.
> I'm going home.

27. He kept on doing this till he disappeared. Now the woman was running to throw herself in the river. Her husband was running off to shoot himself, but they stopped him. Now the whole village was there following.
28. My story, my story. . . .PEKES.

The woman's version was recorded in January 1961, shortly after my first arrival in the field. Following a bit of folkloric folklore I assumed at that time that the best tales were without doubt known and told by old women, for who could better a venerable grandmother as the true guardian of traditional lore? With this bit of wisdom very much in mind I organized a session of tale-telling and three elderly women were invited to perform. Two of them were in their late sixties and the other in her fifties. The former two came drunk and, much to the amusement of the gathered crowd, made garbled attempts at storytelling producing in all a few snatches from distantly remembered tales and songs from tales. The latter, a very sober woman (FJ) of imposing presence told the tale about the Fabricated Child. When she had finished the microphone was passed to a young man in his mid-twenties who turned out to be a brilliant raconteur. After telling a number of tales that held the audience's complete attention another youth, someone in his late teens, took over. Although his performance was nowhere near so brilliant (a number of people in the audience dozed off) there could be no doubt but that he had at his command a very substantial repertoire of tales.

This session made it obvious, as it was borne out later, that tale-telling was the province of young people, and this was surely one of the main reasons for the irregularities in FJ's tale. She was out of practice and probably hadn't told a tale in as many as twenty years.

Some nine years later, in 1970, I asked a friend, AK, who was in his late thirties and who had been present at the original telling, about the tale and its performance. He told me that the main problem with her version was that she had confounded two separate tales. To straighten me out AK gave his version of the Fabricated Child and then followed it with a tale about a Boy and His Herd of Cattle. This latter can be briefly summarized as follows:

A boy's mother dies, and he is left in the care of her co-wife who treats him very badly. She refuses to give him food, to let him bathe, and to let him sleep with his half-brothers. To avoid this treatment he runs away and in the forest meets an old man to whom he tells his story. The old man tells the boy to shave him which he does and eventually on piercing the old man's head he finds a mix of "crossed," soft and regular eggs. The old man instructs the boy to take the crossed eggs and break them on the ground. This he does, and each broken egg produces a cow and a calf. At the very end he breaks a particularly large egg and up rises a particularly large cow. The boy then takes a whistle, mounts onto the back of this big cow, and sets off for home whistling and singing as he goes. The people at home break open the fence and in he rides. Everyone is impressed by the boy's herd, especially his stepmother. But the boy refuses to pay attention to her and divides the milk obtained from the herd with his father only. She persists in her begging and just as the boy is about to give in his deceased mother raises from the ground and reminds him of his stepmother's former mistreatment. "Don't give her anything, don't give her anything!" The mother then returns to her grave and her son follows her advice, refusing to give anything to the stepmother.

The story ends with the following moral comment: "That's why if you have your own child and one that isn't yours you must treat them the same, one as the other."

What FJ did was to interpolate into the Fabricated Child the sequence about the eggs and the cow. I was unable to determine where she got the part about the Hare. But it would be unfair to say that FJ was simply muddled. Quite to the contrary, for what we have here is a creative effort on her part, and if she had been in practice she might have perhaps pulled it off better than she did. That FJ should draw from the Boy and His Herd tale is reasonable, for the two tales have a number of parallels. Of these two important points can be mentioned here. In both tales the villains are the same, co-wives–stepmother, as is the person from whom approval is sought, husband-father. This is revealing, for in any household it is the opposed co-wives (or the wives of brothers) and their respective children that mark the usual place of fission within this basically patrilineal, virolocal society.

The other point: Following FJ's version, the interpolated egg scene plus her other additions are analogically parallel. Although FJ might have failed to link the scenes via any clear-cut story line she has nevertheless made them fit paradigmatically. These parallels, as we shall see later on, give FJ the opportunity to pose an interesting question about sexual roles. They also permit her, when the two tales are considered simultaneously, to make a telling comment not found in AK's version of the Fabricated Child. A boy can win approval by producing cows, a woman cannot and instead must produce children. And if she produces the children magically she is in for trouble. Cows do not worry about their origins, a child does.

There are other places permitting fruitful comparisons, especially if we take into account similar domestic tales. To follow this line of structural analysis further, however, would lead us away from our present task, a close discussion of the Fabricated Child and its central metaphor, the beehive womb.

THE QUESTION OF ESSENCES

A Kujamaat woman, to be considered a properly "legitimate" wife, must have children. This social fact is so basic to the Kujamaat that to belabor it is pointless. A woman on marrying is expected to have children and it is only when she does that her status in her husband's community is assured. The reasons for such stress on having children are quite the usual ones. Socially, children maintain their father's lineage and his position in it and provide a means through marriage for forming alliances elsewhere in the wider community. Economically, they are a source of labor both in the fields and at home and assure that their parents will be properly cared for in their old age.

Not to have children is not to be a woman, and a childless woman is stigmatized, being at once a distress to her husband and an object of both pity and ridicule for her co-wives and other in-married peers.

But childbearing, childbirth, and early child care are all dangerous and difficult business. Infant mortality rates are very high, and miscarriages, stillbirths, and until recently death in childbirth have not been uncommon. It is therefore not at all surprising that most of the women's religious and ritual activities directly concern control over these matters. Thus in the region there are three spirits, controlled by women, that have to do with problems of childbirth. One called *bulúnt* has to do with excessive reproduction and enlarged genitalia (male and female) and is controlled by women who have had twins.[4] Another, the reverse of *bulúnt*, called *dofe*, is responsible for stillbirths and death in

4. I introduce here a simplified orthography for Kujamaat (Diola-Fogny). In my grammar (Sapir 1965) I isolated ten distinctive vowel phonemes, of which five are lax, or relatively open, and the other five are tense, or relatively closed. When combined with tense vowels, lax vowels via vowel harmony become tense. To simplify matters and to avoid redundancy I have, in this chapter, marked as tense (*i,é,á,ó,ú*) only those vowels that are tense before the application of the harmony rules. Thus *bulúnt* is pronounced *búlúnt*, etc. Further, the palatal and velar nasals are here respectively marked as *ny* and *ng*, and the velar nasal plus g cluster as *ngg* as in *bulánggánggab*, "bush spirit."

childbirth, and the third, *kubos,* assures the separation at parturition of women from men and from girls who have not yet given birth.

A barren woman, as a substitute for her own children, will often take under her care a brother's child. If the child is a girl, as is usually the case, she will be expected to marry into the community where she has been brought up and to produce children in place of her father's barren sister. Women who are not barren but who have difficulty having children will go to great lengths to assure that their children will live. One tactic is to assume a liminal role called *-nyalen,* where the woman, to protect a newly born child, will become a buffoon. She will assume for herself and/or for her child a derogatory name, will wear at public gatherings men's clothing that she has decorated in various bizarre and colorful ways, and she will carry with her a multicolored stick. This wearing of the motley, the Kujamaat say, is so that God will take pity on her and prevent her child from dying, or more precisely, so God will "leave her child in peace" (*emitey ekato masúúmay*). The derogatory name for her child, such as "trash heap" or "garbage" is to avert from the child the untoward attention of witches who prefer "nice things."

Witches are always a problem when it comes to raising children, not only for those who lose many but for others as well. In fact a woman who has had the good luck to have many healthy children must take precautions against the jealousies and ill-feelings of her less fortunate neighbors, especially her co-wives and her husband's brother's wives. These women might either accuse her of being too lucky (via witchcraft) or might themselves try to do some harm to her children (also via witchcraft).

If childbearing and childbirth are difficult periods for most women in general, they are particularly so for beginners. Since they are not permitted, because of *kubos,* to witness and assist at the birth of others' children they come to their own first delivery with no prior experience. Today this is less of a problem due to maternity services available to and systematically used by all women. In the past, however, it certainly was a difficult period for a woman was expected to deliver her child on her own, receiving help only in emergencies. Further, since traditional Kujamaat (though no longer the case today) expected a bride to come to her marriage as a virgin, she had to confront for the first time not only her new surroundings and the problems of producing a child, but also the novel experience of having sexual intercourse with her husband. Not that the Kujamaat are or ever were particularly prudish. Although I am sure that for an Ajamaat (sing. of Kujamaat) girl the "first night" was never the ordeal it is supposed to be for an occidental *jeune fille rangée,* it was nevertheless an important and potentially troublesome first encounter.

Thus, virgin or not, marriage was, and still is, an important event. A girl must leave her mother and her agnates and, to establish herself in her new home, she must produce a child. To do this she must bed with her new husband and then survive pregnancy and childbirth. It is such a newlywed that is the subject of our tale.

The Kujamaat take the "sang" in consanguine seriously, a crucial point in the case of the Fabricated Child. A child is a product of his parents' blood, blood that is mixed during sexual intercourse (Sapir 1970). Consanguinity entails some kind of linkage, demonstrable or assumed, of blood mixtures. Thus parallel cousins(terminologically "same" or "opposite sex siblings") are consanguines because one of each of their respective parents were both issues of the same blood mixtures. Now to be legitimate, and I use the term legitimate to mean having a proper and recognizable place, is to have consanguines. To be illegitimate is therefore to have no kin at all, as a foundling, a complete stranger, or a war captive. The Kujamaat call such a person *asúkáten* (which can also apply metaphorically to any orphan), and they cannot conceive of treating him as anything other than a slave (*amikel*). In their songs he is stigmatized as being "easy to kill" and "easy to judge," for he is someone who lacks kin to represent his interests and to protect him from those who might wish him harm.

These notions about consanguines and blood mixtures have a number of implications. First, when strangers take up residence in a community, which they frequently do these days, considerable effort will be made to demonstrate that they, the stranger and his hosts, are on some level of generality actual consanguines. For example, in the quarter where I lived a young man from another village had been a resident for several years, living in the quarter for reasons of health. That he had a right to be there was always argued in terms of consanguinity. His father's mother and the mother of his particular host were both of the same patronym as well as being from the same quarter of a third village. Following Kujamaat kinship terminology his host was his "father." Since the host and his father were the sons of classifactory sisters, they were matrilateral parallel cousins and thus referred to each other as brother. And, since one's brother's son is terminologically one's own son, the designation in this case of the host as father was correct.

More to our present interest, however, are adoption and children born out of wedlock. To begin with, the Kujamaat do not adopt children in the sense of taking a child of other parents and considering it as one's own. A child is yours only when you had a direct hand in the mix that produced it. A direct corollary is the absence of a true levirate. Although a man will often inherit his deceased brother's widow, any children produced from this new union will be his own and never those of the dead brother.

Of course the Kujamaat take care of children whose parents, one or both, are missing. Here the major problem, especially if the children are young, is to make sure that the woman who takes care of them is a consanguine. Thus a thoughtful widower, even when he has another wife, will very often place his motherless children in the care of one of his own female consanguines, a sister, mother's sister, or mother's sister's daughter, anyone of whom, just because of the consanguinal link, would be expected to take her obligations as a surrogate mother more seriously than one of the widower's other wives. A childless consanguine, mentioned already, would be ideal. An alternative, more for an older child than for an infant, is to place him with one of his mother's kin, her sister for instance, but very often her brother.

The relationship of a child to his father's other wife, particularly when she has her own children to worry about, is not likely to be ideal. Not only is she not the child's real mother, but further she is not even a consanguine. Such a relationship is evoked in the Boy and His Herd tale, as well as in a good many other tales. It is simply better to live away from home with a consanguinal mother surrogate than to stay put with someone who is no way linked by blood.

When a man dies one of his agnates, preferably a brother or the son of his father's brother, takes responsibility for his children. The widow will usually opt to remain and marry, as we said, this next of kin. She stays for the sake of the children, for if she chooses to return to her own agnates or to marry elsewhere she must leave the children behind.

AK himself gives us an excellent example of the various possible solutions available for taking care of children missing a parent. He lost his own mother in his early adolescence. After her death he started spending a great deal of time, amounting in total to five or more years, with his mother's brother. His relationship with this mother's brother and with others of the uncle's household as well has remained particularly close. Later AK's wife died leaving him with three boys. The middle child, about four years old at the time, was placed with one of AK's mother's sisters in a neighboring village. The other two, an infant and a child of about seven, were kept at home, but under the care of AK's older sister who had, after a series of unsuccessful marriages, taken up permanent residence with her agnates. Some four years later one of AK's brothers who had been living elsewhere died after a long illness. His four children, all girls, passed into AK's care. Under considerable pressure from his agnates AK consented to marry the widow with whom he subsequently had a son. After another three years the next eldest of the girls (about eleven years old) was farmed out to one of AK's other sisters who was married in another village. We thus have in the space of eight years AK placing four children, three with sisters and the fourth with a mother's sister. During this same period he took charge of his brother's children and widow. At no time were any of the children put under the care of women who were not their consanguines.

A child born out of wedlock will always find a proper place with his mother's agnates or, if appropriate payments are made, with those of his father. Although his position will be somewhat ambiguous, he is called an "outside child," he will always be guaranteed basic rights both in his childhood and later on. There is never any question about his legitimacy.

I go into these details so as to place in relief the sorry plight of the Fabricated Child. If a child who has lost a parent or who is the product of an outside union is nevertheless considered legitimate, the Fabricated Child is, in contrast, just about as illegitimate as Kujamaat could be. As a child of dubious mixture and certainly not the mixture of his parents' blood, he is someone with no consanguines at all. He is a foundling in the full sense of the word and has little more to expect from life than to be treated as a "slave."

One other unstated belief figures indirectly in the tale. Exceptional luck, such as being particularly successful—having many children, being an expert hunter or farmer, etc.—or as being a particularly beautiful person, is all the result of some kind of supernatural intervention that in some way or another must be paid for. Given the Kujamaat's strong egalitarian beliefs (they represent a perfect example where the notion of "limited good" finds full expression), paying for supernatural intervention will almost always entail taking, or stealing, from someone else, a neighbor or more commonly a close relative. In songs a frequent refrain tells of a person's beauty being paid for with a heifer. Informants interpret these lines by saying that in order to have a beautiful child a woman pays something to a spirit, such as the bush spirit in the tale, for the necessary supernatural help. They will then invariably add that the heifer in the song is a euphemism for a young girl. Thus a mother will sacrifice a close kin, even a young sister or a girl child of her own or one of her co-wives', to the spirit so that she may have a beautiful child. Needless to say a woman acting in this way will be thought of as a witch (*asay*).

One reason, clearly stated in AK's version and briefly alluded to in FJ's (21), that the man accepts with enthusiasm the Fabricated Child is that he is physically perfect while the others, the ones he rejects, have only one eye (*katapang*).[5] To the jealous co-wives the perfection of the Fabricated Child, in contrast to the imperfection of their own, could be the result of only one thing, witchcraft. They might be thought of as asking, "If the bush spirit gave her the child, what did she give

5. *Katapang* refers to having only one good eye, the other being defective in one way or another. It is a very common phenomenon with the Kujamaat and serves as a good indicator of physical imperfection.

the bush spirit in return?" Thus added to the child's stigma of illegitimacy is the stigma of perfection.

Taking these various beliefs together, about having children, having consanguines, and about suspicious perfection, we can read the tale's essence as a kind of imaginative experiment with the impossible. Since having children in the natural way is both inconvenient and dangerous what would happen if a child was produced externally? It would certainly solve the dilemma of the woman's problem, stigma/danger, and would also provide her with a guaranteed "perfect" result. But this will not work, for it only transfers the problem from the mother to her child. This child of external origin finds himself face to face both with his own illegitimacy and with a hostile social milieu consisting of the jealous co-wives who have had their own legitimate, if imperfect, progeny rejected. To avoid this irresolvable problem the Fabricated Child has little choice but to "go home." In the beginning of the tale the woman says that she is "going to run away and lose herself" in the forest (AK, 3). Her adventures get her what she wants and she returns home. She in a sense "finds herself" again. All to no avail for after the denouement everyone except the co-wives permanently "get lost": the child, "And there he was losing himself in the ground, there he was getting lost and he entered under ground. Yes there he was losing himself in the ground" (AK, 19); the parents, "She ran and lost herself in the bush, not to return. His father also ran off to lose himself" (AK, 21).

Although a moral is not appended to either version of the tale, as for the Boy and His Herd, we could easily infer one to be: "There is only one, natural, way to have a child. To use other means will raise questions of legitimacy not to mention the jealousies of others, and will result with the child being lost." Or, to make a succinct English pun: "grin and bear it." The accompanying diagram sums up the essences (Figure 1).

FIGURE 1

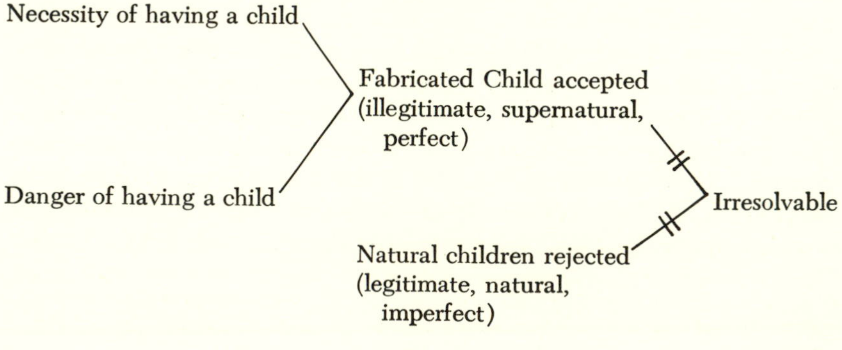

Necessity of having a child

Fabricated Child accepted
(illegitimate, supernatural,
    perfect)

Danger of having a child

Irresolvable

Natural children rejected
(legitimate, natural,
imperfect)

THE TEXT: NOTES ON ITS LINEAR STRUCTURE

Both versions of the Fabricated Child divide into five sections: (1) an initial home scene where there is a command for and a lack of a child; (2) and (3) the bush and the second home scene where the child is sought after and produced; (4) the presentation of the children where the Fabricated Child is accepted by the man and the one-eyed children are rejected. Sections (2) and (3) are developed at length by FJ and passed over quite rapidly by AK. The reverse is true for section (4), with FJ giving it only a couple of sentences (line 21). Finally there is a coda (5) where the Fabricated Child is confronted by the co-wives.

Of these five the first four go together and deal with a change of state, the physical production and then acceptance of a child that resolves the woman's stigma/danger problem. It starts with the child's absence and ends with his presence. What we have is the common narrative sequence that runs, in Dundes's (1968) terms, from lack to lack liquidated. A command is given and instructions are followed so that a change of state will be achieved. In direct contrast the coda, which concerns the child's problem of legitimacy, starts, rather than ends, with a change of state. The child learns from his father's other wives about his origin and all subsequent action proceeds from there. In both parts information is conveyed. In the first, it is information that tells how things *should be* and how things should be done to achieve it. It serves to put things (the child) together. The coda is quite different. The information states how things *are* and serves, not to put things together, but rather to take them apart.

Much of the tale's dramatic impact has to do with this inverse symmetry that sets the two parts off from each other. Looked at abstractly the tale starts with a minus state, absence of the child, and goes via commands and instructions to a plus state, presence of the child. It then finishes by going from a new plus state, knowledge of the child's origins, to the final minus state; the dispersal of the major actors.

The final dispersal is inevitable. The child leaves because he simply does not belong where he is, and his "parents" leave, or attempt to leave, because of their distress on losing their "child" and also because of their shame for having the irregularities to which they were party become public knowledge, to their "son" as well as to everyone else. FJ's version is not clear as to exactly what happens at the end to the "parents." The man attempts to shoot himself, but is stopped. The woman runs off to drown herself, and it is never certain if she succeeds. What we do know is that the tale ends in a general commotion. . ."now the whole village was there following." AK is a lot clearer about what happens. The boy disappears into the ground. He goes "home" (*inje bóót*, as he says in his song) by joining the dead who are the only people who live below ground, "those of below" (*kati tentam*) as the Kujamaat put it. Actually the boy rejoins the dead, the Kujamaat having a cyclical notion of the link between the living and the dead. The "parents" after trying to kill themselves run off to lose themselves and are thus similar to those people (*apúrapúr*) who on their death are refused by the dead and are doomed to wander the ambiguous and unsocialized bush beyond the outskirts of the village. The symmetry is striking. The legitimate co-wives remain alive in the village, the illegitimate Fabricated Child goes below to the dead and the two who produced the disruption end up somewhere in between, off in the bush. The boy is dead, the co-wives alive, and the "parents" socially dead but physically alive.

THE BEEHIVE

Central to the tale is the Fabricated Child's place of creation, a beehive. It is an apt metaphor for several reasons. First there is a direct parallel between a beehive and a womb. Both contain something that gestates, something that is created internally over a period of time, honey and a fetus. They of course differ. Most importantly, from the woman's point of view, one is internal to herself while the other external. This allows her to solve her problem, to have a child without bearing it herself. By transferring the fetus to the beehive she is provided with a convenient "external womb." Another important point is that the beehive = womb is very much an ambiguous entity, like the child himself. It is neither a beehive nor a womb but something new. It is a mixture of the two, a beehive with a fetus. The beehive provides the container, the womb provides what is contained. A cultural object, the beehive, that has been made to contain natural and non-human bees and their work, is used here supernaturally to fabricate a human child.

Since honey very often plays an important role in the cosmology of many peoples in Africa and elsewhere it is tempting to assume that this is equally the case for the Kujamaat. Unfortunately it is not. Honey is economically marginal and, as far as I could ascertain, of no importance in religious activity, nor does it occupy any place in their general cosmology. At times mead can substitute for palm wine in making libations to various spirits, and in one particular case "last year's" honey serves to initiate a ritual. Beyond this it serves no other recorded ritual purpose. Anyone, man or woman, interested enough and willing to take the trouble will make a hive and suspend it from the lower branches of a tree near his compound, or place it in the yard in back of his house. Sometimes a woman will put a hive in the rafters of her cook house. There are two types of hives one called *yungat*, made by hollowing out a log, and the other more common one and the one appearing in the tale that is called *futukany*. It is made of palm leaves woven into a cylindrical shape. Placed in this type of hive is a stick that runs from the mouth inward. The bees build their nest around the stick. In AK's version of the tale recall that it was such a stick that the bush spirit spirit gave to the woman with instructions to place it in the hive. Honey obtained from the hives or from nests found elsewhere in trees is eaten as is, made into mead, or used as a sweetener for rice or millet porridge. The availability of sugar and the conversion of the vast majority of the Kujamaat to Islam (hence abstinence from drinking mead) has reduced their interest in honey.

The only direct (metonymic or contiguous) link between the production of honey and sexuality acknowledged by the Kujamaat is the predilection of one variety of bee (*bayoyompen* or *bayopa*) for the sweat (*ejena*), that is, the lubricant (?) of a woman's vagina. These are small bees that produce a rather tart form of honey and are not to be confused with *faj*, the common honey bees that occupy beehives.

Of more direct interest to our tale is the Kujamaat understanding that honey is made from a mixture of water, nectar from tree blossoms, and tree gum (this latter needed, they say, as a "glue"). The best water for honey is said to come from springs in the rice fields. The reason given for preferring spring water is that it retards spoilage. We might also add that this water is entirely "natural" in that it does not come from a man-made well. The Kujamaat will always say that spring water from the rice fields tastes better and is better for you, and there are a fair number of rituals that prescribe its usage. Honey is thus derived from substances obtained from two natural sources, trees and springs, with each of the sources optimally occupying separate and contrasting areas in the local geography, the bush (*karamba*) for the nectar and gum and rice fields (*biit*) for the water. It is the mixture of separate substances from separate sources that augments the aptness of the womb = beehive metaphor, for quite as with honey, the fetus, as I have already mentioned, is similarly the product of a mixture of substances (blood) from separate sources, the father and the mother. This all can be stated as an analogy, water from the rice fields:nectar and gum from trees::blood from one parent:blood from the other (rice fields and the bush are *not* sexed by the Kujamaat).

Now the tale makes an interesting variation on the notion of mixture, for the substance added to the beehive container is cooked rice (*sinaang*) that in the "real" world is associated with the gestation of neither a fetus nor honey. It belongs to another, third, domain and consequently doubles the metaphor. That rice is involved is clearly stated by AK in the instructions given the woman by the bush spirit, "when you cook rice take some and put it inside [the hive]" (8). FJ's version is a bit different. There the woman is told by her father's sister only to "serve out and put it in the beehive" (17). We can assume, however, and without risk, that FJ had rice in mind, for the word -gab, "serve out food into a bowl or dish," is used almost exclusively with reference to rice, the staple food.

If cooked rice is one of the substances we can infer that honey is the other, and of the two it is the cooked rice that is surely the one equivalent to semen. In terms of the metaphoric parallel it could not be otherwise, for like semen the cooked rice is introduced from the outside into the container (beehive) to mix, as a sweetened porridge (!), with the already present honey. But there are other reasons for the parallel as well. To begin with, like rice, semen is white. Also, like rice, it is a basic form of sustenance. To the Kujamaat semen not only serves in conception, the original mixture that gets things going (semen and blood considered the same in the context), but also helps in the maintenance of the fetus. Intercourse throughout pregnancy and up until the last weeks is thought to help the fetus grow and develop. That rice itself is central to Kujamaat ideas of sustenance cannot be underestimated. It is their principal food crop and is eaten in one form or another at almost every meal. Since the Kujamaat will start feeding rice to a baby almost immediately after its birth, we can think of it as taking over where semen leaves off.[6]

A child made from a mixture of cooked rice and honey is an odd and ambiguous creation, obviously, for he is not made from his parents' blood. But more than this, he is the product of substances that are themselves mixtures, a detail underscoring his fabrication. A normal child is made from the mixture of two substances that are, to the Kujamaat, irreducible. But the Fabricated Child is twice removed from basic and irreducible substances. He is made from cooked rice (sinaang), which itself has been prepared by boiling rice (emaanay) with water (mumel). This cooked rice is then mixed with honey, itself a mixture of water with nectar and gum (cf. Figure 2).

6. A parallel to semen on the beehive side of the metaphor comes with a custom, according to at least one informant, of spitting either palm wine or milk into the beehive to improve the honey's quality. Since I do not have any information on this custom I have not worked it into the analysis. However, like semen and cooked rice, milk and palm wine are also white and are likewise important elements to Kujamaat ideas of sustenance. In this regard, since the conversion to Islam, milk has tended to replace palm wine.

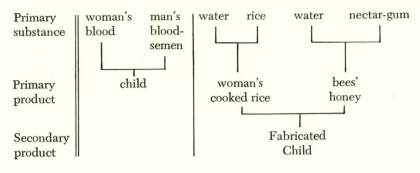

FIGURE 2

The entire ambiguity becomes more complex if we consider the woman's role. For in the creation she performs as a male. Thus as a man inseminates and sustains through intercourse an external object, a woman's womb and its fetus, so the woman places a stick in an external beehive and sustains its growth into a child by "inseminating" the hive with cooked rice. But throughout all this she maintains a certain feminine quality, she places cooked rice in the hive. Now to the Kujamaat rice is associated primarily with women. Although a man prepares rice fields for cultivation, the women do all the rest. They weed rice nurseries, transplant the rice, harvest it, store it, and finally cook it. It is they who command the technical knowledge about rice varieties and their growing patterns. An average Kujamaat woman knows and can quickly identify about ten to fifteen varieties, while a man can at best differentiate the two major species. So, for male semen the tale gives us woman's rice.[7]

FJ, by her innovations—the interpolation from the Boy and His Herd tale plus other rather vague additions, complicates the story considerably. The final image and the metaphor it develops are common to both versions: the woman inseminates a beehive with rice to produce a child. However, before presenting the metaphor and the ambiguous resolution of the woman's problem it implies, FJ offers a number of parallel images that, though similar, are quite obviously different from this main beehive = womb equation. It is worth our while to consider these differences for it seems to me that the sequence of images marks a development that is not at all clear in FJ's story line which, as I noted earlier, is subject to a series of starts and jumps.

7. Referring back to note 6, both milk and palm wine are, like semen, irreducible substances associated with men. It is only the men who tap palm wine and milk cows. Following out the parallel, therefore, we have male semen, milk and palm wine, in the real world, being introduced into a gestating container, while in the story they are replaced by woman's secondary cooked rice.

What FJ has done, in this part of the tale, is to line up a group of images without troubling to tell us in any clear way how one image dissolves into the next. One minute we hear about eggs and the next we are told about whistling for a cow. We never find out what happened to the eggs and whether or not these eggs had anything at all to do with the cow. A cow simply replaces the eggs. In contrast AK's version of the Boy and His Herd tale makes a clear cause and effect linkage. The eggs are broken and out of the pieces emerges the herd. Following Roman Jakobson's notion of the "poetic function" (1960: 358), FJ has simply and without recourse to causal linkages projected a group of paradigmatic images onto what Jakobson calls the syntagmatic or combinatory axis. It is the absence of linkages that gives FJ's version its surrealistic quality. To follow her story we must consider the sequence of images, not the sequence of events. Let us see what we can make of the images.

First I take as a premise, quite as I did in establishing the aptness of the beehive metaphor, that each of the images is a variation on the "real" world model of human intercourse, conception, and gestation, not so farfetched when we keep in mind that the tale *is* about making a child. The constituents of this model are: a male *agent* inseminates a woman's womb (*container*) by means of a male substance (semen) and *activity*, penetration. The result is a *mixture* (male semen/blood with woman's blood) that creates and sustains the *contained* fetus. Recapitulating and augmenting the alterations for the beehive scene we have: the agent becomes female as does the activity, serving for penetration. The container is now the inanimate beehive and the child results from the mixture of secondary substances. The contained fetus remains constant. What about FJ's additions? Recall first the images: bringing something down with a stick, shaving a woman to find eggs, blowing a whistle to call a cow, penetrating a compound astride the cow, and finally, serving into a beehive. Now consider each of these in terms of the basic constituents.

1. The *agent* throughout is the woman, and thus this variable remains constant.

2. The *activities* vary from scene to scene. The first, following from the bush spirit's initial instructions and which the woman fails to carry out, is hard to place. I got the translation as follows. The verb *-lang* when coupled with the "toward the speaker" suffix *-úl* refers to knocking something down with a stick, usually fruit from a tree. Thus *nulangúlom* (you-knock-hither-for-me) gives us "knock it down for me with a stick." Obtaining fruit, or anything else for that matter, in this way is neither a particularly masculine nor feminine activity. However the remaining activities, until the woman serves into the hive, are

masculine, or mainly so. Shaving hair and beards is generally considered a male activity especially for ordinary occasions. However women will shave other women on certain ritual occasions, at funerals and as part of a girl's initiation that involves a form of cliterodectomy. This latter ritual is a recent addition associated with Islam that has been borrowed from the neighboring Manding and Fula peoples. Kujamaat also say that in the remote past women shaved their husband's beards and hair, but no longer do so, not even in anyone's living memory. These albeit important exceptions admitted, shaving nevertheless remains primarily men's work. And cultural norms aside, the very image of shaving, cutting, penetrating has a strong resemblance to the male role in coitus. Recall the man's original threat at the beginning about cutting the girl's throat.

Whistling with a whistle is done only by men and only at certain times: at a wrestling match when a wrestler shows off before encountering his opponent, during a number of dances performed by a male initiate at the time of his circumcision, and by a herdsman or herdsboy who will often whistle a call that designates one of the cows in his charge (Sapir 1969:188). The last, since the woman blows the whistle to obtain a cow, is directly relevant to the discussion. The only time a woman will use a whistle is when she imitates a man (in dress as well) as part of the liminal role she assumes (-*nyalen*) to protect her children, and that I have briefly mentioned above. Otherwise for a woman to whistle, even with her lips, is thought of as bad taste.

In bringing home the cow the woman, still whistling and now singing as well, continues performing a man's job, for cows and their care including the milking is exclusively a male activity. She also enters the compound, not through the gate but by having the fence broken open ("...and they broke open the fence, wooo..."[16]), which recalls, as it did with the shaving, the man's role in sexual intercourse. Her song emphasizes the penetration, "Papa, father, open so Bajending can enter" (14), where instead of cutting into a manlike woman's head she now has a man open up his compound, which is, to the Kujamaat, a container of male agnates.

3. The initial scene does not designate a *contained* object, although we might infer from the verb -*langúl* that FJ had some kind of fruit in mind. From this empty (or plant) constituent we then move to eggs which are potentially animal, to the cow which is fully animal and of greater value than the eggs, to an actual human child. The reference to eggs is curious but nevertheless appears to be a common motif. The euphonic phrase *faaf falaándore, faaf fajone, faafu fakane búkabúk*, "one that's crossed, one that's straight, one that goes *búkabúk* (is soft)," is a formula that appeared in both recordings, FJ's tale and AK's rendi-

tion of the Boy and His Herd, where in the latter instance one of the listeners whispered the phrase in unison with AK. I was told that crossed eggs are of irregular shape and often have double yolks, in contrast to straight eggs which are ordinary. Crossed eggs are considered auspicious and if given the choice you would pick one of these rather than an ordinary one. They are a sign of something good. As one informant put it, "If there were ten ordinary eggs you wouldn't know which one to pick, but if there was a crossed one among them you'd pick it." In contrast soft eggs are inauspicious—"something dangerous is likely to be inside, such as a snake."

4. The initial scene also fails to mention a *container*, although we might want to infer a tree as a container of fruit. The egg-scene provides a very clear container, the old woman's head (or womb-vagina, it is not clear which). Then there is no container at all, for the cow just materializes. The next scene has the agnatic male compound that in Kujamaat thought is very much a self-contained unit. Traditionally, and very frequently today, a compound consists of a tight circle of houses placed around a courtyard with a fence in back of the houses encircling the whole affair. Access to the compound was or still is through a main gate (*fulímet*) and through one or more smaller openings in the fence. These entrances are closed up at night. The Kujamaat have many complex ideas about entering, exiting, and penetrating compounds, for to them inside versus outside the compound has an important place in their concepts about social space (Sapir, forthcoming). Further, until quite recently and even today in other Kajamaat areas, cows were kept at night in the courtyard to protect them from thieves or to make sure, during the rains, that they would not wander into the rice fields. A cow in a courtyard is therefore as forceful a representation of a container-contained image as a fetus in a womb, bees and their honey in a bee-hive, or, as in our tale, of eggs inside an old woman's head.

5. Unlike the final beehive where we have cooked rice combined with honey there is no indication at any point of a *mixture* of substances, although we might want to make something of the crossed eggs as a kind of mixture.

There are two other variables not yet mentioned that should be considered. One qualifies further the woman's activity, which we have so far shown as moving from neutral to masculine to feminine serving into the beehive; and the other has to do with the relative position of the woman vis-à-vis the other constituents.

6. Taking the latter first we have here a kind of spatial oscillation reminiscent in a modest way of the ups and downs, forwards and backings up, spotted by Lévi-Strauss (1958b) in his key study of the North American *Asdiwal* myth. In our tale the oscillation has to do with the position of the woman with respect to other actors and objects. At the

very start of the tale the man goes up into the sky, up there, since *emit* glosses as "God" as well as "sky," with the creator. (FJ's line *panijaw bet emitey,* "I'm going up to the sky (up with God)" was met by the audience with amused approval.) This up/down spatial separation marks the social and personal distance between the man and the woman, and it is a separation that the woman, with the aid of her helpers, attempts to mediate. The initial position of the woman vis-à-vis the man also correlates with the understood point of departure, sexual intercourse. The Kujamaat very emphatically consider the "Missionary position," that is, the man on top, as the norm.

In the bush, when the woman assumes the role of agent, her initial relative position is unchanged. She is below and is told to "knock it down. . .with a stick" (6). Immediately there is a change, for in the following egg scene she is, with respect to the old woman, neither above nor below. They are on equal ground. Then she is climbing up. First she is told by the old woman to "climb up (on) something." The verb used is -*rembor,* a reflexive variant of the causative -*remben,* "place something up on something, as on a table or shelf" (cf. also *buremben,* "a stand for drying rice, etc.," usually about five feet in height). In describing the woman's response FJ does not have her putting herself up onto something, but instead she is described as climbing "up and up and up," where the verb is -*nyito,* "climb up (as a tree)," cf. also *bunyito,* "mount, as a bull mounts a cow in copulation." At this point she is very much in the man's position (the bull's as well?). As the man at the beginning went up into the sky leaving the women to listen for him, so the woman finds she has climbed "way up here listening for God," as she tells the Hare. (FJ refers unambiguously to God with *ati jamit,* "(person) of the big sky," a common expression for God used by Muslims and Christians.) The woman then comes down and puts herself up on the cow, *awalum arembor,* "she came down and climbed up" (13). Up on the cow she is still above, but less so than before. Here above is with respect to the cow and the compound. The final scene has her where she was in the first place, below, serving up into the beehive.

7. The final variable has to do with a movement, on the woman's part, from distraught passivity to creative activity. At the start she does nothing at all. Her co-wives cook and she is told to wait up for the man. When he arrives to ask about the child she sits "quietly" for a long time before answering. In the bush she tells the bush spirit that she is crazy, *airair,* that is, disoriented, head spinning. The initial instructions seem to straighten her out and she goes off to do things, to be active: to find out what it is she must knock down, to shave the old woman, to fetch the whistle, to climb up and then blow the whistle so as to call the cow. Then astride the cow she enters the compound. To this point, although she has been active, she has not been creative (we do not know if she

	Coitus	A.	B.	C.	D.	E.
Agent	male	woman	woman	woman	woman	woman
Activity	penetration male	knock down with stick neither male nor female	penetration shaves male	whistles male	penetrates compound whistles, rides cow male	serves female
Contained	fetus	nothing (fruit?)	eggs	cow	cow	fetus/child
Container	human woman's womb	nothing (tree?)	human old woman's head (vagina?)	open area	inanimate compound, container of male agnates	inanimate beehive, container of insects, honey
Substance	primary mixture of woman's blood, man's semen, and blood	none	none	none	none	secondary mixture cooked rice and honey
Position of agent	above	below	neither above nor below	above, way up high	above, on the cow	below
Quality of activity	active creative	passive-active uncreative	active uncreative	active uncreative	active uncreative	active creative

FIGURE 3

216

finds or makes the whistle). She *finds* eggs, *calls* and *rides* the cow, but she creates neither. It is only at the end, when she serves into the beehive to produce the child, that she is both active and creative.

What can we make of this sequence of variations on the theme of sexual intercourse (cf. Figure 3)? To begin, the major and essential beehive variation, common to both versions of the tale, offers a complete transformation of the initial point of reference. The central constituent, a child, is unchanged but around this constant just who does what and to whom or which undergoes a systematic inversion. This is immediately evident when we consider the diagram (Figure 4).

AK's version of the tale simply makes the inversion without dwelling on it at any length. The woman receives her instructions from the bush spirit and carries them out directly. What interests AK is rather the presentation of the child, the competition between the woman and her co-wives, and the final confrontation that results from the child's predicament. The woman places the child in a room. This scene echoes the beehive, for the woman continues to provide rice for the child who is now contained in the room rather than the hive. Then the child is made pretty, decorated with beads, and presented to his father. The entire section refers to the period after birth when a mother and her newborn infant remain in seclusion in order to avoid polluting (via *kubos*, cf. above) the father with the "birth blood." The string of beads threaded by the woman and attached around the baby's waist represents his first item of clothing.

FJ ignores this scene entirely. In her version the child comes out of his beehive with his waist beads already in place and hence he emerges both physically complete and culturally dressed as well, "she. . .served and pushed it in and she saw there the beads" (20). FJ thus conveniently gets the woman and the child past not only the difficulties of pregnancy and birth, but also past the particularly dangerous first weeks following the birth.

As we have come to see, FJ's focus is less on the child's adventures than it is on the whole business of his fabrication. What she does, and

	sexual intercourse	*beehive scene*
contained	child	child
active agent	+ male	— male
activity of agent	+ male	— male
container	+ human (female)	— human (inanimate)
mixture	primary	secondary
position of agent	above	below

FIGURE 4

does at some length, is to explore several possible sets of relationships that mediate between the real facts of procreation and the beehive alternative. This final beehive solution is unisexual, for it eliminates the man entirely from the procreation. The woman to solve "her problem" and to produce a child external to herself might act as a man, but everything else is going to be female or inanimate. She is guided by helpers who, albeit superordinate and malelike or male linked, are nevertheless primarily women. She acts from the woman's position by performing a woman's activity on an inanimate object constructed to house insects, not humans, let alone men. The result will be a child fabricated out of secondary substances also unconnected with men: woman's cooked rice and bee's honey. Before setting out this completely unisexual solution, however, FJ offers by way of her mediations a number of exaggerated variations. In the bush, with the exception of the vague first scene, each of the images has the woman doing something that makes her more malelike than she actually is in the end. The egg scene, the most pointed exaggeration of the lot, has the woman penetrating a socially malelike old woman, pregnant with eggs, by performing the primarily male activity of shaving. This really has the act of intercourse turned around, although it is diffused somewhat by the woman's equivocal position, neither above nor below, and of course because the object/helper, malelike that she is, is still a woman and not an old man as was the case in the Boy and His Herd tale. Whistling as a man for a cow takes the woman way up high and into the man's position. But now there is no container, human or otherwise. Then acting as a herdsboy the woman brings the cow in the compound, with with herself still above, astride the cow. The major shift now is that the container has become inanimate which diminishes considerably the exaggeration of the egg scene, although, unlike the beehive, it is a container made by men to house, not insects, but a group of male agnates.

Putting the three images together we see that in FJ's extended experiment she raises the possibility, always disguised, of a woman actively penetrating a passive though instructing male by doing a male activity and operating from the man's position. In a word she asks the question, "why cannot a woman, in satisfying a man's demand for a child, change places with the man?" A very good question to ask.

CONCLUSION

To pull the discussion together let me end by taking stock of what I have tried to do in this analysis. Throughout I have operated under three main a priori assumptions. First, the tale should be considered in its entirety and this entirety should hang together as a structure. Second, any interpretation as to what the tale is about must be made, in so far as possible, with reference to the culture and society of the people who tell it. Tales do not exist in a vacuum and regardless of origin the people who tell them and respond to them will do so in terms of their own cultural understandings. Third, the first two assumptions go hand in hand.

Recapitulating the highlights in terms of these assumptions we have the following points. The overall linear structure of the tale, which goes first from lack to lack liquidated and then to a confrontation, or more abstractly from an absent to a present state and then back to an absent state, provides the framework for acting out two sets of essences brought into conflict. Thus the link between the cultural reference, notions about legitimacy, and the tale's structure is direct and close. The beehive metaphor came at the crucial and ambiguous turning point in the tale, the shift from the woman's to the child's problem. To explore the ambiguity of the metaphor we took a good look at its own internal, paradigmatic, structure. Since the relationship between domains implied by a metaphor is seldom if ever spelled out, and the beehive = womb is no exception, it was necessary to bring into consideration Kujamaat notions about beehives and gestation in order to supply the other unstated constituents. The tale gave us only the beehive and the child. To this we added the complementary honey and womb, thus the container/contained parallel. Also important was the Kujamaat understanding that both honey and a fetus are the product of the mixture of separate substances. To add to the ambiguity, the tale mentioned cooked rice, a women's product that substituted for man's semen. Further, the cooked rice and the honey as well were themselves the product of mixtures. Thus in contrast to a fetus and to honey the beehive child was doubly fabricated.

My analysis of FJ's version entailed another more particular assumption. The interpolation from the Boy and His Herd tale was not the result of FJ being muddled. On the contrary, it was the result on her part of a creative effort. By importing a set of parallel images from a tale about male activities FJ was able to develop a linear progression to the beehive metaphor. The movement in this progression was from male activity (shaving, whistling, herding) and a male position (above) to female serving from a female position (below). These additions permitted FJ to make her exaggeration about sexual roles and hence to elaborate further the entire ambiguity of the Fabricated Child's creation.

I cannot say that the interpretation offered here is the correct reading. As Thomas Beidelman has convincingly argued (1971; 1975), it is impossible, quite as it is with literary texts, to give a definitive statement about the meaning and import of a folktale. An aesthetic representation, be it verbal, musical, or visual, is never its paraphrase. In fact, strictly speaking, it cannot be paraphrased at all. We can only be satisfied in this instance that the text was analyzed in terms of the culture of its tellers and for this reason the interpretation offered here should be congenial to the Kujamaat themselves.

There remains one other last assumption. The tale was motivated. I framed this motivation in terms of an imaginative experiment with the impossible. Whether this experiment served to purge the emotional melancholy or the speculative intellect of its tellers and listeners is rather hard to answer. It probably did both. In fact the radical opposition between the depth psychologist who would say it was the former and the Lévi-Straussian structuralists who would insist on the latter seems to be quite a non-issue. Although I leaned in my analysis toward the structuralist position, it permitting a more exhaustive statement, I do not doubt for a moment that basic emotions were at play. The Fabricated Child might have been an intellectual exercise, but it was an exercise that took as its point of departure the problems of having children and of being somebody other than a "slave." Surely these are issues that touch the Kujamaat's deepest sentiments.

APPENDIX

Anyiilaw Batuker, man's version

1. Lako lako, ilako nen emeng kujaora (kwa). 2. Bon. Asekaw kuyaboyabor di anínaw. Kusekak kono kubaakir. Ubuku kubabaj kunyiilaku, uma abajut anyiil. Bon. Anínaw nalako, alako, alako, alako, alako. 3. Nane, "Inje bet ejaw be kajauburung, bare napilaanyúm kajauburungak anoan abajutum anyiil panirámulol." Bon. Ubuku kabajum kunyiilak anoan jinyolo jikíl jakón, katapang. Uma abajutum anyiil nane, "Inje etey ijím."
4. Natey, atey, atey, atey, atey, aríng di karambaak kamámak di kukámbor di bulánggánggab. Bulánggánggab di bono, "Asekaw, be nuje bot?" 5. Nane, "Inje ataom aje kajaburung, mannane napalaanyúm apabajutum anyiil panarámúlo. Ban inje ibajut anyiil. Kupaalom kubabaj. Anoan jinyolo jati katapang." 6. Bon. "Nyer inje ibajut, inje itey ijím bala aríngú manarámulom. Mokami nen dete-ey." Nanom, "Mo ce mo?" Nano, "Ey." Nano, "Jol." Najol, asekaw ajol, ajol, ajol, aríngú. 7. Nanol, "Mati jinyiilaj ceb mo mom dekaniey manutey ujím?" Nane, "Ey." Nane, "Ukob, man inje ikani panubaj jinyiil." Nane, "Jakumubuntom." Nano, "Malegen." Nano, "Jakumubuntom." Nano, "Malegen." 8. Najaw, ajaw aminú jigolaj. Nano, "Jigolaj uje janiseni nye, ujaúmom uríng, nungar unen di futúkanyaf. Manusíl sinaangas nungarú ukandó, usíl sinaangas nungarú ukandó, usíl sinaangas nungarú ukandó.

9. Napulakom nike elóngey pambujam jinyiilaj di jinganúl di futúkanyaf. Napijinganúm di futúkanyaf nutey utebúl ujo unen di kajimak."
10. Mo nakam eno. Natebú jinyiilaj . . . enday . . . jigolaj eringú nanen di futúkanyaf. Jojoró, jojoró, jojoró, jojoró. Fulay fakón alako elóngey ceb najam jigolay di jinganúró nen jinyiilaj. 11. Natey aríng, jinyiilaj. Natebúl, atebúl aríngú nanen di kajimak. Nasíl sinaangas nanen dó, asíl sinaangas nanen dó manjiri.
12. Di kupaalo kuloren bamaalab, o po naloren bamaal; kunyes silolas o po nanyes silolas. Kupaalo di kone, "Wai, jikob mambujukal, an abajut anyiil, o naloren bamaalab, nanyes eloley bet ebujey ataolal. Mbujukall!" 13. Nan fulayaf furíngum anínaw aríngúm ceb, ubuku kabajum kunyiilak di kujítum anoan eilolol, kujaw kuís ataii. O po najítum eilolol, ajaw aseno. Dikukoofor wanafaalo. "Jiker umu abajut anyiil naja akan nen man walal ukanam eno. Jikob mbujuka jat o kootum karámulak!" 14. Nya nankusí sinaangas kuban di kusen kunyolii kujítum. Umu asen anyolol ajítum, umu nasen anyolol O nalako ró manaja asánggen jinyolo di jijak. Natebú sinaangas asenú jinyiilaj. 15. Jon dejoley di batalingab, "firiring fiiriring, fararang fararang, fararang fararang." Nan anínaw ajukulom jinyiilaj aju ceb, nane, "Ubuku kati utapangaw ji-ito, ji-ito, ji-ito! Muyu jilaany be babu di sinyayul, jilaany be babu di sinyayul!"
16. Bon. Mankuri sinaangas di uju, ubuku kanumanjumi kubabaj no mati mutapangam, funyii furiri, súúmutil mati umu manapúrenulom jinyiilaj. Di jijuk, kumamanj jinyiilaj o awolut jo. 17. Bon. Ombo, ombo, ombo, ombo, asekaw ajaw be kamojak di kone jinyiilaj, "Aw batuker! aw numanje aw inyay abajut, aw batuker. Papay, mokami upay najukú aw nabeten ubuku kólólí manane ko utapang." 18. Nyer lako lako nane inyao:

[song]   Inyam, inyam, kubeti kone
            Inje batuker, batuker,
            Inje bóót.
            Upam, upam, kuseki kone
            Inje batuker, batuker,
            Inje bóót.

                    [repeats]

19. Omto najíme tentamaru, ombo najíme, nanoken be tentama. Ey, omto najíme tentama. Nyer inyayol ombo karúlen, upayol ombo karúlen. Upayol ombo dengar epímbeney be kabujoro di kusof. Inyayol etey bet elo deko-longey di kusof. 20. Omto nakane:

[song]   Upam, upam kuseki kone
            Inje batuker, batuker,
            Inje bóót.
            Inyam, inyam, kubeti kone
            Inje batuker, batuker,
            Inje bóót.

                    [repeats]

21. Mam nakam do ajím. Asekaw natey, asekaw akilum anyiilaw akila, natey, natey ajím di karambaak. Alaanyut abajo kotoke. Upayo po natetey ajím. 22. Nyer karegondegom PEKES.

Anyiilaw Batuker, woman's version

1. Anínaw najaumi. Nane, "Panijaw bet emitey." Ajaum aríng bo. Nane kusekaku, "Manijaum nyamo napilaanyúm apitokum manawole jijanga panirámulo." 2. Yo. Nya o najaum awuj be remitey, kusekak di kusof asek am abajutumi anyiilaw. Nanol, "Aw jol, inj'isíl sinaangasu nunen tate manujantenal anínaw." 3. Yo. Kokubo kakíbiria, kokubo kakíbiria, kokubo kakíbiria. Anínaw om babu demitey de' Yo. Be nen naríngulomi. Nakonyenum ban kunyiilak kankubajumi, ban kusúmpulum burám, di ban kuwolumi burám. 4. Nane, "Maninen kabasakaku di fankaf, man apabajutum anyiilaw, o jat, o nijem be karámulaku." Yo. Asekaw omuto manaíne ayento ayajen. Nane, "Inje emitey esenutom anyiilaw."

5. Nyer, najaw katoker. Najajaw be bulánggánggabu. Bujukol di bono, "Asekaw mba manuje nya unoken di karambaaku, wamban?" Nane, "Inje manije bo nye, inje airair. Inj'an abajerut waf. Ifaretérit. 6. Ataóli najaw ajum di emitey. Nye nane napalaanyúmi apabajutum panaramulo. Nye manije bo nya." Nane, "Way, nulángúlom." Nane, "Ilángúli wa? Inje manije nye inje an aja be fulaap." 7. Yo. Nya najaw, najaw, najaw di kulaany kuyajor di jifálum jaju, di jono, "Way anyiilaw nulángúlom tate!" Nanol, "Ilángúli wa? Nen inje manije nya inj'an andey abajerut waf mo en dejay." 8. Nano, "Manujol ukíkom." Nano, "Inj'ikíki iyetut te! Ikíki ja pambikajen." Nano, "Aw ujo ukíkom." Nano, "mba kat usenom manikík, bare pambukanom maniraben." Nya nasenom jilibaju manaje ekíkey, eje'kíkey, eje'kíkey, eje'kíkey. Piyo di kam pá. 9. Nano, "Wo wandó?" Nanol, "Keak koku ró. Faaf faláándore, faaf fajone, faafu fukane búkubúk." Nanol, "Fakan mi búkubúk nuka'ró, fakan mi búkabúk nuka'ró, falándor mi nungarú." 10. Nangarú mi faláándoraf, najaum. Nano, "Mapujaum nya, ujaw ja uríng di karambaaku nubajú . . . enday? . . . jilitaj." Nanol, "Ibaj jilitaju inj'ijum ma ije bo nya mome mbikambu?" Nanol, "Aw ujaw bajú jilitaju mambujuk. 11. Napubajum jilitaju pambiregi manootum ekan enom mbubaj." Najaumi, ajaum, ajaum, aríng to di karambaaku, nabajum jilitaju. Nanol, "Nya nubabaj jilitaj uban?" Nanol, "Ey." Nanol, "Ujaw urembor maniregi." 12. Najaum, anyitom, anyitom aroojumi. Najukumi Jeru nateyúl. Ajol aríng, nano, "Asek ay, manungomumi nyer déru wamah?" Nanol, "Inj'an alenge, man inyitom dére kajanten ati jamit." Nay nanum, "Ulit!" Alitum, alitum, alitumi. 13. Ebé depúrum denganum "maah!" Nalaany alitum, alitum, alitumi. Bajending dejomi, enganum "maah! nyeeh!" Nanom, "Uwalúl urembor." Awalúm arembor, nalit, nalit:

14. [song]   Dinondin, Dinondin
Dinondin, Dinondin
Papa, ampa wambúl Bajendu denoonul.
Dinondin, Dinondin.

15. Nya naremborúl manajol, manajol, manajol, aríngúl:

[song]   Oee, Jirembenum
            Dinondin, Dinondin
            Papa, ampa nuwambúlom Bajendu denoonul
            Dinondin, Dinondin.

16. Nya najol aríngúmi di kufatumi, Kufatumi eluupey wooo man Bandendu enokenum. Ajol aríngú nalako di fankaf. No nanol, "Hani kiti nubajulo sibé sanumanje sikambu, anyiilaw ninyese." 17. Nane, "Wey, asom inje bu panikan?" Nano, "Nyem panugab unen di futúkanyaf. Ugab unen di futúkanyaf mambujukal wan emitey yoote ekaney." 18. Nagab eyus ró, nagab eyus ró, nagab eyus ró, najukúl ukámánaw. Nagab eyus ró, nagab eyus ró, nagab eyus ró, najukúl sijulasu. Nagab eyus ró, nagab eyus ró, nagab eyus ró, najukúl kukánaku. 19. Nagab eyus ró, nagab eyus ró, najukúl faraf. Nagab eyus ró, nagab eyus ró, najukúl ure reti fatámafu. Nagab eyus ró, nagab eyus ró, najukúl babe burám. 20. Nagab eyus ró, nagab eyus ró, najukúl babe bamaalab. Nagab eyus ró, nagab eyus ró, najukúl babe nya fukó.

21. Yo, nya namumi, "Inyeme aw enom asekaw ámba, nignagnor konte yoli. Nya bare ubuku burámii kawolum kunyiilak kati kakílak kakónaku, ko burám anoan nasof bungarab bola. Asofut bungarab bola, o koni jem bet esofey irámul." Yo. Abanumi nalaanyum.

22. Nya, di kujaum kone asekaw kulujúl anyiilaw mah. "Aw koey jat anyiil atukituk, aw koey jat anyiilaw atukituk." Baka ewuj ewujey, "Aw koey jat anyiil atukituk." 23. Yo. Anyiilaw nanumi, "Inyam be jat manukanum afarey yoli manubaj inje, inyeme panukonyen banukinum burám mambiregii wa kubeti kuregom inje." 24. Nakonyenil, nakonyenil burám. Kujom kuríngú, najaum ajuro di fankafu. Omuto akane kakímak kanakan mi kati Bajendu:

25.   [song]   Oee jirembenom.
                   None jat ijol jat di kambu yang?
                   Inje inyam kubeto kone
                   Inje batuker, batuker
                   Inje bóót.

26. Yo. Ombo abao ude!

[song]   Oee jirembenom.
            Inyam kubeto kone
             Inje batuker, batuker
             Inje bóót.

27. Nakan makan nayom ajími. Nyer asekaw etey bet elo di falafu. Atao etey be kayaoro di kulum. Nya sisúkas koku babu derentey. 28. Karegondegom, PEKES.

Bibliography

Abrahams, Roger
  1970a *Deep down in the jungle: Negro narrative folklore of Philadelphia.* Chicago: Aldine Publishing Co.
  1970b *Positively black.* Englewood Cliffs, New Jersey: Prentice Hall.
Albisetti, C., and Venturelli, A. J.
  1962 *Enciclopedia Bororo.* Vol. 1. Campo Grande, Brazil: Museu Regional Dom Bosco.
Almond, Gabriel, and Verba, Sidney
  1963 *The civic culture.* Princeton: Princeton University Press.
Anonymous
  n.d. Emiize! MS in the Hans Cory Collection. University of Dar es Salaam Library.
Ardener, Edwin
  1971 The new anthropology and its critics. *Man* 6:449–67.
Arewa, E. Ojo, and Dundes, Alan
  1964 Proverbs and the ethnography of speaking folklore. *American Anthropologist* 66, part II, pp. 70–85.
Aristotle
  1946 *Rhetoric.* Translated by Rhys Roberts. Oxford: Oxford University Press.
  1968 *The poetics.* Translated by L. J. Potts. Cambridge: Cambridge University Press.
Back, Kurt
  1963 The game and myth as two languages of social science. *Behavioral Science* 8:66–71.

225

Barrett, David B.
    1968   *Schism and renewal in Africa*. Nairobi: Oxford University
           Press.

Barth, Fredrik
    1965   *Political leadership among Swat Pathans*. London School of
           Economics. Monograph no. 19. London: The Athlone Press.

Barthes, Roland
    1957   *Mythologies*. Paris: Seuil (Collection Point).
    1970   L'ancienne rhétorique: aide-memoire. *Communications* 16:
           172–229.

Bateson, Gregory
    1958   *Naven*. Stanford: Stanford University Press. (Originally pub-
           lished in 1936).

Beidelman, T. O.
    1966   The ox and Nuer sacrifice: some Freudian-hypotheses about
           Nuer symbolism. *Man* 1:453–67.
    1968   Some Nuer notions of nakedness, nudity and sexuality. *Africa*
           38:113–32.
    1971   Foreword to *Kpele Lala*, by Marion Kilson. Cambridge: Har-
           vard University Press.
    1974   Kaguru texts: the ambiguity of the hare in Kaguru folklore.
           Baessler-Archiv, Neue Folge, Band XXII, pp. 247–63.
    1975   Ambiguous animals: two theriomorphic metaphors in Kaguru
           folklore. *Africa* 45:183–200.

Berggren, D.
    1962–63   The use and abuse of metaphor. *The Review of Metaphysics*
           16:238–58.

Berlin, B.; Breedlove, D. E.; and Raven, R. H.
    1968   Covert categories and folk taxonomies. *American Anthro-
           pologist* 70:290–99.

Black, Max
    1962   *Models and metaphors*. Ithaca: Cornell University Press.
    1968   *The labyrinth of language*. New York: Frederick A. Praeger,
           publishers.

Boas, Franz
    1911   *Introduction to Handbook of American Indian languages*.
           Bureau of American Ethnology, Bulletin 40, part I, pp. 5–75.

Bohannan, Paul
    1955   Some principles of exchange and investment among the Tiv.
           American Anthropologist 57:60–69.
    1959   The impact of money on an African subsistence economy.
           The Journal of Economic History 19:491–503.

Breton, André
    1969   *Manifesto of surrealism*. Translated by Robert Sears and
           Helen R. Lane. Ann Arbor: University of Michigan Press.

Brooke-Rose, Christine
    1958   *A grammar of metaphor*. London: Secker and Warburg.

Brown, Roger
    1958   *Words and things*. Glencoe: The Free Press.

Bulmer, Ralph
    1967   Why is the cassowary not a bird? A problem of zoological taxonomy among the Karam of the New Guinea highlands. *Man* 2:5–25.

Burke, Kenneth
    1945   *A grammar of motives*. New York: Prentice-Hall.
    1954   *Permanence and change: an anatomy of purpose*. 2d ed. Los Altos, Calif.: Hermes Publications. Originally published, New York: New Republic, 1935.
    1957   *The philosophy of literary form*. Revised abr. ed., Vintage paperbacks, New York: Vintage Books. Originally published, Baton Rouge: Louisiana State University Press, 1941. 3d ed., Berkeley: University of California Press, 1973.
    1961   *The rhetoric of religion: studies in logology*. Boston: Beacon Press.
    1964   *Perspectives by incongruity*. S. E. Hyman and Barbara Karmiller, eds. Bloomington: Indiana University Press.
    1966   *Language as symbolic action*. Berkeley: University of California Press.
    1969   *A rhetoric of motives*. Berkeley: University of California Press. Originally published, New York: Prentice-Hall, 1950.

Caillois, Roger
    1971   Riddles and images. In *Game, play, literature*. Jacques Ehrmann, ed. Boston: Beacon Press.

Cesard, E.
    1928–29   Proverbes et contes haya. *Anthropos* 23:494–510, 792–816.

Chapin, Mac
    1970*a*   Pab Igala: historias de la tradicion kuna. Panama: Centro de Investigaciones Antropologicas, Universidad de Panamá.
    1970*b*   Tad Ibe gi Namakket. [Phonograph record, with text and commentary, from a performance by Sakla Horacio Méndez.] Panamá.

Communications
    1970   *Recherches rhétoriques*. Vol. 16. Paris: Seuil.

Crocker, Eleanor C., and Crocker, J. Christopher
    1970   Some implications of superstitions and folk-beliefs for counseling parents of children with cleft lip and cleft palate. *The Cleft Palate Journal* 7:124–28.

Crocker, J. Christopher
    1969*a*   Reciprocity and hierarchy among the Eastern Bororo. *Man* 4:44–58.
    1969*b*   Men's house associates among the Eastern Bororo. *Southwestern Journal of Anthropology* 25:236–60.
    1975   The stench of death: structure and process in Bororo shamanism. MS.

Dalton, George
    1967   Primitive money. In *Tribal and peasant economies*. G. Dalton, ed. New York: The Natural History Press. Pp. 254–81.

Dawson, Richard, and Prewitt, Kenneth
    1969   *Political socialization.* Boston: Little, Brown, and Co.

Deese, James
    1965   *The structure of associations in language and thought.* Baltimore: Johns Hopkins Press.
    1974   Mind and metaphor: a commentary. *New Literary History* 6:211–18.

de Saussure, Ferdinand
    1959   *Course in general linguistics.* New York: The Philosophical Library.

Douglas, Mary
    1966   *Purity and danger.* London: Routledge Kegan Paul.
    1972   Deciphering a meal. *Daedalus. Journal of the American Academy of Arts and Sciences* 101, no. 1. Entitled: *Myth, symbol and culture.* Cambridge: American Academy of Arts and Sciences. Pp. 61–81.

Dubois, J.; Edeline, F.; Klinkenberg, J. M.; Minguet, P.; Pire, F.; and Trinon, H.
    1970   *Rhétorique générale.* Paris: Larousse.

Duke, James
    1968   *Darien ethnobotanical dictionary.* Columbus, Ohio: Battelle Memorial Institute.

Dundes, Alan
    1964   *The morphology of North American Indian folktales.* Folklore Fellows Communications No. 195. Helsinki: Academia Scientiarum Fennica.

Evans-Pritchard, E. E.
    1948   Nuer modes of address. *The Uganda Journal* 12:166–71. Reprinted in *The position of women in primitive societies and other essays in social anthropology.* London: Faber and Faber. Pp. 197–204.
    1956*a* *Nuer Religion.* Oxford: Oxford University Press.
    1956*b* Sanza, a characteristic feature of Zande language and thought. *Bulletin of the School of Oriental and African Studies* 18 (part 1):161–80. Reprinted in *Social anthropology and other essays.* Glencoe: Free Press.

Fernandez, James W.
    1965   Symbolic consensus in a Fang reformative cult. *American Anthropologist* 67:902–29.
    1966*a* Unbelievably subtle words: representation and integration in the sermons of an African reformative cult. *Journal of the History of Religions* 6:43–69.
    1966*b* Principles of opposition and vitality in Fang aesthetics. *Journal of Aesthetics and Art Criticism* 25:53–64.

1967 Revitalized words from the Parrot's Egg and the Bull Who Crashes in the Kraal: African cult sermons. In *Proceedings of the American Ethnological Society.* June Helm, ed. Seattle: University of Washington Press. Pp. 45–63.

1969*a* Fang representations under acculturation. SSRC-ACLS Conference. MS.

1969*b* Microcosmogeny and modernization. *Centre for Developing Area Studies.* Occasional Papers, no. 3. Montreal: University of McGill.

1970*a* Rededication and prophetism in Ghana. *Cahiers d'Etudes Africaines* 10:228–305.

1970*b* Fang architectonics. SSRC-ACLS Conference. MS.

1972 Persuasions and performance: of the beast in every body. . . and the metaphors of Everyman. *Daedalus. Journal of the American Academy of Arts and Sciences* 101, no. 1. Entitled: *Myth, symbol and culture.* Cambridge: American Academy of Arts and Sciences. Pp. 39–60.

1974 The mission of metaphor in expressive culture. *Current Anthropology* 15 (2):119–45.

Firth, J. R.
1950 Personality and language in society. *Sociological Review* 42:8–14.

Firth, Raymond
1966 Twins, birds and vegetables: problems of identification in primitive religious thought. *Man* 1:1–17.

Fleming, Ian
1972 *Goldfinger.* New York: Bantam Books.

Fox, James J.
1971 Sister's child as plant; metaphors in an idiom of consanguinity. In *Rethinking kinship and marriage.* Rodney Needham, ed. Association of Social Anthropologists. Monograph no. 11. London: Tavistock. Pp. 219–52.

Frake, Charles O.
1964 A structural description of Subanum religious behavior. In *Explorations in cultural anthropology, essays in honor of George Peter Murdock.* Ward H. Goodenough, ed. New York: McGraw Hill. Pp. 111–29.

Freedman, Maurice
1967 *Rites and duties, or Chinese marriage.* London: G. Bell.

Garfinkle, Harold
1967 *Studies in ethnomethodology.* Englewood Cliffs, New Jersey: Prentice Hall.

Geertz, Clifford
1966 Religion as a cultural system. In *Anthropological approaches to the study of religion.* M. Banton, ed. Association of Social Anthropologists. Monograph no. 3. London: Tavistock.

1972 Deep play: notes on the Balinese cockfight. *Daedalus. Jour-*

nal of the American Academy of Arts and Sciences 101, no. 1.
Entitled: *Myth, symbol and culture*. Cambridge: American
Academy of Arts and Sciences. Pp. 1–38.

Genette, Gerard
  1972   *Figures III*. Collection Poétique. Paris: Seuil.
Goffman, Erving
  1967   *Interaction ritual*. New York: Doubleday Anchor Books.
Goody, Jack
  1962   *Death, property and the ancestors*. London: Tavistock.
Gourlay, K. A.
  1972   The ox and identification. *Man* 7:244–54.
Gumperz, John J. and Hymes, Dell eds.
  1972   *Directions in sociolinguistics: the ethnography of communi-
          cation*. New York: Holt, Rinehart and Winston.
Hayley, A.
  1968   Symbolic equations: the ox and the cucumber. *Man* 3:262–
          71.
Holloman, Regina E.
  1969   *Developmental change in San Blas*. Northwestern University,
          doctoral dissertation. Ann Arbor: University Microfilms.
Holmer, Nils
  1951   *Cuna chrestomathy*. Göteborg: Etnologiska Studier no. 18.
  1952   *Ethnolinguistic cuna dictionary*. Göteborg: Etnologiska
          Studier no. 19.
Holmer, Niles, and Wassén, S. Henry
  1958   *Nia-Ikala, canto magico para curar la locura*. Göteborg:
          Etnologiska Studier no. 23.
  1963   *Dos cantos shamanisticos de los indios Cuna*. Göteborg:
          Etnologiska Studier no. 27.
Hopkins, G. M.
  1956   *The collected works of Gerard Manley Hopkins*. New York:
          Penguin Books.
Howe, James
  1974   Village political organization among the San Blas Cuna.
          Doctoral dissertation, University of Pennsylvania. Ann Arbor:
          University Microfilms.
  n.d.   El consejo en la cultura Cuna, to appear in *Hombre y Cul-
          tura*. Panama.
Hyman, E. S.
  1959   *The tangled bank: Darwin, Marx, Frazer and Freud as
          imaginative writers*. New York: Atheneum.
Hyman, Herbert
  1959   Political socialization. Glencoe, Illinois: The Free Press.
Hymes, Dell
  1962   The ethnography of speaking. In *Anthropology and human
          behavior*. Thomas Gladwin and William C. Sturtevant, eds.

Washington D.C.: The Anthropological Society of Washington. Pp. 13–53.

1965 Methods and tasks of anthropological philology. *Romance Philology* 19:325–40.

1971 The "wife" who goes out like a man. In *Essays in semiotics.* Julia Kristeva, ed. The Hague: Mouton. Also in *Structural analysis of oral tradition.* Maranda and Maranda, eds. Philadelphia: University of Pennsylvania Press. 1971. Pp. 49–80.

Hymes, Dell, ed.

1964 *Language in culture and society: a reader in linguistics and anthropology.* New York: Harper.

Jakobson, Roman

1956 Two aspects of language and two types of aphasic disturbances. In R. Jakobson and M. Halle. *Fundamentals of language.* The Hague: Mouton.

1957 Shifters, verbal categories, and the Russian verb. Cambridge: Department of Slavic Languages and Literatures, Harvard University.

1960 Concluding statement: linguistics and poetics. In *Style in language.* Thomas Sebeok, ed. Cambridge: The MIT Press. Pp. 350–77.

Jaros, Dean

1973 *Socialization to politics.* New York: Praeger Publishers.

Jung, Carl and Riklin, Franz

1918 *Studies in word association.* Chap. 2. The associations of normal subjects. London: Heinemann.

Kael, Pauline

1968 The missing west. (The current cinema) *New Yorker Magazine* 44, no. 36, November 16, 1968, p. 127.

Kietzman, D.

1967 Indians and culture areas of twentieth century Brazil. In *Indians of Brazil in the twentieth century.* J. Hopper, ed. ICR Studies 2. Washington D.C.

Kramer, Fritz

1970 *Literature among the Cuna Indians.* Göteborg: Etnologiska Studier no. 30.

Langer, Susanne K.

1942 *Philosophy in a new key.* Cambridge: Harvard University Press.

Langton, Kenneth

1969 *Political socialization.* London: Oxford University Press.

Lanham, Richard S.

1969 *A handlist of rhetorical terms.* Berkeley: University of California Press.

Leach, E. R.

1954   *Political systems of highland Burma.* The London School of Economics, London: G. Bell and Sons.

1964   Anthropological aspects of language: animal categories and verbal abuse. In *New directions in the study of language.* E. H. Lenneberg, ed. Cambridge: The MIT Press. Pp. 23–63.

Le Guern, Michel

1973   *Sémantique de la métaphore et de la métonymie.* Paris: Larousse.

Levine, Robert

1960   The internalization of political values in stateless societies. *Human Organization* 19:51–58.

1963   Political socialization and culture change. In *Old societies and new states.* Clifford Geertz, ed. New York: The Free Press.

Lévi-Strauss, Claude

1958   La geste d'Asdiwal. Annaire 1958–59, Ecole Pratique des Hautes Etudes (Section sciences religieuses). Paris. Pp. 3–43. Reprinted in *Les Temps Modernes* 179, mars 1962. Reprinted with alternations in *Anthropologie structurale deux.* Paris: Plon, 1973. Pp. 175–234. English translation in *Structural study of myth and totemism.* E. R. Leach, ed. Association of Social Anthropologists. Monograph no. 5. London: Tavistock, 1967.

1963a   *Totemism.* Boston: Beacon Press. English translation by Rodney Needham of *Le totémisme aujourd'hui.* Paris: Presses Universitaires de France, 1962.

1963b   The sorcerer and his magic. In *Structural anthropology.* New York: Basic Books. Pp. 167–85. (English translation by Claire Jacobson and Brooke Grundfest Schoepf of *Anthropologie structurale.* Paris: Plon, 1958. Pp. 183–203.) Originally published in *Les Temps Moderne* 41, 1949, pp. 3–24.

1963c   The effectiveness of symbols. In *Structural anthropology.* New York: Basic Books. Pp. 186–205 (pp. 205–26 in *Anthropologie structurale*). Originally published in *Revue de l'Histoire des religions* 135 (1), 1949, pp. 5–27.

1963d   Do dual organizations exist? In *Structural anthropology.* New York: Basic Books. Pp. 132–66 (pp. 147–80 in *Anthropologie structurale*). Originally published in *Bijdragen tot de taal-, land- en Volkenkunde,* Deel 112 (2), Aflevering, 1956, pp. 99–128.

1966a   *The savage mind.* Chicago: University of Chicago Press. (English translation of *La pensée sauvage.* Paris: Plon, 1962).

1966b   The scope of anthropology. *Current Anthropology* 7:112–23. Also separately published: London: Grossman Publishers, Cape Editions 1, 1967. English translation of *Leçon inaugurale.* Collège de France 31, 1960.

1969   *The raw and the cooked.* New York: Harper and Row. (English translation by John and Doreen Weightman of *Le cru et le cuit*. Paris: Plon, 1964).

Levy-Bruhl, Lucien
    1910   *Les fonctions mentales dans les sociétés inférieures*. Paris: Libraries Alcan et Guillaumin.
    1966   *How natives think*. New York: Washington Square Press.

Lipton, James
    1968   *Exaltation of Larks*. New York: Grossman.

Loeb, E.
    1952   The function of proverbs in the intellectual development of primitive peoples. *Scientific Monthly* 74:100–104.

Lorenz, Konrad Z.
    1952   *King Solomon's ring*. New York: Crowell.

Lounsbury, Floyd G.
    1959   Similarity and contiguity relations in language and culture. *Report of the 10th annual round table meeting of linguistics and language studies*. Richard Harrell, ed. Monograph Series in Language and Linguistics, Georgetown University. Washington: Georgetown University Press.

Lowie, Robert H.
    1937   *The history of ethnological theory*. New York: Farrar and Rinehart.

Maranda, Elli Kongas
    1971   The logic of riddles. In *Structural analysis of oral tradition*. Maranda and Maranda, eds. Philadelphia: University of Pennsylvania Press. Pp. 189–234.

Maybury-Lewis, David
    1967   *Akwe-Shavante society*. Oxford: Clarendon Press.

Mayer, Adrian C.
    1965   *Caste and kinship in Central India*. Berkeley: University of California Press (2d ed.).

McCloskey, Mary
    1964   Metaphors. *Mind* 73 (290).

Méndez, Eustorgio
    1970   Los principales mamiferos silvestres de Panamá. Panamá (private printing).

Middleton, John
    1960   *Lugbara religion*. London: Oxford University Press.

Miller, G., E. Galenter, and Pribam, K.
    1960   *Plans and the structure of behavior*. New York: Holt.

Milner, G. B.
    1969   What is a proverb? *New Society* (February 6):199–202.

Murdock, George Peter
    1949   *Social structure*. New York: The Free Press.

New Literary History
    1974   *On metaphor*. Vol. 6, no. 1 (Autumn). Charlottesville, Virginia: University of Virginia.

Nisbet, Robert
  1968   *Social change and history.* New York: Oxford University
          Press.
Nordenskiold, Erland, with Kantule, Ruben Perez, Wassén, S. Henry, eds.
  1938   *An historical and ethnological survey of the Cuna Indians.*
          Göteborg: Comparative Ethnographical Studies no. 3.
Northrop, Filmer S. C.
  1947   *The logic of the sciences and the humanities.* New York:
          Macmillan Co.
Parsons, Talcott
  1966   *Societies: evolutionary and comparative perspectives.* Engle-
          wood Cliffs, New Jersey: Prentice Hall.
Peacock, James
  1968   *Rites of modernization.* Chicago: University of Chicago
          Press.
Peñaherrera de Costales, Piedad, and Samaniego, Alfredo Costales
  1968   *Cunas y Chocos.* Quito: Publicaciones del Instituto Ecua-
          toriana de Antropologia y Geografia, Ilacta no. 25.
Pepper, Stephen
  1942   *World hypothesis: a study in evidence.* Berkeley: University
          of California Press.
Percy, W.
  1961   The symbolic structure of interpersonal process. *Psychiatry*
          24:39–52.
Pike, Kenneth
  1967   *Language in relation to a unified theory of the structure of
          human behavior.* The Hague: Mouton.
Polanyi, Michael
  1958   *Personal knowledge.* Chicago: Chicago University Press.
Rascher, A.
  1967–68 Spruchweisheit der Haya. *Afrika and Ubersee* 50–51.
Rattray, R. S.
  1930   *Akan-ashanti folk-tales.* Oxford: Clarendon Press.
Rehse, H.
  1910   *Kiziba Land and Leute.* Stuttgart.
Reichel-Dolmitoff, Gerardo
  1971   *Amazonian cosmos.* Chicago: University of Chicago Press.
Reining, P.
  1962   Haya land tenure: land holding and tenancy. *Anthropologi-
          cal quarterly* 35 (2):58–73.
Richards, Audrey
  1956   Chisungu. London: Faber and Faber.
Richards, I. A.
  1925   *Principles of literary criticism.* London: Routledge and Kegan
          Paul.
  1936   *The philosophy of rhetoric.* London: Oxford University
          Press.

Ricoeur, Paul
    1975   *La métaphore vive.* Paris: Seuil.

Rigby, Peter J.
    1969   The symbolic role of cattle in Gogo religion. USSCC Conference paper no. 612. Kampala, M.I.S.R.

Rosaldo, Michelle Z.
    1972   Metaphors and folk classification. *Southwestern Journal of Anthropology* 28:83–99.

Roy, Donald
    1960   "Banana time": job satisfaction and informal interaction. *Human Organization* 18:158–68.

Rycroft, Charles
    1974   Is Freudian symbolism a myth? *New York Review of Books* 20 (21 and 22), January 24, pp. 13–16.

Sapir, J. David
    1965   *A grammar of Diola-Fogny.* West African language monographs, no. 3. Cambridge: Cambridge University Press.
    1969   Diola funeral songs and the native critic. *African Language Review* 8:176–91.
    1970   Kujaama, symbolic separation among the Diola. *American Anthropologist* 72:1330–48.
    forthcoming   *Fragments from a cosmology: on the symbolism of Kujamaat Diola religious forms.*

Seitel, Peter
    1969   Proverbs: a social use of metaphor. *Genre* 2:143–61.
    1972   Proverbs and the structure of metaphor among the Haya of Tanzania. Doctoral dissertation, University of Pennsylvania.
    1974   Haya metaphors for speech. *Language in Society* 3:51–67.

Sharpe, Ella Freeman
    1940   *Dream analysis.* New York: W. W. Norton.

Sherzer, Joel
    1970   Talking backwards in Cuna: the sociological reality of phonological descriptions. *Southwestern Journal of Anthropology* 26:343–53.
    1975   *Namakke, Sumakke, Kormakke:* three types of Cuna speech event. In *Explorations in the ethnography of speaking.* Richard Baumann and Joel Sherzer, eds. Cambridge: Cambridge University Press.

Sherzer, Joel, and Sherzer, Dina
    1972   Review article: literature in San Blas. *Semiotica* 6 (2):182–99.

Shibles, Warren A.
    1971   *Metaphor.* Whitewater, Wisconsin.

Shimkin, D., and Sanjuan, P.
    1953   Culture and worldview: a method of analysis applied to rural Russia. *American Anthropologist* 55:329–48.

Sigel, Roberta
    1970   *Learning about politics, a reader in political socialization.*
            New York: Random House.

Southall, Aidan
    1972   Twinship and symbolic structure. In *The interpretation of
            ritual.* J. S. La Fontaine, ed. London: Tavistock.

Spencer, Paul
    1965   *The Samburu: a study of gerontocracy in a nomadic tribe.*
            London: Routledge and Kegan Paul.

Sperber, Dan
    1974   *Le symbolisme en général.* Paris: Hermann (Collection
            Savoir). Translated into English as *Rethinking symbolism.*
            Cambridge: Cambridge University Press, 1975.

Steinen, K. von den
    1894   *Unter den Naturvolkern Zentral-Brasiliens.* Berlin: Verlags-
            bucklandlub Dietrich Reimer.

Stout, David
    1947   *San Blas Cuna acculturation: an introduction.* New York:
            Viking Fund Publication no. 9.

Sundkler, B. G. M.
    1960   *Bantu prophets in South Africa.* Oxford: Oxford University
            Press for the International African Institute.

Tambiah, S. J.
    1968   The magical power of words. *Man* 3:175–209.
    1969   Animals are good to think and good to prohibit. *Ethnology*
            8:423–59.

Titiev, M.
    1944   *Old Oraibi.* Papers of the Peabody Museum of American
            Archaeology and Ethnology, Harvard University. Vol. 22,
            no. 1. Cambridge.

Todorov, Tzvetan
    1970   Synecdoques. *Communications* 16:26–35.
    1972   Introduction à la symbolique. *Poétique* II:273–308.
    1974*a* Recherches sur le symbolisme linguistique, I. Le mot d'esprit
            et ses rapports avec le symbolique. *Poétique* 18:215–45.
    1974*b* On linguistic symbolism. *New Literary History* 6:111–34.

Turner, Victor
    1967   *The forest of symbols.* Ithaca: Cornell University Press.

Van Baaren, Th. P.
    1969   Are the Bororo parrots or are we? In *Liber Amicorum: studies
            in honour of Professor Dr. C. J. Bleeker.* Leiden, Pp. 8–13.

Van der Leeuw, G.
    1928   *La structure de la mentalité primitive.* Paris.

Van Steenburgh, E. W.
    1965   Metaphor. *The Journal of Philosophy* 62:678–88.

Vogt, Evon Z.
    1969   *Zinacantan.* Cambridge: Harvard University Press.

Vygotsky, L.
 1962 *Thought and language*. Cambridge: The MIT Press.
Wallace, A. F. C.
 1956 Revitalization movements. *American Anthropologist* 58:261–
   81.
Wassén, S. Henry
 1938 *Original documents from the Cuna Indians of San Blas,
   Panama*. Göteborg: Etnologiska Studier no. 6.
 1949 *Contributions to Cuna ethnography*. Göteborg: Etnologiska
   Studier no. 16.
Wellek, René and Warren, Austin
 1956 *Theory of literature*. 3d ed. New York: Harcourt, Brace and
   World.
Wetmore, Alexander
 1965 *Birds of the Republic of Panamá*. Smithsonian Miscellaneous
   Collections, vol. 150:1, 2.
Wheelwright, Philip
 1962 *Metaphor and reality*. Bloomington: Indiana University Press.
Whiting, B. J.
 1931 The origin of the proverb. *Harvard Studies and Notes in
   Philology and Literature* 13:45–91.
Zerries, Otto
 1969 Primitive South America and the West Indies. In Krickeberg,
   Trimborn, Zerries: *Pre-Columbian American religions*. New
   York: Holt, Rinehart, Winston.

Contributors

J. CHRISTOPHER CROCKER received his Ph.D. from Harvard University in 1967, and is currently an associate professor in the Departments of Anthropology and Sociology at the University of Virginia. He is pursuing research on the symbolic constituents of individual and corporate identity, and is completing his monograph on Bororo shamanism and beginning another on Bororo cosmology and ritual.

JAMES W. FERNANDEZ received his Ph.D. from Northwestern University in 1963 and is now a professor of Anthropology at Princeton University. He has been using metaphor (and writing about it) in an attempt to advance anthropological insight (and his own career) since 1966.

JAMES HOWE received his Ph.D. from the University of Pennsylvania in 1974 and is now an assistant professor of Anthropology at M.I.T. He is the author of several articles on the San Blas Cuna and co-editor of *Ritual and Symbolism in Native Central America.* Currently he is preparing a volume of Cuna chants and speeches, to be published in Panama.

J. DAVID SAPIR received the Ph.D. degree in 1964 from Harvard University and is currently an associate professor in Anthropology at the University of Virginia. Between 1960 and 1970, Professor Sapir's fieldwork covered descriptive linguistics, folklore, and religious symbolism—the subject of his current publication efforts—of the Kujamaat Diola of the Lower Casamance region of Senegal.

PETER SEITEL, who received his Ph.D. from the University of Pennsylvania in 1972, has recently completed the production of a festival exhibition on American workers' occupational culture and folklore for the Smithsonian Institution. He is currently living in Chincoteaque, Virginia, and preparing a collection of Haya folktales.

Index

(The provenience of unfamiliar words, metaphor texts, etc. has been indicated in parentheses after the entry. The following abbreviations have been used: B. = Bororo, C. = San Blas Cuna, F. = Fang, H. = Haya, K. = Kujamaat Diola.)

241

travesty, 27
tree as a chief (C.), 145–49
trees, fallen, as community problem (C.), 156
trope, 3, 4n, 21, 101. *See also* figure of speech, irony, metaphor, metonymy, synecdoche
semantic domain of, 13
tula (C.), 147
Turner, Victor, 58, 66, 125–27

unaet (C.). *See* admonishments
Uspenskij, G. I., 16n

Van Baaren, Th. P., 165n, 181
Van der Leeuw, G., 165n
vehicle, 7, 54, 70, 104, 105, 113, 151, 155. *See also* discontinuous term
venery, nouns of, 54
vulture, 29–30, 55–56

Wallace, A. F. C., xi
walls, house, as ordinary people (C.), 154

Wassén, S. H., 133, 143n
"we are a trading team" (F.), 109, 110, 114–15, 123–25, 127
"we are macaws" (B.), 10, 11, 32, 41, 54, 69, 71–72, 164–92
"we are of one clan" (F.), 109, 110–11, 115, 123–25, 127
"we are one heart" (F.), 109, 111–12, 123–25, 127
whirlpool as village (C.), 140, 142–43, 143n, 144n, 145, 151
whistling as a male activity (K.), 213, 218
wholeness, indicated by metonymy, 21
"where there is smoke there is fire", 28, 57, 77
Wheelwright, P., 103–4
"wife of Mulalo" proverb, the (H.), 84–87, 89
witchcraft, 93–94, 98, 205
Wittgenstein, L., 36n
womb, external. *See* beehive

zen ngombi (F.), 108, 111